Justifying historical descriptions

Justifying
historical descriptions

◁ ▷

C. Behan McCullagh

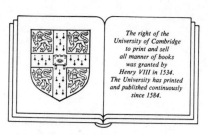

The right of the
University of Cambridge
to print and sell
all manner of books
was granted by
Henry VIII in 1534.
The University has printed
and published continuously
since 1584.

Cambridge University Press

Cambridge
London   New York   New Rochelle
Melbourne   Sydney

Published by the Press Syndicate of the University of Cambridge
The Pitt Building, Trumpington Street, Cambridge CB2 1RP
32 East 57th Street, New York, NY 10022, USA
296 Beaconsfield Parade, Middle Park, Melbourne 3206, Australia

First published 1984

Printed in Great Britain by The Pitman Press, Bath

Library of Congress catalogue card number: 84–7028

British Library Cataloguing in Publication Data
McCullagh, Christopher Behan
Justifying historical descriptions.
1. Historiography   2. History——Philosophy
I. Title
901   D13

ISBN 0 521 26722 6 hard covers
ISBN 0 521 31830 0 paperback

In honour of my parents
Morris B. and Mary L. McCullagh

Contents

Preface

In writing this book I have had two groups of people in mind. First and foremost it is written for teachers and students of history who would like a clearer idea of the conditions which warrant belief in the truth of historical descriptions. There have been occasional discussions of these conditions in previous books and articles, but no systematic exposition of them has previously been attempted. I hope that this will help historians to a better understanding of the logic of their work.

The other group for whom this book is chiefly written are those who have been inclined to agree with Henry Ford that history is bunk, not worthy of belief. In what follows I hope to persuade them that although historical descriptions can never be proved true beyond all possibility of error, it is nevertheless often reasonable to believe that they correctly describe what has actually happened.

My academic indebtedness is to those whose works are listed in the bibliography, together with my teachers, colleagues and students. Of the many teachers who have helped me, two deserve special acknowledgement: Professor G. R. Elton and the late Professor Sir Herbert Butterfield. They provided personal support as well as academic stimulus well beyond the call of duty. Several scholars have been particularly generous in discussing at length the matters contained in this book when it was in preparation: Professors W. H. Dray, Leon J. Goldstein, L. B. Cebik, R. F. Atkinson, Quentin Skinner, Quentin Gibson, Robert Brown and Dr. I. G. Maier. Most of these also commented on sections of the text. I am very grateful to them all. Many others, both colleagues and students, have contributed to my understanding in seminars and in the classroom. I can scarcely have done justice to all the wisdom these people have provided, but without it the book would have been much poorer.

Part of this book was written while I was a Visiting Fellow at the Department of Philosophy of the Research School of Social Studies at the Australian National University in Canberra. I am very grateful to both the Department and the School for the support and stimulation they provided.

My family, particularly my wife Jan, have given and suffered much to help me write this book, and I offer them my heartfelt thanks.

Finally I would like to acknowledge what I believe to have been God's guidance and support in the production of this book. It is just a pity that the clay He had to mould was so recalcitrant! Please praise Him for what is true in it, and forgive me for what is not.

La Trobe University
Melbourne
December 1982

◁ 1 ▷
Introduction:
Truth and justification

In practice most historians assume that when their statements about the past are adequately supported by available evidence, then it is reasonable to believe them true. Precisely what constitutes adequate support is hard to say. Some ideas about adequate justification of historical descriptions can be gleaned from an analysis of historical practice and from a consideration of the logical issues involved, as subsequent chapters will show. Before embarking on that analysis, however, it would be interesting to consider whether historians can possibly be justified in believing that their well-supported descriptions of the past are in fact true. (An historical description is here understood to be a statement which is intended to describe the past, though in fact it may not do so, or not do so accurately.) If truth is an unreasonable goal of historical research, then several widely respected historical practices lack rational justification.

Historians' faith in the truth of their conclusions about the past can only be justified if several assumptions are accepted, assumptions about the nature of reality and our knowledge of it. These assumptions, which are empiricist in character, are very commonly accepted but impossible to prove true. They are:

(1)   An assumption that the world exists and has existed independent of any beliefs about it.

(2)   An assumption that perceptions, under certain conditions, provide an accurate impression of reality.

(3)   An assumption that reality is structured according to most of the concepts by which we describe it.

(4)   An assumption that our rules of inference are reliable means of arriving at new truths about reality.

These assumptions are unquestioned by most people, and upon them rest most of their undoubted beliefs about reality. To reject any one of them would require the rejection of a very large number of beliefs which depend upon it, and would introduce a quite massive dislocation into our system of beliefs about the world. Suppose one rejected the fourth, for example, and said that historical knowledge, which is justified by forms of inference, does not yield knowledge of reality, though knowledge justified by perception is reliable. (Goldstein, 1976, has expressed this view.) This would leave one with a dichotomous view of reality in which descriptions of what can be perceived would be interpreted realistically, but historical descriptions would not. To refuse to accept the third would mean we must refuse to accept most descriptions of the world as providing reliable information about it. To refuse the second is to deny the physical reality of what we normally perceive. And to deny the first is to reject realism presumably for idealism. Recently some have struggled to establish an intermediate position, saying that we should believe both that the world exists independent of our beliefs about it and also that the world is nothing but a function of our beliefs about it. (See Rorty, 1972, 1976, and 1980.) The contradiction here seems inescapable, and fatal.

The truth of these four assumptions cannot be proved, as philosophers have been tireless in explaining. We have no access to reality independent of our beliefs and experiences of it, so we cannot check in a God-like manner upon their truth. We are justified in holding them because it is useful to do so; indeed we may even be psychologically incapable of doing otherwise.

Most historians accept these four assumptions and see themselves as trying to discover what actually happened in the past. That explains why they pay such attention to the accuracy of their observations of evidence and to the adequacy of their inferences from it, and why they refuse to put forward any descriptions of the past for which there is not good evidence. If the pursuit of truth were abandoned as the goal of historical inquiry, then the main reason for insisting upon present standards of historical criticism would disappear. It would then be difficult to resist the pressure to relax those standards and produce history for the purpose of propaganda.

Some historians, acutely aware of the possibility of error, are inclined in their more reflective, theoretical moments to think that the goal of historical research is not truth about the past but coherence with present evidence and beliefs. So long as historical descriptions to some extent imply and are implied by other beliefs we hold, and are contradicted by none, that is enough. But in practice historians demand more than coherence. Good historical novelists respect the requirements of coherence, but go beyond what the evidence warrants. For example, the imaginary conversations provided by historical novelists often cohere well with available evidence but lack sufficient evidential support to be regarded as true. History might well be more colourful, but it would not be as accurate, if present standards of historical inquiry were relaxed.

If historians were to abandon the pursuit of truth and be content instead with coherence, it would be easier to persuade them to produce histories distorted for propaganda purposes. If truth is not the goal, why not go beyond the evidence on occasion or produce a partial and misleading portrait sometimes to secure valued social or political ends? The policy of using history for propaganda purposes, at the expense of probable truth where necessary, has long been adopted in Soviet Russia (see Keep, 1964), and in the last decade or so it has found supporters in the U.S.A. as well (see Handlin, 1979). This tendency will not be checked unless high standards of historical justification are reaffirmed as the only means of getting at the truth.

Why does historical truth matter? History enables us to understand our social and cultural inheritance, our institutions, beliefs and artefacts, and it is vital that it be as accurate as possible. To evaluate our inheritance correctly, we must know why the various elements of our society and culture were created and evolved to their present form, and what functions they have served in the communities in which they have existed. An understanding of the history of useful institutions encourages people to respect them and co-operate with them, rather than resent any restrictions they may impose upon their freedom. Knowledge of the injustices perpetuated by other institutions provides good reasons for their reform or replacement. Appreciation of works of art is much greater if one knows the ideas and values they were meant to express. Generally our attitudes to our social and cultural inheritance will be much wiser if they are based upon an accurate knowledge of its history.

It might be thought that as circumstances alter, so too will the value of institutions, so that a knowledge of their function in past circumstances gives no reliable indication of their value in the present. But this argument takes the historicist doctrine of the uniqueness of each society at each point of time to an extreme. Certainly in any society there are always changes taking place, especially in Western societies where progress in technology has made such tremendous impact. But the problems faced by societies remain remarkably stable – the need for food, shelter, security, justice and freedom, for example. And the effectiveness of certain institutions in promoting these and other goods can be studied, taking careful note of the precise circumstances which made their operation effective. Robert Peel established the Metropolitan Police Force in 1829 to limit crime in nineteenth-century London. The need to limit crime still exists, and the police force has been fairly useful in fulfilling it. Certainly criminals use radios and cars now, as they did not last century, so to be as effective now as they were then the police must use radios and cars too. But the value of the institution can be appreciated by reference to its history, allowing for the changes relevant to its effectiveness which have occurred since it was established.

In practice, then, historians do try to discover the truth about the past, and this is a very valuable endeavour if only because, if successful, it would provide us with the means of better understanding and appraising our cultural inheritance. Historians commonly believe that their well-supported descriptions of the past are true, but can such faith be rationally justified?

1   The truth of historical descriptions

Even if the four basic empiricist assumptions are accepted, it is not possible to prove the truth of any historical description beyond all possibility of error. The reasons for this are familiar to historians. First, it is always possible that the available evidence relevant to a description is misleading, and that if more were available a different conclusion would be drawn. Admittedly, when the evidence in support of a description is very abundant, the chance of more evidence pointing to a different conclusion is very slight. But while it remains a possibility, the conclusion drawn from available evidence is not necessarily true. Second, the premises of all historical inferences are fallible, not necessarily true, so that the conclusions drawn from them are fallible too. Although we might have every reason to be certain that our observations of evidence are correct, the possibility remains that they are not. This possibility only becomes at all worrying when the evidence is indistinct, as inscriptions on old coins or on damaged or faded documents can be. The truth of generalizations used in historical inferences is also strictly unproven, even when they are not doubted. Finally, as will be seen, almost all forms of historical inferences are inductive in form. Inductive inferences are such that, even if all their premises are true, their conclusions could be false. They extrapolate from what is known to what is unknown, and there is always the possibility that what has been extrapolated is false. The only form of historical inference which is clearly deductive and not inductive is that taken by arguments in support of generalizations which proceed from an exhaustive examination of instances. Their conclusions are never necessarily true, though, because their premises are not necessarily true – the instances could possibly have been falsely reported. For these reasons, then, it is always possible that the conclusion of an historical inference is false, no matter how certain it may be.

Although historical descriptions cannot be proved true beyond all possibility of error, they can often be proved probably true, given empiricist assumptions. Assuming that an historian's perceptions of data are very probably accurate, that his general knowledge and other beliefs are very probably true, and that his forms of inference are generally reliable, one can rationally infer the probable truth of many historical descriptions. The probability of the conclusion is just a function of the information available to the historian, but it is normally taken to be a reliable guide to rational belief. When the probability of a conclusion is very high, historians are usually quite confident of its truth.

Is such confidence misplaced? In the chapters which follow, care will be taken to state all the conditions which must be satisfied before faith in the truth of an historical conclusion is justified. Even so, there are two general reasons for doubting their truth which must be faced. One is an argument from science, the other an argument from relativism.

Historians generally describe past events in everyday language, not in scientific terms. They describe objects as having a certain colour or smell and some events as noisy, meaning that these are properties of the objects and events themselves. According to accepted scientific theory however, secondary properties such as these are not properties of things in the world at all, but merely properties of our perceptions. Molecules have no colour or smell, and sound waves no sound — the colours, smells and sounds are just aspects of human perceptions of these things. So from a scientific point of view, many everyday and historical descriptions are strictly false. Since scientific knowledge is, on empiricist assumptions, more likely to be true than are our everyday beliefs, it would seem to be irrational to believe those everyday descriptions true which ascribe secondary properties to physical objects and events.

It is interesting to notice that although these scientific views about the nature of secondary properties have been accepted for a long time, indeed since John Locke stated them in the seventeenth century, very few if any people have ceased to attribute such properties to things in the world in everyday contexts. The reason would seem to be a practical one. For everyday, rather than scientific, purposes it is very useful to speak of things in the world having secondary properties which we can accurately perceive under normal circumstances. Predictions based upon such descriptions can normally be readily verified. Our everyday beliefs about the world may be strictly false, but for practical purposes it is useful to accept them as true.

There are practical reasons too which justify our accepting well-supported historical descriptions as true, even though they are couched in everyday language so that we know them to be strictly, scientifically, false. The historical world is an extension of the present everyday world, and conceived of in the same terms. If President Lincoln's jacket is red today, it was red when he wore it. If Churchill's radio broadcasts are vibrant on tape today, they were vibrant when he gave them. We understand much of the present in terms of the past, and such understanding is most readily achieved if the past is described in terms of the same concepts as we use to describe the present. The fact that such descriptions are judged to be strictly false is outweighed by their practical utility, which justifies their acceptance as true.

If practical utility warrants belief in historical descriptions which are known to be strictly false, should we believe history which has poor evidential support but which is useful for propaganda purposes? Why should we confine belief to those historical descriptions which have satisfied quite demanding standards of rational justification? The answer to this question seems to be that it is not useful to believe just any historical description for practical purposes, but only those which will prove reliable in the long run. Those are the ones which satisfy the standards of rational justification set out below. Predictions based upon them are more frequently verified than those derived from other, less well-justified historical descriptions. Historical descriptions provided by writers of historical fiction or propaganda which are not well supported by evidence are open to ready falsification by the discovery of new evidence, and so are not at all reliable. In practice it is usually to one's disadvantage, not one's advantage, to accept them as true.

Is this to abandon truth for coherence as an ideal of historical inquiry? There are two points to be noted here. The first is that reliability is a stronger requirement than coherence. Historical descriptions which are reliable are not only consistent with other beliefs and perhaps implied by some of them, but are so well-supported that they are unlikely to be falsified for some time to come.

The second point is that if the empiricist assumptions are accepted, then the conditions which justify us thinking an historical description reliable also justify us thinking it true. Roughly speaking, an historical description is reliable if it can be inferred from available evidence; and if our rules of inference are reliable means of arriving at new truths about reality, as empiricists assume, then historical descriptions inferred from observable evidence provide us with new truths about what really happened in the past. So to pursue reliable historical descriptions is to pursue true ones.

The trouble with this second line of argument is that empiricists have reason to doubt some of their own initial assumptions. The assumption that our perceptions normally provide an accurate impression of reality has had to be modified in the light of scientific discoveries built upon empiricist assumptions (including that one), so that scientists now deny that physical objects and events really have the secondary properties we ascribe to them. That modification to empiricist theory has already been noted. But there are further, more damaging facts which must also be acknowledged. These are the implications of relativism.

Historians and anthropologists, working with empiricist assumptions, have discovered facts which cast doubt upon the truth of two of them. The history of science shows that some concepts which were once accepted as reflecting the structure of reality, are no longer accepted as doing so. And the history of thought shows that standards of inference once thought reliable for arriving at truths about reality are no longer judged to be reliable. For example, historians have become much more critical in their use of 'authorities' and 'testimony' than they once were (Collingwood, 1946, Pt V, §3). The problem is that in future years many of our present concepts and standards of inference will probably be thought inadequate, and there is at least a fair logical probability that they are.

One may be tempted to reply to this objection that historians write about everyday matters, and concepts about them have not changed much over time. In fact, however, even man's ideas about everyday objects have changed radically. Some have regarded, and still do regard, physical objects as inhabited by supernatural spirits, and natural events as the work of supernatural powers. At the other extreme, as has been said, scientists are inclined to teach us that in reality things do not have the secondary qualities we attribute to them, qualities such as colour, temperature, sound or smell, those being just features of how things appear to us. Our everyday belief that physical objects are not indwelt by spirits and that they do have the secondary qualities we imagine is not as immutable as we would like to think.

Because an historian's conclusions employ concepts which probably do not correspond to reality and are justified by standards of inference which are probably not very reliable, it is reasonable to think that even those which are well supported by evidence do not provide an accurate account of the past. This is the worrying implication of the facts of cognitive relativism. (See McCullagh, 1984.)

What options remain open to us? As I see it, there are two. The easy way out is to deny that reality is independent of our beliefs about it and to affirm that, on the contrary, it is constituted by those beliefs. The only reality, on this view, is the reality we believe in. As our beliefs about reality change, so too does the reality we believe in. The past is constituted by historians' descriptions of it, according to this theory, and is changed with the changes warranted by historical research.

The most disturbing feature of this theory is that to avoid total scepticism it denies a very deeply held human conviction, namely our conviction that reality exists quite independent of anyone's beliefs about it. We cannot seriously believe, for example, that what has happened in the past can be altered by historians' discoveries in the present.

The alternative is to retain faith in the four empiricist assumptions despite the evidence of the falsity of all but the first, and justify that faith on practical grounds. As a framework of belief and knowledge, those assumptions have enabled us to relate very successfully to our physical environment, to predict and control it to our advantage, and to delight in it with awe and wonder. Faith in empiricist assumptions is not enough, I believe, for a happy life. The reality of human consciousness and the triune God must also be acknowledged. But empiricism is a part of our cultural inheritance which has been of such spectacular value in helping us to understand and control nature that it would seem foolish to abandon it. There is no better framework of beliefs about the world which we could adopt instead. It is not sensible to reject empiricist assumptions because of evidence that they are false when they have served us so very well in the past, and when we have nothing better to put in their place. In a philosophical context we may acknowledge that empiricist assumptions are inconsistent with the empirical facts of cognitive relativism. But for other practical purposes we should accept them as true just the same.

Assuming, then, that the empiricist assumptions are retained for practical reasons, we may reaffirm the conclusion that when historians produce reliable descriptions of the past it is reasonable to believe those descriptions true, in a correspondence sense.

2   The meaning of 'true'

Before concluding these introductory remarks it may be useful to explain briefly what is meant by calling an historical description 'true', in a correspondence sense. What does it mean to say that an historical description accurately portrays past events? Precisely what is being described when the description is of invisible beliefs, attitudes and social institutions?

In general terms it can be said that our descriptions of the world are conventionally related to sets of possible truth conditions, and that a description of the world is true if one set of its possible truth conditions does exist or has existed in reality. There are, for example, many possible sets of events which could be correctly described by the sentence 'Caesar's army crossed the Rubicon'. We have an idea of the range of possible meanings from our knowledge of the language. There are many ways the army might have crossed the river, and many points at which it might have crossed. The description is true if one of the many possible sets of truth conditions occurred in reality, that is, if what actually happened resembled one of the sets of events which are conventionally associated in our minds with the sentence (see O'Connor, 1975). The description would be false if none of its sets of possible truth conditions occurred in reality.

It is easy to see that although one might know an historical description to be true, one might not know precisely what events it describes. We might know from an honest and accurate eye-witness observer that Caesar's army crossed the Rubicon, but not know how or where it did so. The more brief and abstract the description, the less certain can one be of how it was instantiated. If all we knew, for example, was that Caesar overthrew the Roman republic by force and established a dictatorship, the range of ways in which this might have occurred is enormous and so our knowledge of precisely what happened would be extremely uncertain. To know that that statement is true would not involve a very detailed knowledge of past events. Rather it would be to know that one of a large range of possibilities was true.

There are several kinds of statements whose truth conditions it is especially difficult to specify. Some of these employ technical terms from law, politics, economics, sociology and so on, whose definition is the province of the relevant expert. Some are statements of an everyday kind whose truth conditions philosophers try to discover, such as past-tense statements, and negative sentences, like 'Napoleon Bonaparte did not die in France'. None seems to pose insuperable difficulties. It is true that an event occurred in the past, for example, if it occurred before other events which have been identified as present. A negative sentence is true if its positive equivalent is false: if, for instance, it is false that Napoleon died in France. The refinement of analyses like these is the work of philosophical logicians. (A good introduction to such analyses is Quine's *Elementary Logic*, 1965.) They unearth the understanding of truth conditions which we all display in knowing how to use such sentences correctly.

More uncertainty exists about the truth conditions of statements which make essential use of mental terms. Histories abound in statements such as these. Not only are there descriptions of people's beliefs, desires and values; there are also statements about political institutions and social structures whose truth depends essentially upon people's beliefs and attitudes. To describe someone as 'a dictator' in a certain society, for example, is to describe him as having the powers, rights and responsibilities customarily accorded a dictator. Having those rights and responsibilities involves having them respected by the people, and to say that the people respected them is to describe some of the people's beliefs and attitudes.

The truth conditions of statements which use mental terms is uncertain because it is not entirely clear whether mental terms refer to states of the mind, patterns of behaviour or structures of the brain. Philosophers are still debating the question. There is considerable unanimity, however, in agreeing that mental states, whatever they might be, are often expressed or otherwise manifest in verbal and non-verbal behaviour. Thus a person who, in an honest manner, says that Caesar became dictator, probably believes that Caesar became a dictator; and when Caesar had his own statue erected on the Capitol beside those of the seven previous kings of Rome, he clearly manifest his own belief in his sovereign authority. To say that a person had a certain belief or attitude, therefore, is to say at least that it would have been manifest in his or her behaviour on relevant occasions. The variety of ways in which a belief or attitude can manifest itself is enormous: Caesar exercised his assumed authority in a host of ways, and his subjects acknowledged it in many different ways as well. To say that a person had a certain mental state is not to say exactly how it was manifest, but often the reader can imagine many of the ways in which it might have been.

It can be seen that the possible truth conditions of many historical descriptions cannot be specified in detail, though people often have a rough idea of what they are. That is enough for them to have some idea of what the past must have been like if historical descriptions of it are true.

3   Justification of historical descriptions

The purpose of this inquiry is to discover the logical conditions under which people are justified in believing historical descriptions to be true. That certain pragmatic conditions are also essential to justify such belief, has already been explained. Without a practical reason for committing oneself to the truth of historical descriptions, one might rest with the knowledge that no matter how well supported they are, they are probably false, given the facts of cognitive relativism. From a practical point of view it is more reasonable to believe well-supported descriptions of the past than poorly supported ones, as the former are less likely to be falsified than the latter. From an empiricist viewpoint also it may be more reasonable to believe the former true, as they are more strongly implied by our observations of the present data than are the latter. If in fact the world is not at all as we perceive it or as we conceive and describe it, then well-supported descriptions might not provide more accurate descriptions of reality than poorly supported ones. But if, as normally happens, we accept all four empiricist assumptions as true for everyday and historical purposes, then there is reason to suppose that well-supported historical descriptions do get close to the truth.

The logical conditions which justify faith in the truth of historical descriptions are precisely those conditions which warrant us calling a description 'well-supported'. These conditions are commonly called 'justification conditions'. Singular descriptions, general descriptions and descriptions of causal relations all have their own sets of justification conditions, and an attempt will be made to state these in the chapters which follow.

Justification conditions are quite different from the truth conditions of historical statements. The truth conditions are states of the world which existed in the past, and so cannot be appealed to as evidence justifying historical descriptions. Justification conditions are reasons which we have at present for thinking historical descriptions true. Thus, for example, the truth condition of the sentence 'Captain Cook sighted Australia on 21 April 1770' is a past event in the world which corresponds to this description, the event of Cook sighting Australia on that day. The conditions which justify the statement, on the other hand, are documents, such as Cook's *Journals*, from which it may be inferred.

The justification conditions to be investigated are conditions which are rationally related to the claim that historical descriptions are true. There may be procedures of historical inquiry, 'historical methods' they are often called, which, if followed, are likely to yield true conclusions. Consulting Cook's *Journals* might be the most reliable method of discovering when he first sighted Australia, but the fact that an historical statement is the result of applying a reliable historical method does not always justify one in believing it to be true. For example, Cook recorded his sighting of Australia as occurring at 6.0 a.m. on 19 April 1770, and someone who consulted his *Journal* might be led to offer that as the correct date of the event. In fact, however, it is not, because Cook reckoned days in the nautical manner as beginning at noon, and because he had been sailing west from Europe and had not corrected his time since departing. For these reasons Ernest Scott put the date forward to 20 April (Scott, 1920, p. 34); and it could even be argued that it was the 21st. By following sound historical methods historians are more likely to produce descriptions of the past which are true than they would be if they did not follow them, but observance of these methods is not always enough to justify belief in the truth of the conclusions drawn as a result. The justification conditions to be examined here provide much better reasons for believing historical descriptions true than do the usual historical methods.

From a knowledge of the justification conditions of historical descriptions it is easy to see that certain general historical methods are useful in helping to elicit the information the historian needs to reach a justifiable conclusion. Some methodological recommendations thus might follow from the discovery of justification conditions. But useful historical methods are not the main topic of this investigation.

To answer the question 'When is an historian justified in saying that a description of the past is very probably true?', it will be necessary to adopt an approach to historical reasoning which is partly descriptive and partly critical. Historians over the centuries have become more and more discerning in their judgements about historical truth, and the standards of justification which they currently respect are often very high and clearly deserve close consideration. Occasionally, however, other interests besides an interest in truth lead historians to accept judgements as probably true without adequate reason. It is necessary, therefore, to examine historical practice critically in trying to answer our question. The grounds upon which historians in practice accept an historical description as true will not necessarily suffice to justify that acceptance.

Historical practice is one source of ideas about what would justify historical descriptions, and another source is the work of philosophers who have discussed the justification conditions of the kinds of statements historians make. Philosophers are far from being agreed about these, in most cases, but they have produced some interesting models of the sorts of argument which might justify the different kinds of historical descriptions. Although these models are often very helpful, they are sometimes inadequate, and both their virtues and their shortcomings will be described in our search for the highest standards of justification which historians could be expected to adopt.

The qualification added at the end of the last sentence is a rather inadequate excuse for the failure of this work to present forms of justification which would appeal to experts in probability and decision theories, logics of various kinds, and statistics. Some historians would probably be equipped to follow arguments in terms of these theories, but not many. Nor does it seem necessary that they should do so in many cases, with the one exception that expertise in statistics is now required for making some historical generalizations. In all other cases, the standards of justification to be recommended here seem to be adequate and are readily attainable, data permitting, by most historians. There is little doubt, however, that they could be further refined by experts in the appropriate branches of logic.

Some misgivings might be felt towards a study which considers the justification conditions of different kinds of historical description separately, and apparently does not recognize that the acceptance of the individual statements in a work of history depends to a large extent upon acceptance of the whole. Would it not be better to consider the conditions which determine the acceptability of whole works of history first?

In response to this question, several points must be made. The first is that the acceptability of a whole history depends much more upon the acceptability of the statements which compose it, than the other way round. The acceptability of the individual statements in a history depends upon whether or not they are adequately supported by the evidence. Certainly judgements about the truth of individual statements are constrained by other beliefs, themselves based upon evidence, so that, for example, if one document supports statements which contradict many others which are strongly supported, then the document might itself be judged unreliable. Historians certainly seek a coherent account of the subject they are studying. But they also require that its elements are strongly supported by the evidence, and more strongly supported than any other, incompatible, account of the same subject. For then their account is more likely to be true. So to understand the conditions for a whole history to be acceptable, one must first understand the justification conditions of its parts. In examining these justification conditions, due allowance will be made for the importance of individual historical statements cohering with other historical beliefs in judging their truth.

There is no doubt that an historian's evolving idea of the structure of the whole history he is producing directs his inquiry all the time. It directs him to look for evidence relating to matters which pertain to that overall structure, and when he finds that evidence, to concentrate upon its implications for the overall study he wishes to present. But the historian's idea of the overall structure of his work does not determine the truth of the inferences he draws from the data, if the historian is interested in truth. Rather, when the inferences he draws from his evidence yield information incompatible with the structure he had in mind, he does not deny the truth of the inference but modifies his conception of the structure of the whole. Thus an historian's respect for truth, or for intelligibility, constrains his choice of overall interpretation, and not vice versa. This is not the case, of course, when history is written for propaganda purposes. In those cases the overall thesis is preserved by ignoring or even destroying evidence which points to facts contradicting it.

The reason why an historian's idea of the general structure of an historical process is modified in particular contexts by the implications of historical evidence, and not vice versa, is that those general ideas do not have the status of universal truths, or even of limited scientific laws, but are no more than descriptions of patterns of change which frequently have occurred in slightly different ways on several occasions, and which might be repeated in the case in question. E. P. Thompson made the point by saying that

These concepts [of the historical process], which are generalized by logic from many examples, are brought to bear upon the evidence, not so much as 'models' but rather as 'expectations'. They do not impose a rule, but they hasten and facilitate the interrogation of the evidence, even though it is often found that each case departs, in this or that particular, from the rule.   (Thompson, 1978, p. 237)

It is a moot point how much variation from a pattern or 'expectation' can be tolerated before that pattern has to be abandoned and another one found. The support available for particular descriptions, by contrast, often warrants a high degree of confidence in their truth, much higher than the belief one is entitled to accord high-level generalizations about the course of history. It is more reasonable in many cases, therefore, to allow exceptions to a generalization than to abandon faith in a singular description.

B. C. Hurst (1981) has argued that historical evidence can never provide independent support for an historian's descriptions of the past because its interpretation is always dependent upon the narrative being written. His argument reduces to the observation that in deciding the historical significance of evidence, an historian must take into account other beliefs he has about the historical subject in question, and try to draw a conclusion consistent with those beliefs. Since those other beliefs will be very largely incorporated in the narrative the historian is writing, the historian's judgement about the implication of the evidence is not independent of the narrative to which it is thought to relate. For example, a 'fresco in Rome in the style of Fra Angelico is attributed to a follower or member of his studio, as Fra Angelico is known at the time of its painting to have been in Florence' (pp. 282-3).

Hurst describes historical inference as a process of forming hypotheses about the past which will fit with an historian's other beliefs about what was going on at that time. Selection of a hypothesis seems to depend entirely upon which best fits with other beliefs about the course of events at the time. What Hurst overlooks is how the hypothesis is arrived at in the first place. Why consider that a painting was produced by Fra Angelico or one of his school? Surely because it has observable, independently identifiable features which are believed to be characteristic of paintings by him or his followers. These features, together with general knowledge of their significance, make it very likely that the painting was created by him or one of his school. Thus historical conclusions can be drawn from evidence which is described without reference to the narrative being constructed by the historian. The fact that Fra Angelico was not in Rome at the time it was painted is a reason for thinking only that it was not the master but one of his pupils who produced it. Without the observable, independent evidence of the features of the painting, such a conclusion would scarcely be warranted.

Hurst could point out that our general knowledge about the origin of those paintings which in several respects resemble the painting in question is itself the product of an interpretation of the historical significance of all the paintings involved. That is true, and is a point which will be taken up later. Here it is enough to note that if the paintings in question did not have observable features in common, then the historical hypothesis about their common origin would never have been formed. It is not a myth to think that the initial descriptions of the evidence used by historians are independent of the hypotheses which they devise to explain them.

As this book springs from an interest in the truth of written history, it will examine the justification conditions of historical descriptions, but not the justification conditions of historical interpretations and explanations. Historical descriptions are true or false, but interpretations and explanations are only more or less adequate. They may include true or false descriptions, but as interpretations or explanations they are just more or less adequate. So it is only the justification of historical descriptions which will be studied here.

The kinds of conditions which warrant belief in the truth of historical descriptions, differ according to the kind of description involved. For convenience historical descriptions can be classified as of four kinds: singular descriptions, general descriptions, and statements about the causes and effects of historical events. The justification conditions for each of these kinds of descriptions will be considered in turn.

2

Justifying singular descriptions:
I Arguments to the best explanation

Singular statements are those which can be true of only one thing on one occasion, whereas a general statement is about a kind of thing or event which can have more than one instance. The things of which singular historical descriptions can be true are very varied: individuals, groups of people, material objects, institutions, states of affairs and events are all included.

The grammatical form of a sentence is not a sure guide in deciding whether it is singular or not. If the subject refers to a class, and not to the individual members of that class, it is singular even though it looks general. 'White-collar workers are more numerous than before' clearly refers to the class of white-collar workers, as it is nonsense to speak of individuals each being 'more numerous than before'. On the other hand if the subject of a sentence refers to individual members of a class, even though it appears to be about the class itself, it is general. 'The working class is better educated and housed than before' appears to be a singular statement, but in fact is general, being about the members of the working class, as it is nonsense to think of a class being educated or housed.

Even sentences whose subjects are named with a proper noun can be disguised generalizations. Consider the statement 'In the eighteenth century the British Prime Minister was a puppet of the Crown'. This appears to be a singular statement, about one political office in the eighteenth century. Its truth, however, depends upon the truth of a generalization like 'In the eighteenth century British Prime Ministers followed the wishes of the Crown, in order to retain their office'. We shall take singular statements to be those whose truth does not entail the truth of some corresponding generalization.

Should all statements attributing dispositions to individuals be regarded as generalizations? If dispositions are nothing but patterns of certain kinds of behaviour in certain kinds of context, then probably they should. If, on the other hand, some dispositions are real mental states or events, such as beliefs, motives and intentions, then statements ascribing them to individuals are singular. Rather than consider all the arguments in favour of each analysis, let us stipulate that dispositions of which the people who have them have or can have immediate knowledge are real mental states, but that others, like habits, are not, yet may be given a purely behavioural analysis. This is not to suggest that habits lack a cause, even a psychological cause. It is just to adopt a familiar ground for distinguishing those dispositions which we regard as mental states from those which we do not.

Statements about the causes and effects of events can be singular, stating for example that one event was a cause of another, or that one event was an effect of another. The justification conditions of descriptions of causal relations are more complicated than those for simple singular descriptions, however, which is why they will be discussed separately.

When a person sets out reasons which justify him in calling a description of the past 'probably true', one can say that the description can be inferred from those reasons. In the case of historical descriptions, as was pointed out in the last chapter, the inference never necessitates the conclusion, but just renders it credible to some degree. A theory about the kinds of reasons which warrant belief in the truth of an historical description, then, can be called a theory of historical inference.

Philosophers who have considered the nature of historical inferences to singular descriptions of the past, have put forward three main theories about them. The most popular theory in recent years has been that historical inferences are arguments to the best explanation of a body of available evidence. C. S. Peirce (1934) described historical inferences as being of this sort, and although R. G. Collingwood did not formulate such a theory explicitly, one of his models of historical inference, his story 'Who Killed John Doe?', exemplifies it (1946, Pt V, §3). Alan Donagan (1956) and Leon J. Goldstein (1962), reflecting on Collingwood's theory and practice of history, arrived at this account of historical inference. Arthur C. Danto (1965, ch. 5) and Murray G. Murphey (1973, ch. 1) have since adopted this theory almost without question.

The second main theory of historical inference has received little philosophical support in recent years, though it was the one which David Hume adopted when discussing the credibility of miracles (Hume, 1777). That is the theory that historians justify their descriptions of the past by estimating their probability, and showing that it is great. Such estimates of probability rely heavily upon statistical generalizations, and for that reason they may be called 'statistical inferences'. It will be argued that when historians calculate the probability of historical descriptions, they do not make use of Bayes Theorem (see pp. 57–8), but produce arguments which resemble C. G. Hempel's account of statistical inferences (Hempel, 1965, ch. 2).

The third theory of historical inference is the most recent of them all. It has been forcefully defended by L. B. Cebik (1978), and employed by Jonathan Gorman (1982). This can be called a criterial theory of historical inference, as it suggests that historical descriptions are justified if the criteria for their truth are satisfied.

There is a fourth theory of the nature of historical inference which must also be considered, which describes historical inferences as arguments from analogy. It will be shown that when arguments from analogy are successful it is because an argument of another sort has been provided or is assumed. Otherwise arguments from analogy do not warrant belief in their conclusions, and so are not a useful form of historical inference.

Each of the three main forms of historical inference can, under certain conditions, warrant a high degree of belief in the conclusions reached by it, as will be explained. Quite often, however, the conditions for their successful use in isolation are absent, and then they are used successfully in combination, to reinforce one another. Sometimes they are used alone, but quite often in combination.

Each of the three main theories of historical inference stresses a different aspect of historical knowledge, and can be related to well-known theories of justification. The theory that historical inferences are arguments to the best explanation would appeal to those who are interested in a holistic view of beliefs, emphasizing their coherence with one another as their most desirable feature. The theory that historical inferences are statistical inductions from well-established data, draws attention to a fairly solid foundation for historical knowledge, ultimately an empirical basis in the real world. Finally, the criterial theory focuses upon the important part played by linguistic conventions in justifying historical descriptions, which the other theories tended to overlook.

A study of instances of historical inference shows that all three forms of inference are used from time to time, separately and together. The aim here is to show that these forms of inference are capable of justifying belief in the truth of historical descriptions. To this end, each theory of inference will be described and illustrated in turn, and the conditions which justify belief in the truth of its conclusion will be specified as accurately as possible.

1 The nature of arguments to the best explanation

Most philosophers of history in recent years have said that the arguments by which historians justify their singular descriptions of the past, are some form of argument to the best explanation. Murray G. Murphey has asserted this most sweepingly: 'All historical inquiry arises from the attempt to provide explanations of some present phenomena ... The whole of our historical knowledge is a theoretical construction created for the purpose of explaining observational evidence' (Murphey, 1973, pp. 14, 16). It will become clear that these statements are not true. Although historians often try to explain observational evidence, they do not always do so. Sometimes they use evidence as the basis of inferences of quite different kinds, serving quite different purposes. Be that as it may,

Murphey's statements reflect the confidence with which it is currently believed that historical inferences are inferences to the best explanation.

Are inferences of this sort capable of justifying belief in the truth of historical descriptions? Sometimes they do, and sometimes they do not, as will be seen. The questions to be answered now, therefore, are, first of all, what are arguments to the best explanation, and second, when do they justify belief in the truth of their conclusions?

When philosophers have written about arguments to the best explanation, they have sometimes called them 'hypothetico-deductive' (e.g. McCullagh, 1977). This title, however, refers to only two features of arguments to the best explanation, and might give the impression that those two features are all that matter, which is wrong. The two features in question are those upon which Sir Karl Popper has placed so much emphasis in his descriptions of scientific inference, namely the formation of an explanatory hypothesis and the deduction, or inference, of testable consequences of that hypothesis (Popper, 1968, ch. 10). A hypothesis is explanatory, on this theory, if it enables one to infer the data to be explained. And it is acceptable, it is suggested, if none of its other implications is false. If two hypotheses are both unfalsified, Popper said, then one should prefer that which has the greatest explanatory scope, which is most open to falsification.

The simple theory of inference just stated does not describe inferences whose conclusions are always probably true. The basic reason for this is that the truth of the implications of a hypothesis does not entail the truth of the hypothesis itself. The logical mistake of assuming that it does is called 'the fallacy of affirming the consequent'. An example illustrates the mistake clearly. Sir Thomas More said that two little English princes, sons of King Edward IV, were killed at the instigation of Richard III, suffocated in their beds in the Tower of London and buried 'at the stair foot, meetly deep in the ground under a great heap of stones' (Kendall, 1955, pp. 398-9). In 1674 two skeletons were in fact discovered beneath a staircase in the precincts of the Tower, and some have thought that this establishes the truth of More's account. But P. M. Kendall, Richard III's biographer, shrewdly observed:

Can it be seriously argued that the discovery of the skeletons vouches for the essential reliability of . . . [More's tale] . . . simply because one detail [of it] seems to correspond with the truth? There were many staircases in the Tower. The correspondence may well be coincidence (which is often a weakness in fiction but is even oftener a condition of real life). (pp. 495–6)

There could be any number of explanations for the existence of those two skeletons. The fact that an historical hypothesis neatly accounts for some available evidence does not entail the truth of the hypothesis. There may well be another explanation of the evidence which is the true one, and which no one has as yet thought of.

A simple hypothetico-deductive form of historical inference, then, does not warrant belief in its conclusion. Can this form of inference be developed so that its conclusions are probably true? Perhaps arguments to the best explanation are the sort required.

A fully intelligible account of arguments to the best explanation cannot yet be given, as some of the concepts involved have proved very difficult to analyse. It can, however, be made sufficiently clear for present purposes. It might be useful to summarize it first.

The theory is that one is rationally justified in believing a statement to be true if the following conditions obtain:

(1)   The statement, together with other statements already held to be true, must imply yet other statements describing present, observable data. (We will henceforth call the first statement 'the hypothesis', and statements describing observable data, 'observation statements'.)

(2)   The hypothesis must be *of greater explanatory scope* than any other incompatible hypothesis about the same subject; that is, it must imply a greater variety of observation statements.

(3)   The hypothesis must be *of greater explanatory power* than any other incompatible hypothesis about the same subject; that is, it must make the observation statements it implies more probable than any other.

(4)   The hypothesis must be *more plausible* than any other incompatible hypothesis about the same subject; that is, it must be implied to some degree by a greater variety of accepted truths than any other, and be implied more strongly than any other; and its probable negation must be implied by fewer beliefs, and implied less strongly than any other.

(5)   The hypothesis must be *less ad hoc* than any other incompatible hypothesis about the same subject; that is, it must include fewer new suppositions about the past which are not already implied to some extent by existing beliefs.

(6)   It must be *disconfirmed by fewer accepted beliefs* than any other incompatible hypothesis about the same subject; that is, when conjoined with accepted truths it must imply fewer observation statements and other statements which are believed to be false.

(7)   It must exceed other incompatible hypotheses about the same subject by so much, in characteristics 2 to 6, that there is little chance of an incompatible hypothesis, after further investigation, soon exceeding it in these respects.

This list of conditions whose satisfaction is thought to make a hypothesis credible is quite a conventional one. Variations of it can be found in most descriptions of this form of inference. There are only two conditions which sometimes appear on other lists which are not included here. These are that the hypothesis should be simpler than any competing hypothesis, and that it should be of a greater degree of falsifiability than any other. There are several ways in which the requirement of simplicity can be interpreted (see Sober, 1975; and Hesse, 1974, ch. 10), and for ensuring the truth of singular historical descriptions the sort of simplicity required is the minimum of *ad hoc*ness. The less an historical hypothesis goes beyond what is already known, the more likely it is to be true.

Maximum falsifiability is a virtue in hypotheses which are generalizations, since it implies a maximum of explanatory scope and power, and often also a maximum of simplicity. Broad generalizations are usually simpler than narrow ones, because generalizations are made narrower in scope by having qualifications added to them. In singular hypotheses, however, maximum falsifiability, while certainly implying a maximum of explanatory scope and power, usually also implies a maximum of complexity and *ad hoc*ness. Scientific generalizations of great explanatory scope are credible if they have been tested in a variety of conditions and have not been disconfirmed. It then looks as though things really do happen in the world the way the generalizations say that they do. Complex historical descriptions, however, cannot be tested in anything like the same way. The fact that they are not falsified by available evidence by no means warrants the belief that they are true. Historical novels, which have been written carefully to conform to the relevant evidence, contain many such complex *ad hoc* explanations, which are certainly not regarded by anyone as true. In history, singular hypotheses are preferred which imply a larger variety of actual observation statements than any competing hypothesis, but they are not preferred if they imply a larger variety of materially possible, but not actual (or practically possible) observations. This is because in history, unlike some sciences, possible observations cannot be made actual by experiment. If the evidence for an event has not survived, there is no way of discovering it. Historians, therefore, prefer hypotheses which imply the very probable existence of more available evidence which will either confirm or disconfirm them than is implied by any competing hypothesis; but they do not prefer hypotheses which present a long *ad hoc* story accounting for a few observations, such that although the story could conceivably be confirmed or disconfirmed by a large number of observation statements, in fact the number of actual observations it implies is very small. The second condition on the list, of greater explanatory scope, should be interpreted in the first of these senses therefore, referring to actual rather than conceivable observations, and not in the second. And it is in that first sense that historians prefer hypotheses which are of greater falsifiability than others. They prefer hypotheses capable of being falsified by a large number of actual observations, not merely a large number of conceivable ones. There is no need to add this as a further requirement, for it is already expressed by the condition of greater explanatory scope.

Before discussing these conditions any further, we should perhaps help to make them more intelligible by illustrating them. The illustrations also help to bring out some of the points to be made in subsequent discussion.

One example which illustrates the conditions most vividly is discussion of the Christian hypothesis that Jesus rose from the dead. This hypothesis is of greater explanatory scope and power than other hypotheses which try to account for the relevant evidence, but it is less plausible and more *ad hoc* than they are. That is why it is difficult to decide on the evidence whether it should be accepted or rejected. Discussion of the resurrection hypothesis and of alternatives to it is very complex, however, and a simpler example has been chosen as more suitable for present purposes. (Many of the issues involved in deciding whether Jesus rose from the dead are clearly explained in Marxsen, 1970 and Evans, 1970.)

An interesting example of an inference to the best explanation is provided by Christopher Brooke's discussion of why William II (William Rufus) died, in his book *The Saxon and Norman Kings* (1963, pp. 178-96). William II died when he was shot by an arrow during a hunt in the New Forest in Hampshire on 2 August 1100. Brooke says that the two fullest accounts of the incident, by William of Malmesbury (*c.* 1125) and Orderic Vitalis (*c.* 1135), both declare that the arrow was fired by Walter Tirel, and that it was aimed at a stag and hit the king by accident. The truth of this story would help to explain both why those reports narrate it and why the king died, so we can take it as the first explanatory hypothesis to be considered. There are two quite reliable sources, however, which report Walter Tirel's denial that he killed the king, or indeed that he was in the same part of the wood as the king when he died. And since the king was generally judged to be a wicked man, Brooke believes Tirel would not have wished to deny that he had been God's instrument in killing him, if that had been the case and he had not murdered him deliberately. So Walter Tirel's denials cast doubt upon the truth of the hypothesis. As Brooke says: 'If William of Malmesbury was right in saying that the king and Walter were alone, only Walter could have told the story. Yet Walter firmly and frequently denied it. The contradiction is baffling' (p. 180).

A second, different, hypothesis has been suggested by Dr Margaret Murray in her book, *The God of the Witches*, and it is this which Brooke considers next. Chronicles of the king's death report many strange portents of its coming. The night before he died the king dreamed of his death, as did a monk; and it is said that St Anselm knew of it in France immediately by angelic messenger. Dr Murray thought the king was a devil worshipper, and attributed his death to witchcraft. Brooke comments: 'The cunning of Dr Murray's explanation is that it does, indeed, explain the warnings and prognostications, even the king's dreams. Everybody knew he was going to die! Unfortunately, her explanation involves a number of assumptions for which there is no evidence, and which are wildly improbable' (p. 181).

There is no evidence of William II's being a devil-worshipper or involved in witchcraft; it is possible that Luciferians existed in the eleventh century, since we have evidence of their rites in the twelfth century, though only in Germany which William did not visit. Brooke thinks the stories of portents surrounding the king's death are better explained as embellishments typically added by the ecclesiastical chroniclers to express their sense of divine judgement upon the man, at whose hands many of their houses had suffered. Brooke concludes: 'Her theory, in fact, can be dismissed as fantasy' (p. 185).

The third hypothesis is one which Brooke puts forward himself, namely that the king was murdered as a result of a conspiracy involving his younger brother and successor, Henry, as well as Walter Tirel. This would explain Henry's extraordinarily prompt action following his brother's death in seizing the royal treasure, which was conveniently close to the New Forest at Winchester, and then being anointed and crowned king in Westminster three days later, on 5 August. This was just a few weeks before his elder brother Robert returned from the First Crusade and sought the throne for himself. In Brooke's opinion such a quick coronation could hardly have been secured without preparation, and without a nucleus of supporters already formed. The conspiracy hypothesis also explains why Tirel's wife's family, the Clares, were so well patronized by Henry after he became king, and why many bishoprics and abbeys, previously retained by the crown, were bestowed upon the families of his supporters. Fear, or hope of favour, might even have moved the early chroniclers tactfully to overlook Henry's part in William II's death, if they knew of it. This hypothesis is consonant with Henry's known disposition to cruelty, and is itself perhaps explained by his declared belief that he deserved the crown rather than his brothers, since he alone had been born when his father was king. And finally, this hypothesis would explain why, although it was agreed shortly after William's death that Walter Tirel had shot him, Tirel himself denied any role in what he presumably knew to be a traitorous plot.

Thus the third hypothesis is contradicted by no observable data. It certainly explains more than the first, and seems less *ad hoc* than the second, so it is the one to be preferred according to the present theory. But Brooke is too good a scholar to think, as some philosophers of history would have him think, that the third hypothesis is therefore acceptable. 'The circumstantial evidence against Henry can be piled up; but of positive evidence there seems to be none. The verdict must be "non-proven" . . . The most we can say is this: if Rufus's death in August 1100 was an accident, Henry I was an exceptionally lucky man' (pp. 195, 196).

The seven conditions whose satisfaction warrant belief in the truth of an historical hypothesis help us to understand why Brooke preferred the third hypothesis, his own, ot the other two.

(1)   All those hypotheses explain the death of William II as it was reported by early chroniclers. The three hypotheses are incompatible, however. The first is that Walter Tirel shot the king by accident; the second is that he died (presumably by an arrow) because of witchcraft; and the third is that Tirel shot him deliberately as part of a conspiracy. Only one of these hypotheses can be true, though possibly none is.

(2)   *Explanatory scope.* Each hypothesis explains additional facts besides the report of the king's death. The first explains why William of Malmesbury and Orderic Vitalis recorded the details of Walter Tirel's action the way that they did; the second explains chronicled reports of 'the warnings and prognostications, even the king's dreams'; the third explains the promptness with which Henry secured the royal treasure and the throne for himself after King William's death, Henry's munificence to Tirel's wife's family, the Clares, and to other supporters shortly after ascending the throne, and even Tirel's denial of any involvement in King William's death. The third hypothesis explains three kinds of evidence, whereas the first two explain only one kind each, in addition to the death of King William.

(3)   *Explanatory power.* Although the first and third hypothesis imply the facts they explain quite strongly, the second does not. If King William did die by accident, as the early chroniclers said, then it is quite probable that they would have said so in writing their chronicles. And if his death was the result of Henry's conspiracy to seize the throne before the return of his brother Robert, then, too, the other facts about Henry's behaviour which Brooke describes were quite probable. But the king's being a devil worshipper, which is the second hypothesis, does not make it likely that he would have been killed by an arrow fired by Walter Tirel, or, more to the point, that his death would have been recorded in this way. There is no reason to think that the existence of devil worshipping and witchcraft made the king's accidental death at all likely.

(4)   *Plausibility.* The accounts of William of Malmesbury and of Orderic Vitalis make it to some degree probable that the first hypothesis is true, since chroniclers often tell the truth, but reports of Walter Tirel's denial that he killed the king by quite reliable sources, make the same hypothesis improbable. The first hypothesis, therefore, is neither plausible nor implausible.

As for the second hypothesis, a decision about whether the evidence which it explains also renders it probable to any extent, depends upon one's views of the occult. Do dreams and portents of events which subsequently occur make it likely that evil powers were at work, or not? If the answer is that they do, then the reports of those dreams and portents do confer plausibility upon the second hypothesis; but if the answer is negative, then the reports do not contribute to its plausibility. A belief that, quite generally, evil powers of the devil and of witches do not exist, would actually render the second hypothesis improbable, and so implausible, though this is not an argument Brooke uses. Instead he argues that as it is improbable that King William even met any Luciferians, it is also improbable that the King was engaged in devil worshipping, as the second hypothesis states. Brooke clearly judges the second hypothesis implausible, 'wildly improbable', for this reason.

The events which the third hypothesis explains do not make it at all probable. The fact that Henry I secured the throne quickly after William II's death does not imply that he conspired to murder him. The only facts which render this hypothesis plausible are Henry's known disposition to cruelty combined with his belief that he deserved the crown, though the likelihood that these would result in a conspiracy to murder is surely not great. Indeed the horror and danger of such a plot must render its existence somewhat improbable. Thus the third hypothesis is really no more plausible than the first.

(5)   *Ad hoc*ness. As none of the hypotheses is clearly rendered probable by the total available evidence, all must be regarded as *ad hoc*, specially created to account for reports of King William's death. It is tempting to say that the second hypothesis is more *ad hoc* than the others because it is so implausible, and that the third hypothesis is less *ad hoc* than the others because of its much greater explanatory scope. But that would be to confuse *ad hoc*ness with other characteristics of the hypotheses.

(6)   *Disconfirmation*. Brooke clearly believed that Tirel's denial of having shot the king 'contradicts' the first hypothesis. His argument is that if the first hypothesis were true, Tirel would have admitted killing him, and of having thus rid the world of a king who was generally judged to be wicked. This implication of the hypothesis is disconfirmed by the evidence, however, for reliable sources report Tirel's repeated denial of involvement in the king's death.

Brooke can point to no facts which disconfirm the second hypothesis, except perhaps the absence of any evidence of King William's involvement in devil worship or witchcraft. He is inclined to use this lack of evidence to emphasize the *ad hoc*ness of the hypothesis, as one which is implied by no known facts and 'can be dismissed as fantasy'. It could also be used to disconfirm the hypothesis, if it were believed that the truth of the hypothesis made probable the existence of some evidence in the chronicles of the king's reign of his involvement in devil worship and witchcraft. The absence of such evidence would then contradict this implication, thus disconfirming the hypothesis, or the additional assumptions about the knowledge and interests of the chroniclers.

Brooke mentions no facts which disconfirm the third hypothesis. Notice how Tirel's denial of involvement in the king's death, which might have been thought to be incompatible with his participation in the plot, is cleverly accommodated by extending the hypothesis in such a way as to demonstrate its compatibility. If there was a conspiracy, then Tirel would want to deny any part in it for fear of being charged with treason.

(7) *Relative superiority*. The third hypothesis is clearly superior to the other two on the criteria which have been described. It has much greater explanatory scope than they; it is not disconfirmed as the first is; and it is not implausible as the second is.

Why, then, does Brooke not accept that it is true? It may be observed that the third hypothesis does not so far exceed the others in all the conditions listed that it could not quite easily easily be proved false. One or two well-respected pieces of counter-evidence, such as a reliable report of Henry's grief and anger over his brother's death, plus a reported confession by Tirel, that he had denied shooting the king for fear of punishment under the law, the accident being such a remarkable one – these would be enough to make the third hypothesis less acceptable than the first. An historical hypothesis which could be so easily overturned does not deserve to be believed.

Brooke's own reason for refusing to affirm the truth of the third hypothesis, is different. It is that the evidence for that hypothesis is 'circumstantial' and not 'positive', so 'the verdict must be "non-proven"'. His meaning is clear. Although the third hypothesis implies, and thus explains, quite a lot of evidence about Henry's behaviour, the evidence of his behaviour does not itself imply the truth of the hypothesis. Evidence which is implied by a hypothesis but does not imply the hypothesis is circumstantial. Evidence which implies the hypothesis, is direct. The interesting question is, why do historians not regard circumstantial evidence as implying the truth of their hypotheses, and why do they prefer direct evidence?

The basic reason for historians doubting the value of circumstantial evidence is probably their awareness that there might well be other explanations of the data they are trying to explain besides the explanation they have suggested, and that one of these other explanations might well be the true one. (Examples of this argument are given by Karlman, 1976, pp. 44–9.) Just because an historian cannot think of any better explanation does not mean one does not exist. Kitson Clark has shown that this fact is also respected by courts of law. He said that a jury in Liverpool in 1931 condemned a man, George Henry Wallace, for murdering his wife because the prosecution's hypothesis that he had done so was not matched by any cogent alternative. However a Court of Criminal Appeal quashed that jury's verdict completely 'on the ground that there was insufficient positive evidence to support a conviction' (Clark, 1967, pp. 59–60).

Positive evidence, on the other hand, can give both the historian and the lawyer good reason for thinking that an explanatory hypothesis is true.

Taken together with an appropriate generalization, positive evidence implies the truth of a hypothesis in a way that circumstantial evidence does not. If Brooke had had a letter describing Henry I's conspiracy to murder William II and seize the throne, written by one of the conspirators to a friend, then assuming that people generally tell their friends the truth, especially if it is against themselves, Brooke could have inferred that his hypothesis was probably true. Without such evidence, however, he knows it to be a figment of his fertile imagination, and perhaps very far from the truth.

It looks as if arguments to the best explanation are not much more useful than simple hypothetico-deductive arguments after all. The same reason we have for doubting the truth of the conclusions of hypothetico-deductive arguments has turned out to be a reason for doubting the truth of the conclusions of arguments to the best explanation as well. Does superiority of an explanation in respect of conditions 2 to 6 not ensure its truth?

The short answer is that it does not, but if condition 7 is satisfied as well, that is if one hypothesis is so far superior to the others that can be thought of in respect of conditions 2 to 6, that there is virtually no chance of its being proved false soon, then it is reasonable to believe it true. In particular, if the scope and strength of an explanation are very great, so that it explains a large number and variety of facts, many more than any competing explanation, then it is likely to be true. There are some historical events which help to explain so much and such a variety of evidence that there is good reason to believe they could not be superseded by a better explanatory hypothesis. These are what Kitson Clark has called

'the public facts' of history, that is those facts which are so woven into the texture of human history that, unless human affairs are an illusion and all history is false, they are not false.
. . . For instance there can be no doubt that the battle of Waterloo was fought on Sunday, 18 June 1815, and there can be no doubt who won the battle. If the common opinion on either point was wrong then most of the history of Europe in the 19th century would be inexplicable, and a great many contemporary records which allude to the battle, describe the battle, or are concerned with the results of the battle would have to be rejected as spurious. (1967, pp. 41–2)

There can be no doubt that hypotheses whose explanatory scope and power far exceed that of any other incompatible hypothesis about the same subject are generally accepted as true. It is interesting to ask why this should be so. If such an explanatory hypothesis is not itself implied by the evidence it explains, then why should it be accepted as true of the world? One reason is that when such inferences are made about things which can be checked by observation, then they have often proved true. Thus faith in the reliability of this form of inference in yielding true conclusions has been reinforced. But the reliability of inductive procedures cannot be proved without assuming them. So it would not be irrational to ignore the conclusions of such arguments to the best explanation, if one denied the rationality of the form of argument. To ignore them would, however, leave one bereft of knowledge and understanding which could be useful, even if it cannot be proved true. It is better to accept the assumption commonly made that it is rational to believe that the conclusions of arguments to the best explanation which satisfy the stated criteria are correct descriptions of the world.

So far it has been shown that hypotheses of very great explanatory scope and power are accepted as true. Are the other criteria, about plausibility, *ad hoc*ness and disconfirmation relevant, and if so, why? The requirement that hypotheses should be as little *ad hoc* as possible is simply to keep to a minimum the number of statements in hypotheses which are not implied by known facts, and which are therefore more especially likely to be false. The fewer *ad hoc* statements a hypothesis includes, the less likely it is to be false. On the other hand, the more plausible the statements in a hypothesis are, that is the more they are implied by existing knowledge, then the more likely they are to be true.

*Ad hoc*ness and lack of plausibility are not reasons for thinking a hypothesis false, or at least they are not reasons for thinking it is more likely to be false than true. Implausibility and disconfirmation, however, can provide reasons for this conclusion. For a hypothesis to be implausible, our present knowledge of the world must imply that it is probably false. And for a hypothesis to be disconfirmed is for one of its implications to be false, which means the hypothesis itself is probably false. This latter point can be amplified thus. If a hypothesis (H) together with a number of auxiliary statements ($A_1 \ldots A_n$) imply a conclusion (C), and C is true, then H need not be true, because another hypothesis could be the true explanation of C. But if H together with $A_1 \ldots A_n$ imply C and C is false, then either H is false or $A_1 \ldots A_n$ are false. In these cases the auxiliary statements are usually beyond question, in which case H is probably false. Clearly historians wanting to establish the truth of a hypothesis have to take evidence which renders it implausible or which disconfirms it, very seriously, especially if the facts explained by the hypothesis are not very numerous.

There are two more questions which must be considered before this exposition of the nature of arguments to the best explanation in history is concluded. The first is about the relative weight given to conditions 2 to 6. In deciding the merits of explanatory hypotheses, are any more important than any others? The second is a worry about incommensurability. Paul Feyerabend has argued that often two explanatory theories cannot be compared because they do not account for the same set of observation statements. Is this so in history?

The conditions which bear upon the acceptability of arguments to the best explanation can be divided into three groups: those about the explanatory scope and power of a hypothesis; those about the *ad hoc*ness of the hypothesis; and those about facts which render a hypothesis implausible or which disconfirm it. There is a sense in which the third group is the most important. For even if a hypothesis is of greater explanatory scope and power than another, if evidence incompatible with it cannot be explained away satisfactorily, then it is abandoned. Historians simply assume, as do most people, that the world is logically and materially consistent, so that for beliefs about it to be true, they must refer to compatible events and states of affairs. The first group of conditions, about explanatory scope and power, are the next most important, for if two hypotheses are not implausible or disconfirmed, then even if one is more *ad hoc* than another, if it has greater explanatory scope and power it will be preferred.

Feyerabend has said (1975, ch. 17) that competing theories about the nature of the world cannot be compared because each theory provides the terms in which observations relevant to it are to be made, and so there is not any common domain of facts of which it can be said that one theory or hypothesis is a better explanation than another. This is occasionally the experience of historians, when one hypothesis is couched in the context of one world view, and a competing hypothesis in the context of another. Consider the hypothesis, for example, that Jesus had supernatural powers, over against the hypothesis that he did not. Someone urging the first hypothesis is clearly willing to admit the possible existence of such powers, and consequently is willing to interpret the reports of the miracles which Jesus performed as true. Some who deny that Jesus had supernatural powers might also be unwilling to admit the possibility of such powers existing, and consequently would not be willing to admit as relevant evidence any statements about miracles Jesus performed. So what constituted the prime domain of evidence for one historian could be almost entirely denied by another. It would seem that here is a perfect case of the sort of incommensurability which Feyerabend was discussing.

It is not the case, however, that every historical hypothesis brings with it a unique world view. On the contrary, most historical hypotheses are cast within the same, everyday world view. Important differences about what the data are which may be explained are confined almost exclusively to data relating to matters of religious belief. So hypotheses about non-religious topics are almost all commensurable – capable of being compared according to the criteria set out above by reference to a commonly accepted set of data.

The point can be confirmed by looking at cases where historical hypotheses about non-religious subjects are compared, and by noting that the different hypotheses do not reflect basic differences in what observation statements could possibly be admitted as evidence. Most historical hypotheses are expressed in terms of the one, everyday view of the world, which is very widely shared throughout the world. They are, therefore, readily comparable, and by no means incommensurable.

The criteria listed above are those whose satisfaction warrants belief in the truth of a hypothesis, but they do not exhaust the criteria one would list if instead of the truth of the hypothesis one wanted to judge its explanatory adequacy. To be adequate as explanations, hypotheses must also be of the right type – that is, they must refer to the kinds of facts which interest the investigator – and they must be such as to make the data being explained more plausible than some envisaged contrast state (see Scriven, 1966). These two conditions are in fact satisfied by most of the hypotheses judged acceptable by this form of inference, though, as was just remarked, their satisfaction has no bearing upon their truth.

The significance of counter-evidence

It may be of interest to divert for a moment and notice how historians often neutralize the significance of what appears to be counter-evidence. Take evidence which appears to disconfirm a hypothesis, first of all. There are three standard ways of neutralizing it. The first is to show that the hypothesis did not in fact imply a statement which is contradicted by the evidence; the second is to say that the interpretation of the evidence is mistaken; and the third is to find an explanation of facts implied by the evidence which is compatible with the hypothesis. Let us illustrate each of these methods in turn.

Historians do not very often mistake the implications of their hypotheses, but it can happen. R. H. Hodgkin (1952) argued that Cerdic founded the West Saxon kingdom in England at the end of the fifth century. Basing his hypothesis upon the account given in the *Anglo-Saxon Chronicle*, he said that Cerdic and his West Saxon friends landed near modern Southampton in Hampshire and moved north-west into Wiltshire, in which area their kingdom was finally established (see Collingwood, 1937, pp. 397ff.). In discussing this hypothesis, Hodgkin drew attention to 'the archaeological argument which is generally said to be fatal' to it, namely 'the remarkable dearth of heathen Saxon graves in Hampshire and their rarity in Wiltshire'. The heathen Saxons normally cremated their dead, but the graves found in Hampshire and Wiltshire are mostly of bodies which have been buried intact, not cremated. Hodgkin coped with this apparent disconfirmation of his hypothesis by arguing that the hypothesis did not imply that the Saxon graves in those counties would be of cremated remains, as had been widely assumed. For, he suggested, the early Saxons on their trip in Europe may have acquired the practice of burying their dead intact, from Britons or Christian Franks.

The Saxons in Sussex, he said, certainly did adopt this practice. Thus the presence of Saxon graves in Hampshire and Wiltshire containing people intact does not disconfirm the hypothesis about Saxon settlement there, but is quite compatible with it (Hodgkin, 1952, pp. 83–5, 131–2).

For examples of the next two ways of neutralizing evidence which appears to disconfirm a hypothesis, one can hardly do better than use Karlman's example (1976, pp. 40–1) of Jacob Burckhardt's defence of the hypothesis that the emperor Constantine was not a Christian. There is much evidence to suggest that Constantine became a sincere and conscientious Christian in A.D.312 (see Karlman, 1976, pp. 88, 93ff.). Burckhardt maintained the contrary in his book, *The Age of Constantine the Great* (1949). He disposed of some of the evidence to the contrary, for example reports of Constantine's habits of prayer and meditation, as 'contemptible inventions'. Instead of interpreting these reports as evidence of Constantine's religious life, Burckhardt interpreted them as fabrications by the author of the report, who in this case is presumed to have been Eusebius. The kind of interpretation involved here is an interpretation of the historical significance of the document.

The third way of coping with evidence which appears to disconfirm a hypothesis is to accept the veracity of the historical events which documents report, but to create an explanation of those historical events of a kind which is compatible with the hypothesis being defended. As Karlman has pointed out, Burckhardt explained away Constantine's public religious acts as motivated by political ambition rather than by Christian piety. Burckhardt wrote:

Before we proceed further we may briefly dispose of Eusebius' other reports of the alleged Christianity of his hero. After the war with Maxentius Christian priests always attended him, even on journeys, as 'assessors' and 'table companions'. At the synods he took his seat in the midst of them. *These facts are easily explained.* It was essential for Constantine to have intelligence of the viewpoints of the contemporary Church: he had his own informants who delivered reports on the individual sects . . . No clever and energetic ruler could let the praesidium of the synods out of his hands, for they were a new power in public life which it was unwise to ignore. One may deplore and condemn such egoism, but an intelligent power, whose origin is ambiguous, must of necessity act in this manner. (Burckhardt, 1949, pp. 298, 299)

It can be seen that these three ways of neutralizing the effect of apparently disconfirming evidence have much in common. Each involves creating an explanation of the evidence which is compatible with the hypothesis being defended. It looks as though, with sufficient ingenuity, almost any hypothesis could be rendered immune from disconfirmation this way. Bishop Whately (1819) once defended the hypothesis that Napoleon Bonaparte did not exist by explaining away evidence to the contrary. He was criticizing, in an amusing way, those who doubted the historicity of Jesus. Lakatos has explained how scientific theories can similarly be defended from falsification (Lakatos, 1970, pp. 100–1). Two questions immediately arise. When are such saving hypotheses, as we might call them, acceptable? And at what point is it reasonable for an historian to abandon a hypothesis in the face of apparently disconfirming evidence, rather than continue to protect it?

The answer to the first question is not difficult to find. When an historian offers a new explanation of a piece of evidence, to make it compatible with his hypothesis, he is suggesting that it is preferable to the old interpretation of the evidence under which it appeared to be incompatible with the hypothesis. The new explanation must, then, be compared with the old, and accepted if it is much superior to the old on the criteria set out above. It might not always be easy to decide. People's intentions are often particularly difficult to determine. How can one tell, for example, whether Constantine was sincere in his religious life or just acting to fulfil a political ambition? If the historian could find much evidence of religious behaviour which would not be explained as done for political advantage – evidence of private devotions, for example – that would give the religious hypothesis greater explanatory scope, perhaps, than the political one. This is why it was important for Burckhardt to dismiss evidence of Constantine's private religious life as invention.

There are cases, however, when the superiority of the new explanation is easy to judge. Marc Bloch (1954) has provided one, concerning a report by Marbot. The hypothesis in question was about the position of an Austrian army bivouac on the bank of the Danube on the night of 7 May 1809, during Napoleon's invasion of Austria, and about the state of the river that night. From many documents which exist – orders, records of march, reports of the opposing armies – it is known that the Austrian corps in question was bivouaced on the right bank of the river, and that the river was not yet in flood. But in his *Memoirs*, Marbot relates how he heroically crossed the river which was in full flood to free some prisoners of the Austrians from their camp on the left bank. As Bloch says: 'On one side, then, we have the *Memoirs*, on the other, a whole batch of documents which belie them. We must now decide between these conflicting witnesses' (p. 111). Clearly the original hypothesis, that the Austrians camped on the right bank and that the river was not in flood, is of much greater explanatory scope than the hypothesis that they were on the left bank and that the river was in flood, which explains only Marbot's witness. But can Marbot's account be reconciled with the first hypothesis? Only by supposing it was fabricated, to add to Marbot's glory. Is this hypothesis more acceptable than the hypothesis that he was telling the truth? It is, because the hypothesis that he was telling the truth is very implausible, there being so many reports implying the contrary, whereas the hypothesis that he invented the story implies a disposition which helps to account for other anomalies in his *Memoirs* as well. So the hypothesis that Marbot was telling the truth explains no more than his single report and is extremely implausible, whereas the hypothesis that he invented the story from an unprincipled desire for glory is not implausible and can be used to explain other facts as well. Clearly, then, the latter hypothesis is superior.

The ability of historians to defend their hypotheses by creating *ad hoc* explanations of evidence which appears to disconfirm them, is limited by the need to make those *ad hoc* hypotheses more acceptable, according to the recognized criteria, than the other interpretations given to the evidence. If this cannot be done, then historians are forced to admit that what had seemed to be a true hypothesis must be false. An example of this happening can be introduced by mentioning another swimming exploit reported by Marbot. J. M. Rose, in the first edition of his great *Life of Napoleon I*, described how Marbot swam into a lake (Satschan) near Tellnitz during the battle of Austerlitz to save a Russian officer from drowning. It was said that hosts of Russian soldiers had rushed across the icy surface of this lake to escape the French, but that many sank into it. Marbot, apparently, chivalrously saved one of them (Rose, 1919, vol. II, p. 41). The hypothesis that numerous Russians had drowned in the lake, though supported by an impressive variety of evidence, was proved false by the discovery that its observable implications were false. In the third edition of his book, Rose added the following note.

The account given . . . of the drowning of numbers of Russians at the close of the Battle of Austerlitz was founded upon the testimony of Napoleon and many French generals; the facts, as related by Lejeune, seemed quite convincing; the Czar Alexander also asserted at Vienna in 1815 that 20,000 Russians had been drowned there. But the local evidence (kindly furnished to me by Professor Fournier of Vienna) seems to prove that the story is a myth. Both lakes were drained only a few days after the battle, *at Napoleon's orders*; in the lower lake not a single corpse was found; in the upper lake [Satschan] 150 corpses of horses, but only two, some say three, of men, were found. Probably Napoleon invented the catastrophe for the sake of dramatic effect, and others followed the lead given in his bulletin. The Czar may have adopted the story because it helped to excuse his defeat. (Rose, 1919, vol. II, p. 50)

Clearly Rose believed that he could not easily explain away the testimony of those presumably disinterested people who examined the lakes after they had been drained, and since this was clearly incompatible with the implications of the hypothesis that many Russians had drowned there, that hypothesis was abandoned.

Imre Lakatos has suggested that in science one theory is not abandoned until another theory, of greater explanatory scope than the first, has been discovered (Lakatos, 1970, p. 116). Indeed he can think of no other rational grounds for giving up a theory, even if it has been disconfirmed conclusively, as the last example shows. Rose hinted at alternative explanations of the evidence which the original hypothesis had explained, but did not demonstrate their superiority before dismissing it as 'a myth'. It was the counter-evidence produced by Professor Fournier which, he said, 'seems to prove that the story is a myth', not the superiority of an alternative explanation of the original evidence. He only mentions possible alternative explanations of that evidence at the end, to show that the evidence could be interpreted differently.

2 The theory criticized

It was said in the last section that historical descriptions which satisfy all seven conditions listed above are descriptions which it is reasonable to believe true. It was also said that many facts of history deserve to be believed on this basis. Both these assertions have been seriously challenged, however, and the challenges must be considered. Murray G. Murphey, although opening his book *Our Knowledge of the Historical Past* declaring that historical inferences are all arguments to the best explanation, closed it with two chapters setting out gaps in historians' knowledge which are so severe that, he concluded, no satisfactory inferences to the best explanation are possible. Even if all the information necessary were available to produce inferences of this type, however, Sir Karl Popper and Imre Lakatos have argued that such inferences could never establish the truth of their conclusions. Popper's point is not one we have ever denied, but it bears further investigation. Murphey's arguments are much more disturbing, and they must certainly be considered very carefully.

Murphey's arguments against the possibility of an argument to the best explanation in history

It has been seen that for an explanatory hypothesis to be accepted as true, it must be possible to point out a large number of observation statements which it, together with some auxiliary assumptions, implies, and to observe that these observation statements are true. As Murphey remarks, if historical descriptions are explanatory hypotheses, one would 'expect historians to be engaged in deriving predictions from their "theories" and in testing these predictions against systematically collected data' (Murphey, 1973, p. 134). But, Murphey goes on, that is not what historians appear to do. Indeed, he argues, they cannot do this, because they cannot derive observation statements from their hypotheses about the past. And they cannot do this, because they do not know any generalizations which would enable them to predict what evidence of past events at present exists; and even if they did know of any, they could not prove that the generalizations were true.

To elaborate a little, Murphey says that to predict what evidence now exists of some past event, one would need to know generalizations about (i) how people interpret and respond to the situations they witness; (ii) under what conditions they will record descriptions of those situations or leave a record of their responses to them; and (iii) when the records will be preserved. Murphey admits that although there are no universal laws about these things, there are some limited historical generalizations which historians can use to predict the present existence of records or traces of events described in their hypotheses. We know that certain societies have regularly recorded births, marriages and deaths in certain ways; and that many institutions, especially those relating to the judicial, legislative and executive arms of governments, have regularly recorded their decisions and sometimes even their deliberations in certain ways. However, Murphey goes on, generalizations like these are of limited use. For many historical hypotheses are designed to account for documents such as comments in journals and letters whose existence could hardly be predicted from the hypotheses themselves (p. 144). And the preservation of documents over any appreciable length of time can be affected by so many chance conditions that it really cannot be predicted either (p. 146). 'Accordingly, no historian formulates his endeavour in terms of testing hypotheses by deriving from those hypotheses consequences concerning what should be observed in the data. The chances are that the predicted observations cannot be made' (p. 147). Or, to put it more accurately, the chances are that the predictions cannot be made.

It would seem, then, that, if historians do justify their descriptions of the past, it cannot be by means of an argument to the best explanation. This, however, is not the conclusion which Murphey immediately draws. Rather, he comments that instead of beginning with a hypothesis and then looking for data implied by it, historians usually begin with data and form hypotheses specifically to account for them (p. 148). Historical theories 'are usually of an *ex post facto* character' (p. 152). Having formulated a hypothesis in this manner, an historian might then look for further evidence implied by it. But to begin with, historians restrict the hypotheses they form to ones which account for data already known to them.

Even if this is how historians form their hypotheses, the question still remains as to whether it is possible for the existence and character of the evidence which those hypotheses are designed to explain to be inferred from them? Consider an example Murphey uses. Helen Morgan was able to reconstruct what took place in Virginia's House of Burgesses on 30 and 31 May 1765, because a French traveller happened to visit the House on these days and leave an account of its proceedings in his journal. Apparently no other record of the proceedings is available. But does Morgan's reconstruction entail the record upon which it is based? As Murphey admits, it was pure chance that the traveller was there and recorded what he witnessed. (Vernon Dibble has avoided this difficulty by interpreting the inference from the traveller's journal to the events in the House of Burgesses as statistical. See Dibble, 1963, pp. 205–6.)

The possibility of arguments to the best explanation being confirmed is not retrieved simply by pointing out that they are of an *ex post facto* character. In concluding his chapter Murphey hints at a solution in the following sentence: 'Any historical theory must contain within itself the principles necessary to relate the events and objects postulated in the theory to the observations which serve as the evidence for the theory, and this involves an immensely complex structure of rules' (pp. 152–3). But can such rules even be formulated, with any plausibility? What rules would relate the activities of Virginia's House of Burgesses in 1765 to the note-taking of a French traveller? Is there any rule by which the former will entail the latter?

Murphey is perhaps unwilling to pursue this question further because he is anxious to point out, in the following, concluding chapter, that even if appropriate rules could be formulated, there is no way they could be confirmed. Historians sometimes do refer to generalizations relating their hypotheses to their data, he says, but 'although they believe them to be true, they cannot prove them to be so'. He explains: 'We may distinguish five methodological problems which beset the historian in his efforts to confirm law-like statements – the problems of quantity, aggregation, sampling, informant bias, and measurement. Of these, the first two are the only ones for which there is at present much hope of a solution' (pp. 155–6). Since the generalizations by which historians might relate their hypotheses to their data cannot be proved, it seems that we cannot tell whether those hypotheses really explain the data or not. Murphey concludes: 'It seems clear that historians are unable to use the methods or meet the standards for the confirmation of hypotheses and theories which are prevalent in the contemporary social sciences, and . . . this inability is a function of the character of historical data and of the problems respecting confirmation which they generate' (p. 205). In Murphey's opinion, then, even if an argument to the best explanation could be formulated, it could not be confirmed.

Murphey's critique of the possibility of justifying historical descriptions by means of an argument to the best explanation is so impressive, that it makes one wonder whether this is a commonly used form of justification after all. It has already been noted that Vernon Dibble interpreted the inference from the French traveller's diary about the events in the House of Burgesses as statistical in form, and it will be argued later that this is a much more common form of inference in history than philosophers have recently admitted.

The only way in which one could defend the possibility of justifying many historical descriptions as providing the best explanation of the evidence which supports them, is by adopting a model of explanation different from that assumed by Murphey. As Murphey repeatedly admits, he likens historical inference to scientific inference, and so has viewed historical explanations as like those which C. G. Hempel called 'deductive-nomological' or 'inductive-statistical' (Hempel, 1965, ch. 12). These are explanations in which statements describing events to be explained are inferred from statements about antecedent conditions by means of universal or statistical laws. There is, however, another view of the nature of historical explanations which has developed in contrast to Hempel's models, and this sees historical explanations as characteristically describing a process of historical change. Processes are typical sequences of events. Let us suppose, then, that when historians explain observable data, they do so by describing some historical processes, usually a sequence of processes, which resulted in its being where and as it is.

The two kinds of explanation can be illustrated by using Murphey's example of the French traveller's journal notes for 30 and 31 May 1765. Murphey knew that these had been used to infer events in the House of Burgesses in Virginia on those dates. Assuming (i) that the form of inference was an argument to the best explanation, and (ii) that the form of explanation was according to Hempel's models (see Murphey, 1973, ch. 3), he naturally expected there to be a law or generalization which related the events in the House to the existence and contents of the journal. But he could think of none, none at least which could be confirmed. A different way of explaining the existence and content of the journal would be by postulating a series of historical processes. The first process would be of the French traveller who wrote the journal visiting the House of Burgesses in Virginia on 30 and 31 May 1765, witnessing the proceedings there, understanding them according to his ability and, according to habit, faithfully recording them in his journal. The second process would describe how the journal was preserved over the years, until it ended up wherever it now is, unaltered since the day it was written. The decisions to store the journal safely, to pass it on to descendants, and to put it in a library, were probably made for sensible reasons. So the links in the process are often supplied by rational explanations, sometimes by generalizations about a person's habits, but almost never by generalizations of the sweeping scope envisaged by Murphey.

It is true that historians seldom spell out explanatory hypotheses in terms of processes like this. But often they have investigated the history of their documents, which suggests that that is important in judging their significance. Indeed if the process relating the events described in a document and its present content and existence is found not to be as assumed, and a different causal history of the document is found to be true, then the document may no longer be taken to be evidence of the real existence of events it describes. There is, for example, a document known as 'The

Diary of a Public Man', which describes events supposed to have occurred in Washington between December 1860 and March 1861. When it was found to be a hoax written by one Sam Ward, then even though some of the facts it describes are known to be correct, 'yet for the historian [of that period] – except the one who writes Sam Ward's biography – the document is worthless' (Barzun and Graff, 1970, p. 126).

The analysis of historical processes is a subject deserving careful research. It seems that their logical structure is like that of 'genetic explanations', as Hempel called them (1965, pp. 447–52). To an initial situation are added further facts which, taken together with that situation, are sufficient to cause another situation, and so on. The transition from one situation to the next can be mediated by rational as well as other kinds of causal explanation. But there is more to processes than this, it seems. Quite often they exemplify typical patterns of change, though how often this is so, is hard to decide; how typical the patterns of change are is hard to decide too. Still, enough should have been said about them by now to give a rough idea of the kind of explanatory hypotheses historians provide when they justify a singular description of the past by means of an argument to the best explanation.

Once a process explanation has been offered for one event or piece of evidence, it can be extended, by the addition of further processes, to explain more data. Recall Brooke's hypothesis that William II was deliberately shot by Walter Tirel as part of a conspiracy by Henry I to seize the throne before the return of his brother, Robert. This story accounts for the ancient reports of Tirel's shooting the king, and by adding a sub-plot about Tirel's fear of being charged with treason, it also accounts for his repeated denials of involvement. One of the virtues of the hypothesis, however, is that it also helps to explain Henry's immediate securing of the royal treasure, his quick coronation, and his beneficence to the Clares and other supporters. How does it explain those things? Not by means of a generalization relating a conspiracy to kill the king with those events. There are no such generalizations. It explains those events by being easily extended to include them. If Henry did want the throne, then how reasonable of him to have behaved in those ways in the circumstances. Thus a part, that is one statement, of the original explanation, when taken together with other statements believed true of the period, yields new processes which account for more facts.

The generalizations which mediate the stages of process explanations are of various kinds. There are some generalizations about habits of rational thinking, relating beliefs, goals and actions, which will be set out later; there are some generalizations about the dispositions of individuals or groups of people; some about institutional customs of various sorts; and even some physical laws. Most of these are much narrower in scope than the sorts of generalizations Murphey was considering, being true of only individuals or groups of people, or about customs within individual institutions. Often these are quite well confirmed by known data. When they are not, the explanatory power of the hypothesis is weak. Thus singular historical descriptions may be justified by arguments to the best explanation, but those arguments do not have the logical structure which Murphey had imagined.

Are the conclusions of arguments to the best explanation probably true?

Sir Karl Popper and Imre Lakatos have been at great pains to explain that we have no reason to think that just because an explanatory hypothesis has proved superior to others which were designed to explain the same data, that it is true, probably true, or even closer to the truth than they. As has been said before, one cannot prove that the inductive procedures we commonly respect do generally yield true results, so one has no reason for saying, on any particular occasion, that the use of one of them will yield a true conclusion.

Popper said: 'Our science is not knowledge (epistēmē), it can never claim to have attained truth, or even a substitute for it, such as probability . . . *We do not know: we can only guess!*' (1968, p. 278). Even if a hypothesis satisfies all the criteria, it could still be false. As Lakatos has reminded us, even Newtonian physics, a theory which explained so much that it seemed bound to be true, was superseded by Einstein's theories, so that 'now very few philosophers or scientists still think that scientific knowledge is, or can be, proven knowledge' (Lakatos, 1970, p. 92).

Popper's opinion about our ability to know the truth of scientific theories has been sometimes obscured by his talk of 'verisimilitude'. He described the relative proximity of two theories t_1 and t_2 to the absolute truth in terms of their 'verisimulitude', which is a function of their truth-content and their falsity-content. This in turn is a function of the classes of true and false statements entailed by the theories. If one theory entails more true statements and fewer false statements than another, then its verisimilitude is greater, and it is closer to the absolute truth, said Popper (1963, ch. 10). This may be so, but it is no reason to think that a theory which entails more propositions believed to be true and fewer believed to be false is closer to the truth than another. For when a few more observations are made, it may be that what was previously the better-confirmed theory becomes the less well confirmed. Even if the absolutely true theory is a theory confirmed by all possible observations in the universe, as Popper believes (1974, vol. II, p. 1106), the degree to which a theory is at present confirmed is no indication of its approximation to such an ideal theory.

Popper does not always make this fact entirely clear. For example, having explained the notion of verisimilitude, Popper asked 'How do you know that the theory t_2 has a higher degree of verisimilitude than the theory t_1?' He replied: 'I do *not* know – I only guess. But I can examine my guess critically, and if it withstands severe criticism, then this fact may be taken as a good critical reason in favour of it' (1963, p. 234). In favour of its being what? Of greater verisimilitude, one supposes, or why did he introduce the concept? But this conclusion is not warranted. All that a critical examination of the theories would yield, would be a judgement about what Popper calls their 'empirical content', which is roughly speaking their explanatory value (see the six criteria for determining empirical content, ibid., p. 232), not their degree of verisimilitude.

If there is no good reason to think the hypotheses which are proved to be the best explanations at a certain time are true, then the question arises, what reason is there for assuming that these hypotheses are true in preference to any other description of the past we may care to make? If satisfying the seven criteria set out above does not establish the truth of historical descriptions, what merit, if any, is conferred upon those historical descriptions which satisfy them?

There is no doubt that hypotheses which are superior on the basis of the seven criteria listed will be more closely integrated with our existing beliefs about the world than those which are inferior. Historical descriptions designed to explain some facts about observable evidence, at least those descriptions which have been considered here, have gone beyond our present beliefs about the world, suggesting new descriptions of historical processes which may be true. The seven criteria ensure that those explanatory descriptions we finally adopt are more closely related to our existing beliefs than any others which can be thought of. Inconsistencies, introduced by hypotheses which are implausible or disconfirmed, are to be minimized, indeed to be eliminated by being explained away if possible. Novelty, in the form of *ad hoc* hypotheses, is to be kept to a minimum. And the preference given to hypotheses of greatest explanatory scope and power is to ensure that those which are accepted have as many and as strong logical ties with present beliefs about the world as possible.

The seven criteria thus minimize the chance of an explanatory hypothesis being accepted which is inconsistent with existing beliefs. But doing that does not ensure its truth, nor even provide reasons for holding it to be probably true. According to the traditional view, the conclusion of an argument to the best explanation is not rendered probable by the data it explains. Popper was adamant about this, and presented this form of argument as a substitute for Humean verificationist (as opposed to falsificationist) forms of induction.

Despite Popper's arguments, there does seem to be a convention that hypotheses for which there is a large amount of circumstantial evidence, and which satisfy the seven criteria, may be accepted as true. This does not mean that they will never be abandoned – the convention of accepting them as true is not as conservative as that (see Lakatos, 1970, pp. 104–5 on conservative conventionalism). But they are not abandoned until either decisively disconfirmed by data which cannot reasonably be explained away, or until new discoveries make a different, incompatible explanation superior to it.

What justification is there for this convention? It is hard to be sure. The most obvious justification is the fact that in many cases, hypotheses which have been accepted because they satisfy the seven criteria are confirmed, rather than disconfirmed, by further observations. Charles Darwin presented his hypothesis about the evolution of species by natural selection as the best explanation of a number of accepted facts, and he defended this form of argument by saying that it regularly yielded reliable conclusions in everyday life. In the sixth edition of *The Origin of Species* he wrote:

It can hardly be supposed that a false theory would explain, in so satisfactory a manner as does the theory of natural selection, the several large classes of facts above specified. It has recently been objected that this is an unsafe method of arguing: but it is a method used in judging of the common events of life, and has often been used by the greatest natural philosophers. (Darwin, 1872, p. 476)

There is no doubt that belief in the regular reliability of arguments to the best explanation does much to persuade people that it is reasonable to accept the conclusions of such arguments as true. But it is doubtful whether such reliability of those conclusions, allowing it to be a fact, constitutes a good reason for the practice of accepting the conclusions as true. The worry is that the argument presupposes what it is trying to prove. The argument employs the generalization that the conclusions of arguments to the best explanation are usually reliable, from which it follows that the conclusion of any particular instance of such an argument is probably reliable. But how is the generalization itself justified? It may be justified as the best explanation of all the instances of which it is true, in a characteristically Popperian manner. In that case the generalization is not a good reason for the reliability of arguments to the best explanation, for it presupposes their reliability. On the other hand, the generalization might be justified by some principle of enumerative induction, as warranted by the number of cases of which it is true and the few of which it is false. Without an argument to the best explanation to fall back on, however, the principle of enumerative induction cannot be proved reliable, so the justification it provides is limited. It seems that the reliability of good arguments to the best explanation in yielding true conclusions is something we just accept. Once we have accepted it, we then use it as Darwin did, to justify faith in the truth of the conclusion of a particular argument to the best explanation.

Are all historical inferences arguments to the best explanation?

At the beginning of this chapter it was noted that several philosophers believe all historical inferences are arguments to the best explanation.

Murray G. Murphey clearly does, Alan Donagan appears to, and, for all he has said, Arthur Danto does as well. Leon Goldstein has written in a similar vein in the past, though more recently he has cast doubt upon the thesis (1976a, pp. 202ff.). The belief that all historical inferences are arguments to the best explanation has not been systematically defended, though a number of arguments have been put which can be marshalled in its defence. None of these, however, is sufficient to establish its truth, as will shortly be seen. Indeed there are good reasons for thinking it false.

The prevalence of the belief that all historical inferences are arguments to the best explanation is very largely the result of attention paid to R. G. Collingwood's writing on historical inferences, both in the essay entitled 'Historical Evidence', published in *the Idea of History* (1946) and in his little book, *An Autobiography* (1939). Both Alan Donagan and Leon Goldstein's early expositions of the logical structure of historical inferences drew upon Collingwood's work (Donagan, 1956; Goldstein, 1962). Although Collingwood did not call historical inferences 'arguments to the best explanation', from his discussion and examples it is clear that his understanding of these inferences approximated quite closely to this form.

Collingwood called the historical inferences of which he approved 'scientific', contrasting them with the methods of 'scissors-and-paste history' and of 'critical history'. The earliest historians, said Collingwood, were content to record the reports of events by contemporaries, or near-contemporaries, whom they regarded as 'authorities', and to discard all other accounts as unreliable. This form of historical writing Collingwood called 'scissors-and-paste history'. In response to criticism by Descartes and others, in the seventeenth and subsequent centuries historians refrained from using reports by contemporaries until their credibility had been established. Instead of their 'authorities', historians now spoke of their 'sources'. This stage Collingwood called that of 'critical history', though he observed 'that it was still only a form of scissors and paste' (1946, p. 259) since critical historians, like their forbears, restricted their histories to excerpts from reliable sources, and rejected the statements of those they judged unreliable as useless. 'Scientific history' Collingwood thought to be superior to scissors-and-paste history in two important respects. First, it enables the historian to go beyond the testimony of past witnesses, to discover hitherto unsuspected implications of available evidence. By inquiring about the origins of his evidence, an historian is often able to discover more about the past than the evidence itself reports. As he has explained in *An Autobiography*, the 'scientific' form of inference is one which he used successfully as an archaeologist, as well as in teaching the history of philosophy, and which he interpreted by what he understood to be Francis Bacon's method of questioning nature in order to discover new scientific truths about it

(1939, pp. 30, 80–8, 107–9; and 1946, pp. 269–82). This method of inquiry he also found to be exemplified by detectives, who do not rest their case simply upon the reports of reliable witnesses, but ask of all the reports which come their way '"What light is thrown on the subject in which I am interested by the fact that this person made this statement, meaning by it what he did mean?"' (1946, p. 275). In expounding Collingwood's theory at this point, Donagan has said that the questions put by the investigator – be he scientist, historian or detective – are designed to elicit hypotheses which would account for the data being questioned (Donagan, 1962, pp. 150–4, and ch. 8). The examples provided by Collingwood make it clear that this is how he considered scientific history to be written. One example takes the form of a detective story entitled 'Who killed John Doe?', and in it Detective-Inspector Jenkins formulates a coherent set of hypotheses to account for all the reports and all the data he has received. When he discovers further evidence implied by one of the hypotheses, he becomes convinced of its truth. In his autobiography Collingwood has given other examples of this method of inquiry. He reports how he toyed with different hypotheses to account for the ugliness of the Albert Memorial (1939, pp. 29–30), and later how he conjectured upon the purpose of the Roman Wall between Tyne and Solway (pp. 128–30), and upon the reasons Caesar may have had for invading Britain (p. 131). There are several other examples drawn from his study of Roman Britain as well. Each example resembles an argument to the best explanation.

The second feature of 'scientific history' which appealed to Collingwood was the certainty of its conclusions. Critical historians, he argued (1946, pp. 261–2), having judged a source to be reliable, nevertheless cannot be absolutely certain about the truth of the statements it contains. They must adopt the view that 'historical inference . . . is never compulsive, it is at best permissive; or, as people sometimes rather ambiguously say, it never leads to certainty, only to probability'. But 'scientific' historians have often produced 'an historical argument which left nothing to caprice, and admitted of no alternative conclusion but proved its point as conclusively as a demonstration in mathematics' (p. 262).

Although some historical inferences of the kind Collingwood called 'scientific' do have the two merits he ascribed to them, of going beyond the testimony of the evidence and of yielding conclusions of which we can be certain, not all have, and even if they all had, that is no reason for denying that there might be other forms of historical inference which have those merits as well. Many of Collingwood's own inferences yielded conclusions of which he was not entirely certain. For example, in *Roman Britain* Collingwood argued convincingly that the best explanation of the physical features of the ditch or Vallum which ran beside Hadrian's Wall from Tyne to Solway was that it had been constructed by the financial branch of the Roman administration to force traffic across the border to use occasional causeways where Roman customs officers could collect dues. Although Collingwood made this hypothesis convincing, he denied that he had proved its truth. 'There is no proof that this explanation of the Vallum is correct', he wrote, 'All that can be claimed for it is that it fits the facts' (Collingwood, 1937, p. 134). All arguments to the best explanation go beyond the testimony recorded in the evidence, but far from all yield certain conclusions.

What is more to the point, the merits which Collingwood ascribed to 'scientific' inferences are attached to other forms of inference as well. In particular, statistical inferences will be seen to go beyond the testimony provided by evidence, and sometimes to yield conclusions quite as certain as those of arguments to the best explanation. It is not the case that the only good historical inferences are arguments to the best explanation.

Donagan has objected to the suggestion that historians use generalizations to infer facts about the past by pointing out that the generalizations themselves cannot be arrived at without some historical knowledge – knowledge of previous instances of them – so that historical knowledge must be attainable without resort to any generalizations, assuming that it is attainable at all (Donagan, 1962, p. 176; 1975, pp. 83–5). This argument is quite reasonable; but Donagan takes it as implying that no historical inferences can be mediated by generalizations. 'What then is the characteristic method of history? Its negative characteristic has already been established: it does not presuppose that the acts it investigates can be subsumed under universal formulae or laws of nature' (1962, p. 176). He goes on to suggest that historical inferences are hypothetico-deductive in form, and that to infer the implications of the hypotheses they conjecture, historians do not use general laws, but only generalizations which are analytic truths 'about what historical agents will do in certain situations in virtue of what they think', or which are logically implied by 'propositions about what historical agents think' (1962, p. 191; see also, Donagan, 1964).

That the generalizations relating historians' hypotheses to the data they explain are of these kinds may well be doubted, as will be seen later. For the moment what it is important to notice is that it does not follow from the fact that some historical beliefs must be acquired without reference to laws, that all must be. Once historians have acquired some general knowledge, then they can often use it to draw conclusions about the significance of evidence available to them, and to infer causes or effects of known historical facts. Examples of such inferences will be given in the next chapter.

The final reason why philosophers have presented all historical inferences as arguments to the best explanation is that by doing so they depict historical inferences as being similar in logical form to scientific inferences, as these have been described by Sir Karl Popper, T. S. Kuhn, Imre Lakatos and others. Philosophers of science say that scientists discover facts about the world by constructing laws and theories which will best explain the observational data available to them. Several philosophers of history believe that historians do just the same. In discussing one of Collingwood's explanatory hypotheses, for example, Donagan remarked that Collingwood 'claimed for this conclusion exactly what a natural scientist would claim for an hypothesis that satisfied all the experimental tests he could devise' (1962, p. 183). Danto compared historical and scientific knowledge at much greater length, observing that historical descriptions organize and explain both chronological data (in a way that chronicles do not) and documentary evidence available to the historian (Danto, 1965, pp. 79–82, 94–102). Murphey, who stated in the most explicit and unqualified way that all historical inferences are arguments to the best explanation, has also been the most blunt in likening historical inferences to scientific ones. 'What I wish to maintain is that George Washington enjoys at present the epistemological status of an electron: each is an entity postulated for the purpose of giving coherence to our present experience, and each is unobservable by us' (Murphey, 1973, p. 16).

There is a hint of an argument here, to the effect that historians, like scientists, are trying to discover what is unobservable, and that consequently their arguments must resemble those of scientists, or at least they should if they are to be intellectually respectable. The argument is invalid, however, for it overlooks the possibility of other forms of inference being capable of yielding conclusions about what is unobservable, besides arguments to the best explanation. Statistical inferences can and are used by historians for this purpose, and they are in no way rationally inferior to arguments to the best explanation. Scientists who postulate hitherto unknown entities to explain observable events cannot use statistical inferences to infer the existence of those entities, for they have no generalizations relating such entities to such events. Historians, on the other hand, usually explain their data by referring to fairly common, familiar things in the world about which there is quite a lot of general knowledge. (Scientists sometimes do so too – geologists provide many examples.) Historians can therefore use statistical inferences to discover facts about things which are not observable, whereas many scientists cannot. Historians only employ arguments to the best explanation when they lack the general knowledge which would permit them to infer what they want to know directly from evidence in hand.

There is, then, no good reason for thinking that all historical inferences are arguments to the best explanation. Indeed there are very good reasons for thinking that they are not. For many historical inferences are statistical in form, and as shall be shown, these are not the same as arguments to the best explanation.

3

Justifying singular descriptions:
II Statistical inferences

1   The form of statistical inferences in history

It is strange to have to demonstrate that some historical inferences are statistical in form, given that so many of them are, and given that in philosophy of law it goes without question that the implications of testimony are normally discovered by statistical inference. (On use of such inferences in legal contexts, see Eggleston, 1978; and Cohen, 1977, especially ch. 18.) One reason why the prevalence of statistical inferences in history has been largely unrecognized is that the generalizations they employ are seldom stated. They are only stated when they are likely to be doubted, or to be unfamiliar to the reader. Thus, when John Evans compared two British coins of similar denomination but different weight and concluded that the heavier of the two was the older, he explained: 'the weight alone would be nearly sufficient to prove its superior antiquity . . . it being almost universally the case, that the earlier coins of any country are heavier than those of more recent date, though of the same denomination' (Evans, 1950, p. 44).

General knowledge like this is very useful to historians both in suggesting singular hypotheses about the past, and in conferring a measure of probability upon them. Such generalizations usually prove a much more reliable guide to the implications of evidence than do the analogies upon which historians draw for their hypotheses in arguments to the best explanation. That is why historians prefer statistical inferences, and use them when they can. A striking example of their superiority to arguments to the best explanation is given by Henri Marrou. It concerns a Latin inscription discovered on a tombstone in the south of France which ends with the letters V.S.L.M. The local inhabitants, with no general knowledge to guide them, produced an unlikely interpretation of these letters and accepted it for want of any better. They read them backwards as standing for *Marias Iacobi et Salome videbis*: 'you will see the Marys, James and Salome', in support of their belief that these biblical people were buried in a basilica there. Marrou comments:

If the inscription were unique in its particularity, it is difficult to see how it would be possible to interpret it with any certainty. But the final formula V.S.L.M. . . . is one of the combinations of initial letters which we very often encounter engraved at the end of a Latin inscription. We possess thousands and thousands of such inscriptions, coming from all parts of the Roman world. Consequently, we must exclude the possibility that there is question here of some particular allusion to the two Marys of the gospel. It is simply a formula of common usage. Sometimes, indeed, it appears in a less elliptical abbreviation as VOT SOL LIB MER, or even with all the letters: *Votum Solvit Libens Merito*, the pagan equivalent of the *ex voto* formula commonly used today. (Marrou, 1966, p. 123)

The example well illustrates Marrou's general point that 'the more nearly a document resembles a quite homogeneous group of similar documents that are already well known, the more easily and unerringly will its interpretation become possible' (p. 119).

Precisely the same point has been made by G. R. Elton, with a less bizarre example:

That eminent historian, A. F. Pollard, encountering in fifteenth-century royal grants the phrase '*datum de mandatu parliamenti*', concluded that Parliament had authorized the gift; but the words were common form and referred to the dating of the grant which, by a statute of 1444, was appointed to be the date of the delivery of the authorizing warrant into the king's Chancery . . . Every field of history yields examples of this kind, and only training – acquired knowledge – can save the historian from obvious howlers and bad misjudgements. On the other hand, such training saves him with ease. (Elton, 1967, pp. 78–9)

Is it ever reasonable to believe the conclusions of statistical inferences true, and if so, under what conditions? This is the question to be addressed in this section. To answer it, the relatively simple statistical inferences commonly made by historians will be studied. Experts in statistics, probability theory and the logic of support could take the analysis and discussion of statistical inferences much further, but the cases they discuss are often much more complex than those which historians study. It is the truth of the conclusions of historical inferences which is of present interest.

There are several different conditions which must be satisfied before one is justified in believing the conclusion of a statistical inference to be true. Before listing those conditions, however, it would be wise to present the basic form of statistical inferences as clearly as possible.

The form of inference preferred by most philosophers for calculating the probability of singular statements from a given body of observation statements and generalizations is the form of argument called Bayes Theorem, or some variation of it. It appeals to them because it can be derived from the axioms of probability calculus, and although sometimes difficult to apply, it generally yields satisfactory results. (The theorem and its merits have been ably explained by Salmon, 1966. A more sophisticated discussion of its use in estimating the probability of singular statements is to be found in Swinburne, 1973, chs 8 and 9.) We shall later briefly discuss its use in inferring singular statements about the past. But it will not form the chief focus of our attention because virtually no historian has used it and even if any wished to do so, he would probably find it difficult as it requires information which is often hard to obtain. The form of inference used by historians is more closely represented by C. G. Hempel's account of the statistical syllogism (1965, pp. 53–79; and see also pp. 376–403) to which my own discussion will be largely indebted.

To illustrate the logical form of a statistical syllogism, consider the argument used by Marrou above. It can be represented as follows:

(1) In thousands of cases, the letters V.S.L.M. appearing at the end of a Latin inscription on a tombstone stand for *Votum Solvit Libens Merito*.

(2) From all appearances the letters V.S.L.M. are on this tombstone at the end of a Latin inscription.

(3) Therefore these letters on this tombstone stand for *Votum Solvit Libens Merito*.

Each of these statements can be expressed as a kind of probability, as follows:

(1A) The probability of the letters V.S.L.M. appearing at the end of a Latin inscription on a tombstone standing for *Votum Solvit Libens Merito* is very high.

This is a statement of the proportion, or relative frequency, of such letters standing for such words in all cases in which they occur at the end of a Latin inscription on a tombstone. It is derived from the thousands of observations of such inscribed letters already made. It is a statistical generalization.

(2A) Probably the letters V.S.L.M. are on this tombstone at the end of a Latin inscription.

This is a statement of what it is reasonable to believe to be true, on the basis of one's perceptions and general knowledge, especially general knowledge about tombstones and the Latin language. The probability expressed here is an epistemic probability. One of the ideas it expresses is that on the relevant evidence available at the time of writing, it is reasonable to believe the sentence which follows to be true. The word 'probably' is often qualified to express the degree to which it is reasonable to believe the sentence true. In this case we should have written 'very probably', as it is clear that a high degree of belief is warranted.

(3A) Therefore, probably the letters on this tombstone stand for *Votum Solvit Libens Merito*.

This statement also expresses an epistemic probability. It says what it is reasonable to believe true on the basis of the two premises, namely the sentence 'the letters on this tombstone stand for *Votum Solvit Libens Merito*'. The degree of probability, the degree to which this sentence deserves to be believed on the basis of the premises, is a function of the probabilities expressed in the premises. It is, indeed, the product of those probabilities. This is the degree to which the premises support the conclusion. To make it quite plain that the probability referred to in the conclusion is that entailed only by the premises of the argument, and not by any other considerations, Hempel has suggested that the whole argument be written as a statement that the premises jointly confer the probability r upon the statement which follows 'Therefore, probably' in the conclusion (p. 60). This suggestion has not been adopted here as it is assumed that the word 'therefore' will alert the reader to the proper significance of the probability statement which follows.

The form of the argument can be represented schematically thus:

There is a probability (of the degree p_1) that whatever is an A is a B.

It is probable (to the degree p_2) that this is an A.

Therefore (relative to these premises) it is probable (to the degree $p_1 \times p_2$) that this is a B.

The probability of the conclusion does not necessarily express the degree of belief one is finally warranted in placing in the conclusion, for this might be affected by other facts besides those stated in the premises. This point will be elaborated shortly.

For arguments of this form to be acceptable, that is for the conclusion to be warranted by the premises, two important conditions must be satisfied. The first is that the first premise, a statistical generalization, must apply to hitherto unexamined instances which fall within its scope; and the second is that the second, minor premise, a singular description, must truly be of an instance of the subject of the generalization.

Historical arguments can fail to satisfy each of these conditions, though they are more likely to contravene the first rather than the second. It would be useful to illustrate each of them before discussing them further. Lord Macaulay attacked the character of William Penn, the Quaker, several times in his great *History of England*. One of these attacks was based upon a letter addressed to a 'Mr Penne', implicating him in a dishonourable action on behalf of the Maids of Honour at Court. Macaulay's critics objected that the letter could not have been sent to William Penn, as his name was spelt without a final 'e'. The critics' argument depended upon the truth of the generalization that the people to whom letters are addressed spell their own name the way it is spelt in the letters sent to them. It follows that the letter to which Macaulay referred must have been addressed to a Mr Penne who normally spelt his name with a final 'e', and they named one George Penne as its likely recipient. Macaulay's defence was to deny that the generalization assumed by his critics applied in this case. It is true enough of Britain today, but it is not true of Britain in the seventeenth century, said Macaulay, for 'it is notorious that a proper name was then thought to be well spelt if the sound were preserved'. He cited five well-known examples of this, besides pointing out that William Penn's family name was sometimes spelt Pen, and sometimes Penne (Macaulay, 1857, ch. 5). Because the generalization assumed by Macaulay's critics did not apply to instances of its subject in the seventeeth century, the conclusion they had drawn by means of it, namely that the letter could not have been meant for William Penn, did not follow.

Historians seldom interpret or classify their evidence incorrectly. The distinguishing features of some artefacts are so few that their classification cannot be precise. But although the classification of historical remains is sometimes imprecise, it is seldom incorrect. When it is mistaken, this is usually because the object in question is a fairly skilful forgery, made to resemble a class of objects of which it is not a genuine member. One famous forgery is that known as the Piltdown skull. In 1913 some cranial fragments were reported as having been found at Piltdown in Sussex, a human cranium combined with part of the lower jaw and tooth of a modern ape. The latter had been stained to look just like the genuinely ancient cranium, so that the find seemed to provide evidence of the existence of a palaeolithic creature which was part human and part ape. The generalization mediating this conclusion was, roughly, that Pleistocene fossil remains of skeletons are of creatures which lived in the palaeolithic period. The mistake was that of classifying the Piltdown fragments as those of one Pleistocene skull. It was not until the 1950s that scientific tests fully exposed the fake (see Weiner et al, 1953).

Having illustrated the importance of the two conditions which must be satisfied for statistical syllogisms to be valid, a word or two of comment upon them might be useful.

The important question to be asked about the first of them is, when can a statistical generalization be said to apply to hitherto unexamined instances which fall within its scope? It is sometimes thought that for a generalization to be useful in drawing conclusions about the nature of unexamined instances of its subject term, it must be law-like, not accidental. The differences between law-like and accidental generalizations will be stated more fully in Chapter 6. Briefly, however, the subject term of law-like generalizations is meant to refer to all possible as well as actual known instances of it, whereas the subject of accidental generalizations refers only to a set of known actual instances of it. If an historian wants to infer a fact about an unexamined object, it would seem that law-like generalizations would be more useful than accidental ones, since they refer to possible as well as actual instances of their subject terms.

In history, however, many accidental generalizations refer to unexamined instances of their subject term, and can be used in calculating the probability of the predicate of the generalization being true of any particular unexamined instance of the subject. The subjects of many historical generalizations refer to very large numbers of things, to classes with a very large membership. For instance, they can be about the political or religious attitudes of certain large groups of people, or about the degree of wealth or literacy of large social classes. In establishing accidental generalizations with such large reference classes, historians normally use a sampling technique (see Chapter 6, section 2). From what they believe to be a representative sample of the population of the reference class, they infer the proportion of the members of the whole class having a certain attribute. If their sample has indeed been representative, then the chances of any unexamined member of the reference class having the attribute in question can be estimated precisely. Thus some accidental generalizations can be of use in drawing statistical inferences to singular conclusions. The only restriction on their use is that the unexamined instance of the subject of the generalization must be a member of the actual population it has been designed to describe.

It is perhaps worth adding that it is often quite difficult to decide whether an historical generalization should be regarded as accidental or law-like. Law-like generalizations can be derived from natural laws, in theory at least, which is why they are believed to be true of all possible members of their reference class, not just of all actual ones. It is often hard to tell whether a steady correlation between variables, among a large variety of samples, is a matter of chance or is the effect of natural laws (see Chapter 6, section 3).

The generalizations used in historical inferences are often more complicated than those which have been described so far. They often conclude with a disjunction of predicates which could be true of an instance of the subject class, and sometimes they even specify the conditions under which each disjunct is very likely to be true. An example of the latter kind of generalization is appealed to in another of Macaulay's replies to his critics. The critics had complained that his hypothesis that the letter was addressed to William Penn was inconsistent with its tone. The letter implicating Penn in dishonourable behaviour had been written for the Maids of Honour by the Earl of Sunderland. Macaulay wrote:

But, it is said, Sunderland's letter is dry and distant; and he never would have written in such a style to William Penn, with whom he was on friendly terms. Can it be necessary for me to reply that the official communications which a Minister of State makes to his dearest friends and nearest relations are as cold and formal as those which he makes to strangers? Will it be contended that the General Wellesley, to whom the Marquess Wellesley, when Governor of India, addressed so many letters beginning with 'Sir,' and ending with 'I have the honour to be your obedient servant,' cannot possibly have been his Lordship's brother Arthur? (Macaulay, 1857, ch. 5)

Macaulay's critics had assumed that 'In seventeenth century Britain, whenever friends wrote to each other, then they did so in warm and intimate terms'; whereas Macaulay believed the true generalization to be 'In seventeenth century Britain, whenever friends wrote to each other they did so in warm and intimate terms, unless the author was a minister of state writing an official communication, in which case it would be cold and formal, dry and distant.'

One could schematize the form of inference thus:

(1) It is highly probable (in a frequency sense) that if something is *A*, it is also *G*; unless it is *A* and *B*, in which case it is very probably *H*.
(2) This is, in all probability, *A* and *B*.
(3) Therefore, probably this is *H*.

It is interesting to see that statistical syllogisms are sometimes used, as here, to establish the implications of a hypothesis.

Michael Scriven has written interestingly of such complex generalizations which he calls 'normic statements' since they state what is normally the case (1959a p. 465). In at least two essays he has argued that when generalizations are qualified in the way Macaulay qualified the generalization used by his critics, listing the exceptions to the usual, it is possible to convert a statement which began as a statistical generalization into a universal one. 'If the exceptions were few in number and readily described, one could convert a normic statement into an exact generalization by listing them' (Scriven, 1959a, p. 466; cf. Scriven, 1963, pp. 346, 358). An adequately qualified generalization would apply to every instance of its subject, and so be true without exception. Scriven was eager to explore this possibility, chiefly as a way of avoiding what he regarded as a weakness of statistical explanations, namely their failure to state conditions sufficient to have made the occurrence of the event being explained necessary. What must be noted here is that although it is theoretically possible to convert statistical generalizations into universal ones this way, it is not possible to do so in practice. For, especially when the generalization is about human behaviour, an historian can never know that the qualifications he has added to a statistical generalization cover every exception to the rule, and so he is never in a position to declare it universally true. Even when an historian has listed all the possible consequences of an antecedent which he can think of, the most he can claim for the generalization is that it is extremely probable.

If historians have doubts about the adequacy of the evidence for a statistical generalization, they can express their uncertainty by allowing for a margin of error in their probability estimate, suggesting that the proportion of *A*s which are *G*s lies within a certain range. For this reason the probability estimates expressed in the generalizations used by historians are often a bit hazy. Another reason for their being imprecise is that the information upon which they are based has seldom been quantified. Macaulay, for example, did not have an adequate sample of the proportion of cases of people in seventeenth-century Britain who were content to preserve the sound of a name in spelling it, compared with others, who, like William Penn and his father, spelt their names consistently. Consequently the probabilities involved in historical inferences are normally stated in qualitative, rather than quantitative, terms. These terms represent a series of grades ranging from highly improbable through to highly probable. But the fact that grades are used to express historians' probability estimates should not be taken as evidence of their purely subjective, arbitrary character. Their estimates are generally based upon some acquaintance with actual frequencies. The grades they use, like the grades given for students' essays, can often be related to a range of numbers. For most people the equivalents would be roughly as follows:

extremely probable	= in 100–95% of cases
very probable	= „ 95–80% „ „
quite or fairly probable	= „ 80–65% „ „
more probable than not	= „ 65–50% „ „
hardly or scarcely probable	= „ 50–35% „ „
fairly improbable	= „ 35–20% „ „
very improbable	= „ 20–5% „ „
extremely improbable	= „ 5–0% „ „

The first condition which must be satisfied for a statistical syllogism to be valid is that the generalization it employs applies to unexamined instances which fall within its scope. The second is that the singular description must truly be of an instance of the subject of the generalization. The Piltdown skull was not entirely a Pleistocene fossil, so it did not belong to a creature living in palaeolithic times. The interesting question which this second condition raises is, how does one decide whether or not an object belongs to a subject class? Should one decide by noting a number of resemblances between the object and other known members of the class? Should other factors be taken into account, such as known implications of certain possible classifications?

In fact both of these methods of classification are used, though the first is normally the final arbiter. The lower jaw and canine tooth of the Piltdown remains had been shaped and stained to resemble those of a genuine human fossil, which is why they were classified as such at first. Many anthropologists were dissatisfied with this classification, however, as 'the combination of a cranium closely similar to that of *Homo sapiens* with a mandible and canine tooth of simian [ape-like] form seemed too incongruous' (Weiner et al., 1953, p. 30). Because the initial classification of the Piltdown remains did not fit existing evolutionary theories, the bones were regarded as a possible fake, and were then subjected to much closer scrutiny by J. S. Weiner and his colleagues. On close examination they discovered that the shape of the teeth was not like that produced by natural wear but was like that produced by artificial abrasion; the fluorine deposited in the lower jaw and canine tooth was much less than that in the genuine fossil; the nitrogen lost by the bone in the jaw and teeth was much less than that lost by the genuine fossil; and the iron staining of the jaw bone was much less than that of the cranium, and was confined to the surface, unlike the staining of the cranium. In short, the lower jaw and teeth more closely resembled those of a modern ape which had been artificially shaped and stained than they resembled the bones of a genuine Pleistocene fossil, and so they were re-classified accordingly. It is noteworthy that incompatibility with existing theories was not enough by itself to render the first classification totally unacceptable. If an observable object, closely investigated, warrants a certain classification because of its similarity with other members of a class, then it is the theories which are incompatible with it which must be modified, and not the classification. The logic of classification by reference to criteria is further discussed in the next chapter.

Although the conclusion of a statistical syllogism is expressed, normally, as a probability, the probability is nothing but a function of the probabilities of its premises. Even when the premises are true and the syllogism is valid, the conclusion might not be worthy of belief. For there might be other data, not mentioned in the premises, which, when taken into account would alter the probability of the conclusion, and perhaps even suggest another conclusion altogether. An instance of this occurring was provided by Macaulay's discussion of whether or not it was probable that the Earl of Sunderland would have addressed William Penn in a warm and friendly manner. Given just the fact that the two men were on friendly terms, it was probable that their letters to each other would have been warm and friendly. But, Macaulay argued, if one takes into account the additional fact that the letter in question was an official communication written by Sunderland as a minister of state, then the probability is that it will not be warm and friendly but 'cold and formal'.

From cases like this, the conclusion has been drawn that the probability of a statement normally expresses the degree of belief one is warranted in placing in it only when that probability estimate is based upon all the relevant evidence which can be taken into account. This has been referred to as 'the requirement of total evidence' (Hempel, 1965, pp. 63–7, 397). The problem which immediately arises is that of discovering how one should take into account all the evidence relevant to the probability of a statement.

2 Assessing the implications of all relevant evidence

Sometimes, as in the case just discussed, the additional relevant information can be subsumed under a new generalization which specifies the consequent probability. A generalization which refers to a class of things which are both A and B usually has a narrower reference class, having fewer members, than a generalization which refers to things which are just A or just B. Thus, for example, there are fewer letters written between friends which are also official communications from ministers of state than just letters written between friends. It has been suggested that the most reliable estimate of the probability of a singular statement is that which is based upon the narrowest reference class for which reliable statistics can be compiled. (See Swinburne, 1973, pp. 138–9. Salmon (1966) has expressed the same point differently, on pp. 91–2.)

Sometimes, however, even the conclusions of inferences which employ the narrowest possible reference class do not indicate the degree of belief which it is reasonable to adopt. For sometimes there is additional information relevant to the probability of that conclusion whose significance, when taken in conjunction with the other relevant evidence, has never been determined. Such additional information cannot, then, be accommodated by a generalization having an appropriately qualified reference class, because no such generalization is known. Yet because the additional information is relevant to the probability of the original conclusion, which is the hypothesis under consideration, it should if possible be taken into account in reckoning what is a reasonable degree of belief to recommend for that hypothesis.

One qualification must be added to what has just been said. Additional information will only alter the probability of a hypothesis if it is independent of the evidence previously taken into account in determining its probability. To make a difference, an additional fact must not be a consequence of previous evidence, nor must it share a common cause with previous evidence. This point is easily illustrated. Suppose one person witnessed an event and then described it to another. The second person's testimony about the event would then not be independent of the first's, and would add nothing to the probability of the first witness's testimony being accurate. Again, suppose a journalist reported one event and his report was printed in 10,000 newspapers. The probability of the report in one copy of the newspaper being true is not increased by its appearance in the remaining copies. New evidence only alters the probability of a hypothesis if it is causally independent of the evidence already considered.

New independent evidence can either increase or diminish the probability of a hypothesis. Appearances can be deceptive, however. Carnap has shown that two pieces of evidence which individually support a hypothesis can, under unusual conditions, jointly diminish its probability. The conditions under which this happens are so unusual, however, that they need not concern us (see Salmon, 1975, pp. 14–17). Let us first consider additional independent evidence which supports a hypothesis. If this cannot be subsumed under a new generalization with a narrower reference class than that used before, then there is seldom any plausible and practicable way in which an historian can actually calculate the probability of the hypothesis in the light of the old and the new evidence together. To demonstrate this somewhat disappointing fact, the inadequacies of the better-known methods of estimating the joint significance of evidence will be exposed in turn.

(i) *The product and sum of probabilities*

If evidence e_1 confers a probability of 0.5 upon a hypothesis, and independent evidence e_2 also confers a probability of 0.5 upon the hypothesis, the probability of the hypothesis taking both e_1 and e_2 into account cannot be the product of the probabilities of each, for that would be 0.25, and it is implausible to suggest that additional support for a hypothesis reduces its probable truth. Should one, then, add the probabilities which each piece of evidence confers upon a hypothesis? Some have written as though one should. J. P. Day, for example, in his book *Inductive Probability*, suggested something of the sort.

What we do is 'add' the degrees of probability conferred on p by each of the favourable pieces of evidence, also the degrees of probability conferred on $\sim p$ by each of the unfavourable pieces of evidence, 'subtract' the smaller from the larger 'sum', and judge p (or $\sim p$) to be probable in the degree that is the 'remainder'. But although it is natural to use the terminology of addition and subtraction to describe these procedures, it is necessary to remember that the words do not carry their literal mathematical sense in this context. (Day, 1961, p. 57)

What sense the words 'add' and 'subtract' can have other than their mathematical one, Day does not say. To add and subtract probabilities in the way he suggested, however, would yield quite absurd conclusions. The point can be conveniently illustrated by means of an historical example. Consider the following passage.

The excellence of some of the figure sculptures on the great Anglian crosses at Bewcastle in Cumberland and Ruthwell in Dumfriesshire led some scholars to believe that they could not be earlier than the twelfth century, but the art-motifs, the form of the inscribed runes [letters of the earliest Teutonic alphabet used by Anglo-Saxons], and the language of the inscriptions show that they belong to the earlier period of Northumbrian art. (Whitelock, 1952, pp. 227–8)

It may be that in this case the historian knew that the vast proportion of crosses, if not all of them, having together the art-motifs, the form of the inscribed runes, and the language of the incription such as were found on the crosses at Bewcastle and Ruthwell, were Anglo-Saxon. (Whitelock's discussion on pages 228–30 suggests rather that these attributes could be found separately on Anglo-Saxon crosses.) But suppose she had no such general knowledge, and knew only the following:

   (i)   90% of crosses having such fine sculpture were known to be post eleventh century;

   (ii) 60% having their art-motifs were Anglo-Saxon;

   (iii) 70% having inscribed runes of such a form were Anglo-Saxon ; and

   (iv) 80% having inscriptions using such language were Anglo-Saxon.

Now the absurdity of adding and subtracting the probabilities to calculate the probability that those crosses were Anglo-Saxon is patent. If we added the degrees of probability conferred by each favourable piece of evidence, we would get a probability of 210%, which is nonsense, since the maximum conceivable probability is 100%. And if one subtracted 90% from that total, the probability becomes 120%, which is still nonsense. Clearly the joint significance of the different pieces of evidence is not to be discovered by adding and subtracting their probabilities.

(ii) *The mean of the probabilities*

Is the joint significance of independent pieces of evidence given by the mean of the probabilities they severally confer upon a hypothesis? This suggestion yields less absurd results than the last, but they are still quite implausible. Suppose one discovered crosses without the fine figure sculptures of those described by Dorothy Witelock, but having all their other features. Then the probability that they were Anglo-Saxon would be, on this theory,

$$\frac{0.6 + 0.7 + 0.8}{3} = 0.7.$$

But this means that the evidence of the art-motifs and of the language of the inscriptions added absolutely nothing to the evidence of the form of the inscriptions in deciding the probability of their being Anglo-Saxon, and that is implausible. Indeed, on this account the evidence of the art-motifs and of the form of the inscriptions, although quite favourable to the hypothesis that the crosses were Anglo-Saxon, served to reduce the probability of this hypothesis conferred by the evidence of the language of their inscriptions.

(iii) *Bernoullian analysis*

A slightly more complicated formula for calculating the probability which several independent pieces of evidence confer upon a hypothesis was suggested by James Bernoulli. If e_1 confers a probability of p on h, and e_2 confers a probability of q on h, then the probability of h is

$$\frac{pq}{pq + (1-p)(1-q)}.$$

This is a well-known formula expressed by George Boole, but as L. Jonathan Cohen has pointed out, it sometimes yields implausible results when the probabilities p and q are less than 0.5 (Cohen, 1977, pp. 95–7). Suppose e_1 and e_2 are the independent evidence of two unreliable witnesses, both of whom give exactly the same account of an incident. The evidence e_1 might be judged to confer a probability of 0.4 upon a hypothesis, and the evidence e_2 to confer a probability of 0.3 upon it. Then the evidence of both would, on this formula, make the probability of the hypothesis little more than 0.2, whereas the fact that they both told the same story would strike most people as increasing, not diminishing, the probability that the hypothesis was true. Similarly, suppose several people had a mild motive for a murder, and several had had an opportunity to perform it. If one had had both, then he would be more rather than less suspect, though on Boole's formula the probability that he did the deed would be less. These arguments can also be used against taking the mean of the probabilities as indicating their joint significance.

(iv) *Bayes Theorem*

The best-known formula for calculating the significance of additional evidence is Bayes Theorem. It has seldom been recommended as a form of historical inference, because the information required to apply it is often unavailable. A. L. Burns (1949–51) once suggested that it could be used in history, but he admitted that it might be difficult to apply.

Richard Swinburne has presented Bayes Theorem thus:

$$\text{If } P(e/k) \neq O, \text{ then } P(h/e.k) = \frac{P(h/k) \times P(e/h.k)}{P(e/k)}$$

To read this formula, one must understand that $p(e/k)$ means 'the probability of e given k', or 'the probability conferred upon e by k'. Swinburne further explained:

Where h is the hypothesis whose probability we are assessing, k our background evidence and e the new evidence, then '$P(h/k)$' is called the prior probability of h in contrast to '$P(h/k.e)$', the posterior probability of h. '$P(e/h.k)$' ... is a measure of how much the new evidence e is to be expected, for given background evidence k, if the hypothesis h is true. (p. 42)

This equation can be used when estimates are available for the terms on the right-hand side. One needs to know the prior probability of one's hypothesis on the basis of information already considered, i.e. $P(h/k)$. One needs to be able to calculate the probability, or improbability, of the additional evidence (e) being as it is, supposing that the hypothesis (h), together with the background information (k), were true, i.e. $P(e/h.k)$. And finally one has to know the probability of the additional evidence (e) being as it is, given the background evidence alone, i.e. $P(e/k)$.

An historian might think it quite impossible to calculate all these things; but sometimes it is possible to calculate them roughly. Suppose both a socialist journalist and a conservative journalist reported enthusiastically on the success of a new socialist policy, say of Aboriginal housing. Let k be the report of the left-winger, e be the report of the right, and h be the hypothesis that results of the housing programme were as k had described them. Allowing that the socialist journalist might exaggerate the good effects of a policy for which he was enthusiastic, we might estimate $P(h/k)$ as roughly 0.7. Knowing the conservative journalist to be honest, if unimaginative, we might put $P(e/h.k)$ at 0.8. And the frequency with which the conservative reporter described the same facts as the socialist, when reporting the same incident, we might know to be 0.7. So $P(h/e.k) = 0.8$.

Generally, the sort of information required to employ Bayes Theorem is not available to the historian. Revert to the Anglo-Saxon crosses for a moment. Let k be the art-motifs on the crosses and e be the form of the inscribed runes. What is the probability of a cross being Anglo-Saxon which has both these features: $P(h/k)$ is already known; it is 0.6. To calculate $P(e/h.k)$, one would have to know how frequently Anglo-Saxon crosses having such art-motifs also had such inscribed runes. And to know $P(e/k)$ requires one to know how often crosses with such art-motifs, be they Anglo-Saxon or not, had such inscribed runes. Such information is, perhaps, obtainable, but it is seldom readily at hand, and most historians would judge the effort involved in obtaining it to be hardly worth the result.

Apart from the frequent difficulty of estimating the probabilities involved, there is another reason why Bayes Theorem would not commend itself to historians. If, as often happens in history, $P(h/k)$ is high, and $P(e/h)$ or $P(\sim e/h)$ is high, then $P(e/h.k)$ will be roughly equivalent to $P(e/k)$, so that Bayes Theorem will not give a fair indication of the joint significance of e and k. In history, I think more than in science, one often has evidence which strongly implies the truth of a hypothesis, such as a diary entry providing strong evidence of an event it describes. And one often has another piece of independent evidence which strongly confirms or disconfirms the hypothesis, such that if the hypothesis were true it would very probably be true or very probably be false. If nothing more of relevance is known about the initial evidence (k), the hypothesis (h) and the additional evidence (e), then $P(e/h) \simeq P(e/h.k) \simeq P(e/k)$. Given the initial evidence (k), both the hypothesis (h) and its implication (e) are to be expected, so according to Bayes Theorem the discovery that the implication is true adds little to the probability of the hypothesis. But given that the implication of the hypothesis might well be materially independent of the initial evidence for it, since probabilities do not always express causal connections (the diary entry did not cause the event it described, even if the latter caused the additional confirming evidence), this consequence is unacceptable.

Many other ways of estimating the joint significance of independent evidence have been considered by philosophers interested in the logic of confirmation and support, but most require evidence which it would be difficult for historians to obtain, or they have implications which are unacceptable. If an historian has no general knowledge about the joint significance of the kinds of evidence he has at hand, there is no easy way by which he can estimate the probability the various pieces of evidence jointly confer upon the hypothesis which they individually support. The most the historian can conclude, it seems, is that, other things being equal, the probability of the hypothesis is at least as high as the highest probability conferred upon it by any single piece of evidence, and is probably higher. For the frequency with which descriptions of the world are true increases with the number of independent pieces of evidence which render them probable.

This conclusion is not the reasonable one to draw, however, if, in addition to evidence supporting a hypothesis, there is evidence which renders it improbable. For in that case the evidence for the hypothesis is to some extent offset by the evidence against it. The question which now arises is how is the probability of a hypothesis affected by evidence against the hypothesis? How does one calculate the degree of belief which it is reasonable to hold in a hypothesis, given that there is evidence both for and against it?

In some cases these questions are easily answered, and in other cases they are not. It depends upon the way in which additional evidence diminishes the probability of a hypothesis. There are four fairly common ways in which this happens, which deserve to be considered. The first two are easily dealt with, but the last two are not.

(i) New information might reduce the frequency estimate expressed in the major premise of the statistical syllogism, and thereby reduce the probability of its conclusion. There are several ways in which evidence bears upon such frequency estimates, and these will be indicated in the chapter on generalizations. The implications of such a reduction are easily calculated, by means of a new syllogism using the new generalization in place of the old one.

(ii) Additional evidence might be used in conjunction with a new, suitably narrowed generalization, to produce a conclusion with a lower probability. Thus the fact that Sunderland was writing on business as a minister of state was used by Macaulay in conjunction with a narrower generalization to lower the probability that Macaulay would have addressed William Penn in a warm and friendly manner. Frequently, in such circumstances, friends address each other in a cold and formal manner, such as Sunderland had used in his letter.

(iii) New facts might be adduced which contradict an implication of a hypothesis, thereby rendering it improbable.

(iv) Evidence might be found which supports another, incompatible hypothesis.

In order to discuss the significance of these last two kinds of counterevidence, it will be useful to have an example of them. Quite a good example is provided in this passage from J. E. Neale's essay 'The Sayings of Queen Elizabeth'. In reading it, it helps to remember that Mary Queen of Scots was Elizabeth I's cousin, and that Mary's child was likely to inherit the throne of England as well as that of Scotland. That is indeed what happened, when James VI of Scotland succeeded Queen Elizabeth I as King James I of England in 1603. Neale's essay is about Queen Elizabeth.

Now how can historical science, or, to use Lord Bryce's less pretentious phrase, refined common sense, hope to separate the false from the true in the traditional stories about such a woman as this? *Omnis fabula fundatur in historia*, it has been said. Perhaps; but we must examine the foundations, none the less; and it is only by a critical review of our sources that our problem will be solved, if at all. Let me illustrate the point by examining one of the best known of Elizabethan stories. In 1566 Sir James Melville was sent to England by Mary Queen of Scots to announce the birth of her child. Melville tells us in his *Memoirs* that Cecil first whispered the news to Elizabeth in the course of a dance. Thereupon 'all her mirth was laid aside for that night', and sitting down she put her hand under her cheek and burst out with the moan 'that the Queen of Scots was Mother of a fair son, while she was but a barren stock'.
'When men's memories do arise', said Fuller, who was himself a delightfully garrulous offender, 'it is time for History to haste to bed.' Melville's *Memoirs* were the child of his old age, and though he had some of his papers by him on which to rely, fickle memory played its tricks, and his narrative is by no means reliable. If not conclusive proof that this particular story is false, it is at least sufficient to make us pause in believing it, that the Spanish ambassador, Silva, who was not at all one to miss the chance of retailing such a story, and who saw Melville the day after his audience, merely tells Philip that 'the Queen seemed very glad of the birth of the infant': nor had he a different tale to tell, though he was an assiduous collector of Court gossip, when he wrote again four days later. (Neale, 1963, pp. 181–2. Neale's references have been omitted here.)

Clearly Melville's report in his *Memoirs* supports the truth of his story; it describes a dramatic incident which it appears he witnessed in person, so even after a lapse of several years there is a considerable probability that his description of it would be accurate in essence, if perhaps slightly embroidered. But Neale felt confident that, had it been true, the Spanish ambassador would very probably have reported it to his master. It was precisely the sort of event he was fond of recounting, and it was one which Melville would surely himself have communicated to him at their interview the next day, and which others would have described to him in the following few days. But the ambassador did not report the Queen reacting in the way Melville described. So far then, we have the following arguments:

(1)   People who report witnessing dramatic incidents at court are quite likely to report them accurately.
       Melville reported witnessing Queen Elizabeth I being told of the birth of Mary's son, which was a fairly dramatic moment.
       So it is quite probable that Melville's report of the incident was accurate, that is, it is quite likely that the incident occurred as he reported it.

(2)   Most dramatic incidents at the court of Queen Elizabeth I were described in the reports of the Spanish ambassador, Silva (who 'was an assiduous collector of court gossip').

There was an incident at Queen Elizabeth's court as reported by Melville which was dramatic enough. (This is substantially the conclusion of the first argument, whose implication is here being scrutinized.)

So very probably it was reported by Silva.

It was not reported by Silva, so either the first or the second (or both) premises of the above argument is false. Since there is much more evidence in support of the first premise than the second, it is reasonable to think that the second is more likely to be false than the first. Therefore the second premise is probably false.

The Spanish ambassador's report not only contradicts an implication of the hypothesis derived from Melville's *Memoirs*. It also provides evidence for an alternative hypothesis, incompatible with the first. The ambassador's report makes it probable that Queen Elizabeth expressed pleasure at the birth of Queen Mary's son. Since, one gathers, the ambassador's reports were generally accurate, the probability of his report on this matter being true must be quite high. In Neale's opinion it is clearly higher than the probability that Melville, writing years after the event, remembered it correctly. This argument can be presented more formally as follows.

(3)   A high proportion of the Spanish ambassador's reports of incidents at the court of Queen Elizabeth were accurate.

The ambassador reported that the Queen expressed pleasure at the birth of Mary's son.

So very probably this report is accurate: the Queen did express pleasure at his birth.

The conclusion of the first argument is the hypothesis which Neale considered after reading Melville's *Memoirs*. The second argument produced evidence which contradicted an implication of that hypothesis, namely the implication that the incident described by Melville would have been reported by the Spanish ambassador, thereby reducing the probability of its truth. And the third argument used further information in support of a statement incompatible with the original hypothesis. In the light of these arguments, what is the probability of the first hypothesis, to what degree is it rational to believe that hypothesis true?

There are two ways in which historians can arrive at rational answers to these questions, one more satisfactory than the other. The first, less satisfactory procedure is that of balancing the probabilities of the hypotheses. Historians can compare the highest probability which their evidence confers upon the hypothesis with the highest probability conferred upon its negation, or upon another hypothesis incompatible with it (which is logically equivalent to the negation of the first hypothesis), and note which is superior and by how much. The difference would represent the degree to which the superior hypothesis is more likely to be true than false. The point is most easily illustrated if one quantifies for a moment. Suppose the probability of Neale's first hypothesis is 0.65, and the probability of the alternative, presented as the conclusion of the third argument, is 0.80. Assuming that the probability of a hypothesis which is as likely to be true as it is likely to be false is 0.5, then the probability of the second hypothesis is, on balance $0.5 + (0.80 - 0.65) = 0.65$.

The image of a balance of probabilities is to be understood as follows. Imagine a balance, with one hypothesis in each pan of the balance, each of a different degree of probability. The indicator on the balance will incline from the centre (0.5 probability) to the side having the greater probability. The distance it will move in favour of the superior hypothesis will correspond to the differences between the probabilities of the two.

There are several respects in which this procedure is unsatisfactory however. It takes no account of the amount of evidence supporting the incompatible hypotheses. It compares only the maximum probability which that evidence confers upon each of them. Yet it might be argued that a hypothesis which is supported to a moderate degree by many independent pieces of evidence is quite as credible as one which is rendered highly probable by one piece of evidence. How can the amount of evidence be taken into account?

Furthermore, the method of balancing probabilities leaves the inconsistency in the historian's knowledge unresolved. While it remains, there exists reason to believe the superior hypothesis false, so that the truth of the hypothesis remains far from certain. This degree of rational uncertainty is reflected in the relatively low probability which is finally accorded the superior hypothesis, once the alternatives have been balanced.

The other, more satisfactory method of reckoning with contrary evidence is to let each of the different hypotheses which the evidence makes probable become part of a separate explanation of the total relevant evidence, in the hope of demonstrating that one explanation is far superior to the others, and thus worthy of belief. This procedure sometimes avoids both of the shortcomings of the other. If there is much evidence supporting one hypothesis, then as well as contributing to the plausibility of the hypothesis, it might well be explained by the hypothesis and thus increase its explanatory scope. This does not always happen, as not all evidence which supports a hypothesis is explained by it. The causes of an event may increase the probability of the occurrence of an event without being explained by it. But if the evidence in support of a hypothesis is an effect of the event described by the hypothesis, as so much historical evidence is, then it might indeed be explained by that hypothesis.

Furthermore, in developing explanatory hypotheses the historian can often account for evidence which makes alternative hypotheses probable, thereby avoiding any inconsistency in his set of beliefs. In effect this is what Neale did to accommodate Melville's testimony, which ran counter to the story of the Spanish ambassador. He explained it away as 'the child of his old age' and of his 'fickle memory'. If one explanation accommodates all the relevant evidence, and is much superior to the others, then it may be accepted as almost certainly true.

It should not be thought, however, that statistical inferences are all arguments to the best explanation, for they are not. It has been suggested that, because it is not reasonable to accept the conclusion of a statistical syllogism until all the evidence relevant to the probability of that conclusion has been considered, then statistical inferences must be inferences to the best explanation (Harman, 1965, pp. 90–1). But this is not the case.

To begin with, there are quite striking differences between the two forms of argument. The conclusion of a statistical inference is always inferred directly, by means of a statistical generalization, from the data available to the historian; the conclusion of an argument to the best explanation, on the other hand, is often reached by conjecture, usually on the basis of analogous cases. It is possible to calculate the probability of the conclusion of a statistical inference relative to its premises; whereas there is no mathematical way of calculating the probability of the conclusion of an argument to the best explanation. An historian might express his estimate of the degree of reliability of the conclusion of an argument to the best explanation as a qualitative probability estimate, but there is no formula for calculating the probability of that conclusion.

It is true that the conclusion of a statistical syllogism cannot be accepted as indicating a reasonable degree of belief until all available data relevant to the probability of that conclusion have been taken into account. But this fact does not transform a statistical inference into an argument to the best explanation. Sometimes all the relevant evidence can be accommodated within the syllogism itself, by means of a suitably narrow and otherwise qualified generalization. When this is not possible, and the significance of relevant data can only be assessed by means of an argument to the best explanation, the argument is often of a hybrid form, part statistical and part not, owing the credibility of its conclusion very much to the acceptability of a statistical inference by which that conclusion was reached, and rendered to some degree probable, in the first place. Some characteristic hybrid forms of inference will be described in the fourth section of this chapter. These forms of inference often allow the historian to estimate the probability of their conclusions in a way that ordinary arguments to the best explanation do not.

At the beginning of this chapter the question was asked whether it was ever reasonable to believe the conclusion of a statistical inference to be true. The answer which has been presented so far may be summarized thus: When there is no evidence in support of a contrary proposition, the probability expressed in the conclusion of a valid statistical syllogism whose premises are warranted may be taken as indicating a reasonable degree of belief in that conclusion, so long as the generalization employed has the narrowest reference class which the data warrants. When there is evidence supporting a contrary hypothesis, however, it is best to decide which proposition to believe (if any) by judging which provides the best explanation of all the relevant data.

3   Challenges to the rationality of statistical inferences

There are several grounds upon which someone might object to the claim that it is sometimes rational to accept the conclusion of a statistical inference as indicating an appropriate degree of belief. It might be doubted whether the evidence which has chanced to survive of past events is likely to give an accurate impression of those events. It might be thought difficult to establish the independence of the evidence which is available to an historian, and this must be known before its joint significance can be estimated. Finally, it might be argued that historians have no way of knowing whether they have satisfied the requirement of total evidence or not, and so cannot really tell what it is rational to believe relative to all the relevant evidence available. Human interests so easily blinker investigators, preventing them from seeing what they would rather not. None of these worries warrants wholesale scepticism about the conclusion of statistical inferences, but they are of sufficient interest to merit discussion.

The first worry is that the evidence which survives of past events, survives usually as a result of a haphazard series of chances in the course of which much gets destroyed, so that the likelihood of what remains giving a fair indication of its origin is quite small. In fact the depression which this objection arouses is generally not justified. Let it be admitted at once that even when the probability of the conclusion of a statistical inference is very high, it could be false. What the objector overlooks, though, is the fact that quite small amounts of randomly acquired evidence can warrant judgements of which historians have every right to be certain. If the appropriate general knowledge is available, historians can draw certain conclusions from quite small configurations of evidence. We have already seen an example of this at the beginning of this chapter, with the interpretation of the letters V.S.L.M. in a Latin inscription on a tombstone. Here is another example drawn from archaeology:

As but one example we shall quote the many thousands of Iron Age brooches which have been discovered in Britain and on the Continent in association with other trinkets and pottery of the period, often in recognised living-places: if, then, we see a bronze brooch with a fretted catch-plate, a well-moulded bow and double spring, the very brooch-form that is familiar to us from fifty well-attested Iron Age sites, we shall have no difficulty, in general, in suggesting that it may well be of La Tène III type and belong to a late division of the Early Iron Age. (Jessup, 1965, p. 90)

It is not the amount of evidence but the strength of the relevant generalization that is crucial in determining the certainty of the conclusion of a statistical inference.

The same cannot be said of arguments to the best explanation. Paucity of evidence generally does count against the possibility of certainty in those arguments, as the less the evidence, usually the greater the number of possible, plausible explanations of it.

The second objection to the rationality of statistical inferences focuses upon the frequent difficulty of establishing the independence of the historian's evidence. If two independent witnesses gave roughly the same account of an incident, the probability of its having been as they described it is much greater than if the second witness was merely repeating what the first had told him about it. But with two pieces of historical testimony it is often impossible to determine whether they were independent or not. So it is impossible to know what probability they confer upon the occurrence of the event which they both describe, or, more generally, whose occurrence could be inferred from each of their descriptions.

In reply it must be admitted that the degree of independence of testimony can be difficult to determine, but sometimes it is not. Historians often have both internal and external evidence they can use to discover it. Internal evidence consists of features of the testimonies themselves, which, if remarkably similar suggest lack of independence, and if remarkably different suggest the reverse. The turn of phrase, the sequence of points, the paragraphing – all can reveal copying. Repetition of trivial details, omission of important facts, identical commentary upon the events, these can suggest lack of independence between witnesses. External evidence relates to the circumstances under which the witnesses produced their testimony. If the witnesses were for some reason hostile to one another, they are less likely to have collaborated than if they had something to gain by such collaboration. The historian might have detailed information about the activities of each witness which would enable him to decide whether or not their testimony was independent. He might be reasonably certain, for example, that Hansard's report of events in the British House of Commons, and a political journalist's report, produced the same day, were independent, knowing how each was produced and how little chance there was of either copying the other. Thus, although the independence of testimony is sometimes difficult to establish, it is not always impossible to determine.

Finally, can historians ever be sure that they have consulted all the evidence relevant to the conclusion of a statistical inference so as to provide a reliable estimate of what, at the time of writing, it was reasonable to believe? Time and money might be needed to discover all the evidence, but that may be found eventually. A greater difficulty is that of circumventing the historian's natural disposition to overlook or misinterpret evídence which tells against his preferred conclusion. This is a problem of bias, which will be discussed further in the concluding chapter. Suffice it here to say that the likelihood of an historian's conclusions being distorted by bias can be minimized by submitting them to experts, particularly to hostile ones, for assessment. If an historical description has been accepted as true by several experts working in the field, it is probably a reasonable conclusion to draw from the available relevant data.

The objections to the rationality of statistical inferences which have been mentioned have each pointed to a possible difficulty in reaching a rational conclusion by this means; but no difficulty is so common or so great as to warrant general scepticism about the likelihood of historians reaching rational conclusions by statistical inferences.

4   Some hybrid and complex forms of statistical inference

To this point the arguments to the best explanation and the statistical inferences which have been described have been pure and simple in form. As has been seen, examples of these pure forms occur quite often in history. But it is important to recognize that sometimes the statistical inferences used by historians are a little more complex than the statistical syllogisms examined so far. And occasionally, when the conclusions of such arguments are less than certain, historians strengthen them by means of an argument to the best explanation, by showing them to be part of the best explanation of the data from which they have been inferred. Such combined forms of inference can be called 'hybrid'.

Common hybrid inferences

The most common kind of hybrid inference is that in which the historian reaches a conclusion by means of a statistical inference, but is not confident of it, either because the generalization he used was not well enough supported to be entirely reliable, or because the historian knew of two or more incompatible hypotheses, each of which was rendered to some degree probable by the data. An example which illustrates both these causes of uncertainty is provided by L. Gershoy's discussion of the French revolutionary Bertrand Barère.

Barère changed his political colours three times during the course of the revolution, twice to the left and then once to the right. In the Constitutional Assembly, in 1791, Barère supported constitutional monarchy, but in the National Convention in 1792 he voted for the formation of a republic and expedited the trial and condemnation of the king. In the Convention in 1792, Barère began as a friend of the moderate centre party, the Girondins, and did his best to prevent open conflict between them and the more extreme revolutionaries, the Jacobins. But in June and July 1793 he voted with Robespierre and the Jacobins for the arrest of the Girondins, who by then were engaged in civil war against the government in Paris. In July 1794, however, fearful with many other deputies lest Robespierre should have his life, Barère plotted and achieved the arrest and execution of the Jacobin leader. Two hypotheses have been advanced to explain Barère's behaviour. Lord Macaulay, J. M. Thompson and others have thought his motives were purely selfish, that each change of stance was made to save his own skin and maintain or increase his political power. L. Gershoy, on the other hand, in a recent biography of Barère, argues that each of these moves, as well as many of his other political acts, were motivated by a genuine desire to sustain the authority and unity of the revolutionary government in Paris (Gershoy, 1962).

Gershoy has explained that his account of Barère's motives was arrived at by means of a generalization based upon a number of similar cases. In Gershoy's opinion, however, the generalization was not entirely reliable, though it did confer a measure of probability upon his conclusion. Here is Gershoy's own account of his reasoning in this case.

I . . . drew upon the experience of earlier would-be pacificators of history, such for example, as the *Pacifiques* in the religious wars of the sixteenth century. I also looked back to the Barère experience from the dilemmas of hopeful mediators in the tensions of the cold war of today [1962].
. . .
No situation is ever exactly comparable with another, no facts identical. The limits of generalization, even more of prediction, are palpable. Generalizations are bound to be incomplete and inexact . . . They can have no universal validity nor absolute predictive certainty. They do, however, suggest the range of the possible. In them there is a conditional validity, a working measure of probability. (Gershoy, 1963, pp. 68–9)

It is not entirely clear, in the context, precisely what generalization Gershoy had in mind, though the one which seems best to fit his discussion is the generalization that 'people who change their political stance in times of political instability, sometimes do so in order to prevent war and to preserve strong government'. This true generalization not only made Gershoy's hypothesis plausible, but gave it some measure of probability. Clearly, however, the probability was not high enough to make Gershoy certain of the conclusion.

The weakness of Gershoy's generalization was one reason for his uncertainty about the conclusion he drew, but another must have been his knowledge of an alternative explanation of Barère's behaviour, namely the traditional one that such changes of side are often made from a desire for personal security and power. The probability that this was Barère's motive was far from negligible.

To strengthen his hypothesis and to show its superiority to the traditional one, Gershoy demonstrated its superiority as an explanation. He was able to show that it made intelligible a far greater number of Barère's actions than the other did. (Alan Donagan (1969) has analysed Gershoy's argument along more strictly Popperian lines.)

When an historian is able to draw two or more incompatible conclusions from the available evidence, he can sometimes use another form of argument to decide between them, which is often more powerful than that adopted by Gershoy. Suppose Gershoy had known that the alternative explanations of Barère's actions exhausted the possibilities, he might have expressed this by saying that Barère must have acted either for selfish motives or to further the revolution. Had he then been able to show that one of these explanations was very probably false, the consequence would have been to make the other very probably true, without introducing any further support for it at all. The logic of such an argument is simple. If two hypotheses exhaust the possibilities, then the sum of their probabilities must be one. Suppose the *a priori* probability of each to be 0.5. If the probability of one hypothesis is reduced, usually by showing that its implications are false, to say 0.2, then the probability of the other immediately rises to 0.8. This is one form, the most powerful form, of argument by elimination.

A common complex statistical inference

The historian is not always able to infer the information he wants to know about a subject in the past directly, but sometimes he is able to infer other facts about the historical subject from which he can infer the information he wants with confidence. The historian's inferences in these cases are complex because the statistical inference from the evidence does not take the historian straight to the information he wants, but merely provides a set of clues, as it were, about the truth of the matter. Further argument is needed to reach a conclusion of the right sort. Examples will make this plain.

Consider, to begin with, V. H. Galbraith's inference as to 'Who Wrote Asser's Life of Alfred?', which he has offered as a model of historical inference. (It forms the concluding essay in his book *An Introduction to the Study of History*, 1964.)

The *Life* purports to have been written by a contemporary of King Alfred, Bishop Asser, in the late ninth and early tenth centuries, and although the last editor of the work, W. H. Stevenson, had noted some difficulties implied by the hypothesis that Asser was its author, he had finally accepted it as probably true. After further examination Galbraith concluded that the difficulties of reconciling this hypothesis with several features of the work are so great as to render it altogether improbable. Rather, considering the language and prose style of the book, the title given to Alfred in its Dedication, and its references to the diocese of Exeter, Galbraith inferred that it was probably written by 'an eleventh-century Welshman, educated in foreign parts, who was closely interested in the removal of the see of Crediton to Exeter' (pp. 90–9). These are propositions concerning the author of the *Life* which Galbraith thought very probably true.

Galbraith then put forward the hypothesis that the work was from the hand of one Bishop Leofric, observing that 'bishop Leofric, who in fact moved the see [of Crediton] to Exeter, was himself a Welshman, *altus et doctus* among the Lotharingians, and seems to have been brought to England by Edward the Confessor' (p. 99). So all of the propositions noted as true of the author are true of Bishop Leofric. Galbraith found that an additional one is also true, for the range of books borrowed from in the *Life* corresponds roughly to the range of books known to have been in Leofric's library.

Galbraith concluded:

Such are the grounds for attributing the Life to bishop Leofric. The hypothesis, of course, could be and perhaps should be widened to include the possibility that the actual author was an ecclesiastic in Leofric's service, or a Crediton colleague; and, so qualified, seems to me to have strong claims on our acceptance. The evidence, even if largely circumstantial, is many-sided. (p. 102)

The evidence does not allow one to infer directly that Leofric or one of his associates was the author. He is not alluded to as such in the book itself, either directly or indirectly, nor in any other document known to Galbraith. But the facts believed to be true of the author are all known to be true of bishop Leofric, and it is unlikely that so many diverse attributes were possessed by anyone else. Had Galbraith known only that the author was an educated man of the eleventh century, it would have been much harder to justify saying Leofric was probably the man. This is the point in remarking that the evidence is 'many-sided'; the number of people having all of the characteristics believed true of the author of Asser's *Life of Alfred* is known to have been very small. From his knowledge of the sizes of the sets of people involved, Galbraith felt sure that it was highly unlikely that anyone outside Leofric and his close associates was a member of all of them. Indeed Galbraith's knowledge of those closely interested in the removal of the see of Crediton to Exeter is manifestly so detailed and comprehensive that he might well have known them all, so that had any other foreign-educated, eleventh-century Welshman been closely interested in it, Galbraith would have known of him. If this were so, then Galbraith's judgement that Leofric was the author of the *Life* is all the more probably true.

The form of the argument used here may be represented as follows:

(1)   There is a thing (person, object, event) of which the sentence S_1 is a true description (e.g. that he wrote the *Life of Alfred*), of which

other sentences $S_2, S_3, \ldots S_n$ are probably true also (e.g. that he was an eleventh-century Welshman, that he was educated abroad, and that he was closely interested in the removal of the see of Crediton to Exeter.)

(2)　$S_2 \ldots S_n$ are probably true of the thing T_1 (e.g. Leofric).

(3)　$S_2 \ldots S_n$ are not true of any thing other than T_1.

(4)　Therefore S_1 is probably true of T_1.

Statistical inferences are used to reach the conclusion that the thing of which S_1 is true, is a thing of which S_2 is true, and $S_3 \ldots$ and S_n. These inferences are based upon the evidence available to the historian. In this case that evidence included the language and prose style of the book, as well as details of its contents. The second premise (2) is based upon existing knowledge or arrived at by further investigation. The third premise (3) is indispensable, for it rules out the possibility of something other than T_1 satisfying $S_1 \ldots S_n$. There are two ways in which this premise is normally arrived at. If $S_1 \ldots S_n$, or at least most of these sentences, are each known to be true of very few people, then the number of people of whom they are all true is likely to be extremely small, being the intersection of the small sets, as it were. This is the more likely to be the case, the more independent the properties described by $S_1 \ldots S_n$ are. The intersection of the sets of people who are British police constables, who wear blue uniforms and who carry whistles, is not as small as the intersection of the sets of people who are British police constables, who belong to an ornithological society, and who have Spanish wives. If the sets are small, numerous and independent, the number of things which are members of all of them is likely to be very small indeed, often hardly more than one. An even more reliable way of establishing the third premise is to check every member of one of the sets to see whether they are also members of the others. When the sets are small, this is quite practical, so long as the relevant data is available. If only one thing is found to belong to all the sets, so that $S_1 \ldots S_n$ are true only of it, then the third premise has been established.

Clearly this is not a simple statistical inference, but neither is it an argument to the best explanation. Indeed explanation plays no part in it at all, though the conclusion, once established, can sometimes be used to explain much of the data from which it was drawn. It is really just a complex sort of argument about probabilities. It is very commonly used by historians. (Other good examples are provided by N. Denholm-Young's essays 'The Authorship of *Vita Edwardi Secundi*' and 'Who Wrote *Fleta*?', in his *Collected Papers*, 1969.)

Sometimes historians attempting this form of inference cannot establish the third premise, but have to admit that there are two or more things of which $S_1 \ldots S_n$ are all true. Then, to choose between the different possibilities, historians try to reduce the probability of all but one, or, failing that, attempt to show one provides a better explanation of known data than does the other. In short, they look to either an argument by elimination or an argument to the best explanation to assist them. If they use the latter, then the form of inference is hybrid: they reached their hypotheses by means of statistical inferences and chose between them by judging which provided the best explanation of the evidence.

There are possibly other hybrid and complex forms of inference used by historians to justify belief in their descriptions of the past. Those analysed here are very common, however, and the examples are well known.

5 Intuitive inferences

Michael Scriven has pointed out that the generalizations which historians can be supposed to use when drawing inferences about the past are often very complex, stating, for example, several different possible causes of an event, and that sometimes the range of possibilities of which an historian is aware is greater than he can readily state. Furthermore, an historian is often aware of the kinds of circumstances under which each of the possibilities is likely to be realized, but is unable to put that knowledge into words either. For this reason, Scriven said, historians' use of such general knowledge in drawing inferences about the past is often intuitive. They reach their conclusions without having articulated the premises of their arguments, even to themselves. In this respect, Scriven observed, expert historians resemble expert doctors and engineers who diagnose the probable cause of an illness or of an engine malfunction without being able to state precisely the reasons for their conclusions. (Scriven, 1966, pp. 250–4; and Scriven, 1969. The latter article has been discussed by Van Evra, 1971, and Scriven, 1971b.)

There is no doubt that historians do draw inferences from their general knowledge intuitively, just as Scriven said. The role of general knowledge in the formulation of the historical hypotheses used in arguments to the best explanation has probably been largely ignored because such hypotheses are frequently intuited rather than explicitly inferred. It is sometimes thought that explanatory hypotheses are just a product of an historian's imagination, but more often than not it is clear that the imagination which suggests them is an informed imagination, not mere undisciplined fancy. It is almost always possible for an historian to see, once a hypothesis has been produced, that it was logically implied by his general knowledge based upon analogous cases. Scriven did not argue, however, that intuitive inferences yield merely plausible hypotheses, which must then be tested before being accepted as true. He contended that 'empathy is a fine provider of knowledge' (1969, p. 203). Is this assertion justified? Or, at least, is one ever justified in believing historians' intuitive judgements about the past to be true?

There are two grounds for scepticism about historians' intuitive judgements which Scriven acknowledged but did not discuss (ibid., p. 208). First there is the danger that intuitive interpretations of actions and artefacts in cultures other than the historian's will be inaccurate because those things do not have the same significance in the other cultures as they do in the historian's own. The second danger is that once an historian intuitively happens upon a hypothesis which adequately fits the data he is trying to interpret, he might fail to consider another hypothesis which is even more probable or provides an even better explanation, and so is more worthy of belief.

Both of these dangers are likely to be avoided if certain conditions are satisfied. As to the first, there certainly is a danger that an historian who intuitively interprets the behaviour and products of people in other societies will use general knowledge appropriate to his own. This danger can be averted, however, if the historian immerses himself in the conventions of the society he is studying, learning the significance of its words and actions by studying them in different contexts. This is precisely what professional historians do, as J. H. Hexter has fully explained in his essay 'The Historian and His Day' (Hexter, 1961). Hexter regularly spent nine or ten hours a day reading 'things written between 1450 and 1650 or books written by historians on the basis of things written between 1450 and 1650' (p. 6). As a result he found that 'instead of the passions, prejudices, assumptions and pre-possessions, the events, crises and tensions of the present dominating my view of the past, *it is the other way about*' (p. 9). By such intense study, the professional historian builds up a detailed and quite reliable understanding of the community he is studying. Thus Herbert Butterfield wrote of Sir Walter Scott: 'He so soaked himself in the Convenanters that he did not need to remember things about them – he could think their way and feel what they would do or say in various kinds of situations' (Butterfield, 1951, pp. 245–6). Professional historians avoid the danger of interpreting the past by the conventions of the present, by building up a comprehensive knowledge of the conventions and preoccupations of the past.

An historian's intuitive interpretation of past behaviour is not likely to be inaccurate if he has a professional understanding of the period. Scriven allowed that it is only the intuitive judgements of professionals which deserve to be believed. Even professional historians should not be trusted, however, when they make intuitive judgements about events which occurred outside their area of expert knowledge. Leopold von Ranke, for example, deplored Scott's portrayal of Charles the Bold and Louis XI in *Quentin Durward* as quite unhistorical, much as he admired the liveliness of his descriptions. C. V. Wedgwood, having reported this, went on to remark:

Those who are sensitive for the honour of Scott as a student of history may also reflect that if the young Ranke had confined his attention to *Old Mortality, Rob*

Roy, Heart of Midlothian and those novels in which Scott is historically and geographically at home with his subject, he would not have found him playing half so many novelist's tricks with his material. (Wedgwood, 1967, pp. 27–8)

The second reason for doubting the truth of intuitive inferences is that the historian making them might not have given due consideration to all the different possible implications of his data. It is tempting to accept the first hypothesis that fits, and not consider alternatives. Thus several historians accepted the hypothesis that Barère shifted his political allegiance for selfish reasons without even considering the hypothesis which Gershoy defended, namely that he acted to sustain the authority and unity of the revolutionary government in Paris. How can such blindness to alternatives be prevented?

Once historians are aware of this problem they can help to overcome it by conscientiously considering whether there are alternative possibilities every time they draw an intuitive conclusion. The success of this procedure in revealing plausible alternatives cannot be assured, however, especially when an historian's first conclusion fits neatly with his general understanding of the period. Some historians are more flexible in this regard than others. Therefore it is only reasonable to believe those who have a high rate of proven success in drawing intuitive inferences. The success of an intuitive inference is proved when its conclusion is borne out by subsequent investigation, that is when its implications are found to be true and when other beliefs about the past are found to imply its probable truth. A high success rate is a sign not only of an historian's mental versatility but also of the adequacy of his understanding of the period in question.

Some philosophers have thought that no conclusions intuitively arrived at should be accepted as true until proved so by subsequent investigation (e.g. Abel, 1948, and Howard Cohen, 1973). Without the qualifications which have just been described, intuitive inferences often are unreliable and their conclusions do not deserve to be believed without further investigation. When they are made by professionals in their area of expertise, however, and when the professional has a reputation for producing reliable hypotheses in the past, then it is reasonable to believe them true. To refuse to accept them might be to deprive historical scholarship of remarkable insights by learned scholars, and that would be a high price to pay for the right to check all inferences before believing them. In fact it will be found that when experts arrive at their conclusions intuitively, in many cases they can then readily justify them by one of the common forms of inference. The beliefs which warranted the conclusion are seldom entirely beyond identification and description.

4

Justifying singular descriptions: III Arguments from criteria and arguments from analogy

1 Arguments from criteria

The most common ways in which historians infer singular descriptions of the past are by arguments to the best explanation and by statistical inferences. But they use other forms of inference as well. Sometimes they use simple mathematics to calculate people's age or the dates at which certain events occurred. Often they appeal to rules governing the correct use of words to produce new descriptions of the past.

There are two kinds of rule about the correct use of words which it is important to distinguish here. There are rules stating the truth conditions of descriptions, that is rules which state what conditions must exist in the world for a certain description of the world to be true; and there are rules stating the assertion conditions of descriptions, that is rules which state what conditions in the world warrant the use of a certain description. The truth conditions and the assertion conditions of historical descriptions are sometimes the same, but not always. The truth conditions are necessary as well as sufficient for a description to be true, whereas the assertion conditions are merely sufficient. One may assert that a man has died if his obituary is reported in the newspaper; but what makes it true that he has died is the event of his death. The assertion conditions of historical descriptions can be said to be the criteria which warrant their assertion.

Having made the distinction between rules stating the truth conditions and those stating the assertion conditions of descriptions, it must be said that such rules have seldom been formulated by the people who use them, so that many are rules which people follow in practice rather than rules they appeal to in theory. Once an attempt is made to formulate them, it is often found that they are far less precise than had been imagined. Even apparently unambiguous words can usually be applied correctly to a range of things. Lemons, for example, can be large or small, green or yellow, so that there is a somewhat imprecise range of truth conditions for the statement 'That is a lemon'. The conditions denoted by some words, like 'a game', are notoriously difficult to state. These difficulties make one qualify the claim that truth conditions are all necessary for a description to be true: only one set of all the possible sets of truth conditions of a description must correspond to part of reality for that description to be true (see Chapter 1, sect. 2).

If one takes the criteria of a description in a broad sense as any set of conditions which are sufficient to justify the assertion of that description, then the last two chapters, setting out the acceptance conditions of arguments to the best explanation and of statistical inferences, can be seen as stating two different kinds of criteria for historical descriptions. There are two reasons why it might be thought that in the present context such an interpretation of criteria is too broad. The first is that such criteria do not relate specific conditions to specific descriptions, and so cannot be used as rules of language in the way which is here being discussed. To say that a certain description may be asserted if it is the best explanation of certain data, or the one most probably true, is not to give criteria for the use of a description in the normal sense. Second, such a broad interpretation of criteria would make it difficult to distinguish arguments from criteria from other forms of justification of singular descriptions of the past, as may usefully be done.

This contrast can readily be made if one adopts a very narrow interpretation of criteria, regarding them as truth conditions sufficient to warrant a description. These will often be fewer than all the truth conditions of a description. Some historical descriptions are justified by showing that enough of their truth conditions obtained to warrant the description given, according to the normal rules of the language. The act of arriving at a new description in this way is a simple act of classification.

Simple classification

Historians classify data most often at the beginning and at the end of their inquiry. They classify evidence on the basis of its observable characteristics, usually without difficulty. Jonathan Gorman has discussed the use of criteria in this sort of classification in chapter 6 of his book *The Expression of Historical Knowledge* (1982). He points out that historians need criteria to determine that something is a sentence, and that something is a letter, just to be justified in saying that they have a letter containing a certain sentence. Then, after historians have discovered quite a lot about past events, they often classify them under some general concept like 'a revolution', 'a coup d'état', 'an economic depression' and so on (see Dray, 1959; and McCullagh, 1978). What is being classified in both these cases of arguing from criteria is the thing of which all the criteria are true, not each individual property of that thing. According to Gorman, for example, a letter is an object with sentences inscribed upon it which has been written with some characteristic intention (such as to convey information to some specific individuals in a literary manner). It is an object having these properties which is classified as a letter, not the properties themselves. Similarly a democratic political system might be described as a political system with 'a wide franchise, secret balloting and widespread political office holding' (Karlman, 1976, p. 58). Any system which has these features may be called 'a democracy', though the features themselves are not democracies. When the criteria are among the truth conditions of historical descriptions, it is true to say that they are parts of the things described, though the whole is usually much more than the sum of the criteria. A letter, for example, has texture, shape and weight; and a democracy usually has a list of citizens (the electoral roll), wooden boxes (ballot boxes) and other bits of paraphernalia which are not among the criteria of the organization which makes it democratic. Furthermore, the various properties of these wholes are usually related to a function which the whole serves. The criteria which justify a classification are just the distinguishing characteristics of the things classified.

Gorman has presented arguments from criteria as deductive in form, and so they generally are, though one could argue that they should not be. An example of a deductive argument from criteria is as follows:

> Every political system which includes wide franchise, secret balloting and widespread political office holding is democratic.
>
> The political system in pre-revolutionary Massachusetts had these features.
>
> Therefore the political system in pre-revolutionary Massachusetts was democratic.

The first, major premise here is a universal generalization, derived from what is taken to be a rule about the English language. As several writers have pointed out, rules of language are normative. They express what a linguistic community has agreed should be the universal rule, rather than what rule members of the community actually follow in practice (Scruton, 1976, pp. 207–8; Scriven, 1959b, p. 866). To emphasize this fact, Roger Scruton has said the major premise should mention but not use the description which the criteria warrant. In the present example one should conclude the major premise with 'may be called "democratic"', rather than 'is democratic'. The difference, however, is insignificant. If one is warranted in calling a political system democratic, then one may say that it is so without further qualification. Scruton's advice must be followed, though, when stating the warrant for the generalization, which is a rule of language about what may be said and not just an observed fact about political systems.

Although the major premise is commonly construed as a universal generalization, it is not thought to be necessarily true, even within a language, but just contingently so. Rules of language change from time to time, words lose old meanings and acquire new ones, so that the criteria for their use can change. Our understanding of a democratic political system probably differs from that of an eighteenth-century American, so that what they would have judged to be democratic, we might not. They probably thought a property qualification for franchise, and the restriction of office holders to the upper classes was consistent with democracy, whereas we would not. (For further discussion of this example see Karlman, 1976, pp. 57–63, 90–3.)

There is some reason to be dissatisfied with the view that arguments from criteria are deductive, but it is hard to decide whether the objections are weighty enough to make that logical model unacceptable. It is widely acknowledged that adequate statements of criteria for descriptions are very difficult to produce. We use language efficiently without always being aware of the rules we are in fact following. The rules are not very easy to discover, and most formulations of them are a bit tentative. Should that tentativeness be reflected in the generalization? Instead of a universal statement, perhaps it should be a probability statement expressing a relative frequency 'in most cases, things with these properties are of this kind'; or, 'probably a thing with these properties is of this kind'. Even the minor premise should perhaps be a probability statement, expressing what properties it is reasonable to believe that a certain thing has. This qualification is particularly appropriate if the minor premise is itself the product of historical inquiry. Even if it reports sensory observations, however, it is not infallible but could be false. If both premises of the argument were probability statements, then the inference would be a statistical syllogism, an inductive argument, and not a deduction. It would differ from the arguments described in the last section only in that the generalization is derived from a rule of language, rather than from relative frequencies. The conclusion would then be a probability statement, saying what it is reasonable to believe to a certain degree.

The deductive model is clearly misleading, and so probably it should be abandoned. It is a relic of the days when people thought the rules of language were analytic, necessarily true. We now have a different view of those rules. We admit that our formulations of them might well be inaccurate and even that the rules might be superseded. Similarly, the conclusions we draw from them are much more fallible than the deductive model suggests. The conclusion of a deduction is necessarily true if the premises are true. But the conclusions of arguments from criteria are by no means necessary, and it is misleading to represent them as such.

The question might be raised, if an argument from criteria establishes that it is reasonable to assert a certain description, has it provided us with a new truth about the world or has it just demonstrated how we are entitled to talk about what was already known? It is easier to discuss this question if one has a concrete case in mind. Suppose an historian employed a sound argument from criteria to establish that a certain document was a genuine charter giving certain rights to a medieval monastery. Does describing the document in this way provide us with new information about the world?

There are two ways in which it very probably does so. First, it might yield facts about aspects of the object classified which had not been known before. The criteria which justified the classification might not have exhausted its truth conditions. Once an object has been identified, other features of it might be inferred to exist which had not been noticed or understood before. Certain phrases and marks on the charter might become easier to interpret, once its nature is recognized. Second, and even more important, once something has been classified by means of a general term, it is often possible to draw many new inferences about it, using generalizations in which that general term is one of the variables. Once a charter has been identified, then the historian can draw inferences about the rights and privileges of the·monastery under law, and perhaps even draw inferences about its relations with the Crown, its wealth and size, and so about its importance in the land. Thus, although a new description might not itself provide much more information about the internal nature of what has been described, it often makes it possible for an historian to infer a lot of new facts about its relation to other things. Strictly speaking, of course, a new true description is a new fact in itself, but if it implies the existence of no new truth conditions, it does not by itself yield much new information.

Dispositions and actions

The philosopher who has done most to draw attention to arguments from criteria in history is L. B. Cebik in his book *Concepts, Events and History* (1978). Cebik has paid particular attention to the way historians justify statements about people's actions. Normally they do not justify such statements by the construction of arguments to the best explanation or by statistical syllogisms, according to Cebik; nor do they appeal to specific rules of language to justify their descriptions. Rather, they use behavioural criteria of an appropriate kind.

The truth conditions of action-descriptions are in fact of three kinds. First, actions can be described in terms of the intentions with which they were done; second, they can be described in terms of their consequences, whether these were intended or not; and third, they can be classified on the basis of certain intrinsic features they have together with the context in which they were performed, in the manner described above.

Since the last of these ways of justifying action descriptions employs the sort of reasoning which has already been discussed, it will be convenient to explain it first. In certain contexts, certain kinds of behaviour warrant certain action descriptions, according to rules of language, and sometimes rules of law as well, no matter what the intentions of the agent or the effects of his behaviour. Thus, in our society, raising a hand at an auction constitutes a bid no matter whether it was intended as such or taken as such. Similarly, the French took the behaviour of King William of Prussia, as reported in the telegram from Ems which Bismarck had carefully edited before releasing it to the papers in July 1870, as insulting to the French nation. As Erick Eyck said, by editing them Bismarck 'gave the words of the Ems text – "the King had informed the French Ambassador through his A.D.C. that he had nothing further to tell him" – the meaning of a grave and intentional snub' (Eyck, 1958, p. 172). The French regarded the reported cold, deliberate refusal of the King to receive their ambassador as a national insult, irrespective of the King's intentions in doing so. Bismarck's carefully falsified report provoked the French to declare war on Germany. The description of the king's reported behaviour as 'an insult to the French nation' is justified by the criteria for the use of such a phrase. There are various ways in which one country can insult another, and refusing to speak to its ambassador is one of them. Another would be for the government of one country publicly to vilify the national character of another; or to burn its flag and destroy its embassy and other agencies. The Iranian government's behaviour towards the U.S.A. after the overthrow of the monarchy in Iran provides vivid examples of these kinds. Notice that here there are several sets of possible truth conditions of the description, and the satisfaction of any one set is sufficient for the correct use of that description, but the description is not warranted unless at least one set is satisfied.

The other ways of justifying action-descriptions, in terms of the intention with which an action was done or in terms of the effects of the action, appeal to criteria in a different way. They do not refer to a rule of language which relates a particular description and its truth conditions. Rather they appeal to rules of a much more general kind, together with relevant features of the situation.

Action-descriptions in terms of intention, for instance, are justified by the rule that an action may be described in terms of the intention with which it was done, together with a statement of the agent's intention in performing the action in question. Thus the one action of Bismarck's can be called 'publishing a telegram from King William at Ems' and 'provoking the French to war', so long as these descriptions accurately reflect Bismarck's intention in acting. Even if the French had not responded as Bismarck had hoped, and no war had followed, his action would still have been one of provoking the French to war if that was his intention. One person can provoke another, even though the other will not be provoked.

Action-descriptions in terms of effect are justified by the rule that an action may be described in terms of its effect, plus a statement of what its effect was. In that Bismarck's publication of the edited telegram did cause France to declare war on Germany, it may be described as bringing about that effect, whether Bismarck intended it or not. In this case the description of his action as one of 'provoking France to war' can be justified by reference to its effects, as well as its intention. Bismarck's action was also one of angering King William, as this is what it did. Finally, it facilitated the unification of Germany under a central government. This was its most important effect.

In the opening chapters of his book, Cebik makes two interesting points about action-descriptions. The first is that often they do not seem to classify what they describe in the usual Aristotelian way, *per genus et differentia* (p. 22). The analysis just given helps one to see why this is so. Actions described in terms of intentions or effects are seldom seen as members of a class, because those intentions or effects are often quite unique. Only actions classified in the usual way, in accordance with a rule relating the description to sets of general criteria, do appear to be members of a class. There are many acts of national insult, but not many of provoking the government of Louis Napoleon to declare war on Germany in July 1870.

Cebik's second point is that when we describe people's plans or dispositions we are not describing 'new empirical facts' about them but are simply ascribing things to them in accordance with linguistic conventions (p. 29). The conventions in these cases relate patterns of behaviour in context to descriptions of plans and dispositions. Bismarck's energetic support in 1870 of a Hohenzollern candidate for the Spanish throne seems to have been directed to provoking the French to war, as some of his contemporaries remarked (Eyck, 1958, p. 170). (A. J. P. Taylor, 1954, has challenged this judgment, however, on p. 205, note 2). The convention which warrants one ascribing such a plan to Bismarck is the rule that if a person performs a sequence of actions which he would have expected to help bring about an outcome which he desired quite strongly, then he may be said to have acted in accordance with a plan to achieve that outcome. The ascription of a plan to someone in such circumstances, according to Cebik, is not providing additional empirical information. It is just pointing out the significance of what has already been observed. If this is right, then to describe a person's behaviour in terms of his other intentions is not to supply new empirical information about it either. There is one respect in which Cebik qualifies this conclusion. Descriptions of dispositions might entitle us to draw inferences about other events, about a person's future behaviour for example, so they do add something to our knowledge. They are not entirely devoid of additional factual significance. But they do not, in Cebik's eyes, correspond to anything in the world over and above those things which warrant their assertion.

One question raised by this line of argument is the question of the truth conditions of statements describing people's dispositions, and of those describing actions in terms of intentions. The analysis adopted by Cebik suggests that the truth conditions of such statements are nothing other than the observable criteria which warrant them. That opinion is disputed, however, by philosophers who think of dispositions, such as intentions and plans, as real mental states which people manifest in certain patterns of behaviour but which exist independent of that behaviour, and indeed might never be manifest in observable behaviour at all. On this account, observable behaviour might correspond to criteria for ascribing certain dispositions to people, but the truth conditions of such descriptions would be the existence of the states of mind described. There is no consensus yet as to which interpretation of human dispositions and actions is the correct one.

If it is accepted that the truth conditions of statements about people's dispositions are mental states, quite different from the behavioural manifestations of those states which constitute the criteria for ascribing such dispositions to others, then clearly sometimes the criteria for descriptions are not among the truth conditions of those descriptions. Sometimes, as in these cases, the criteria are sufficient to warrant the assertion of a description but do not have to exist for that description to be true. (Some people are in pain but never show it. Many think thoughts and dream dreams but never express them.) Here the word 'criteria' is not being used in the very narrow sense which has been adopted so far, as referring to truth conditions sufficient to warrant a description. Yet this new use can be accommodated without having to adopt the very broad account of criteria as any set of statements warranting a description, which allows the premises of some arguments to be criteria for the truth of their conclusions. Instead one can say criteria for a description are conditions sufficient to warrant that description according to rules of certain kinds, including rules of language and rules relating the intentions and effects of actions to action descriptions, but not according to general rules about the validity of arguments. Such criteria may be truth conditions of the description, but they need not be so.

The logical structure of these two kinds of argument from criteria justifying action descriptions is clearly different from the structure of simple cases of classification, discussed before. There is no need to deny that the generalizations used in these arguments are universal. They may be expressed thus:

(1) If a person's movements were performed with a certain intention, they may be described in terms of that intention. Thus, if a person's intention in moving is 'to ϕ' (e.g. to publish a telegram, to provoke a war), then the movement may be described as 'ϕ-ing' (e.g. publishing a telegram, provoking a war).

(2) If a person's movements caused a certain event to take place (so that it would not have taken place but for those movements and its occurrence was made probable by those movements), then those movements may be described as bringing about (in some way) that effect.

These rules are accepted without qualification. What is sometimes uncertain is what the intentions were with which a person acted and what the effects were of his action. The general criteria for determining intentions are clear enough: a person usually intends to bring about consequences of his action which he can predict as following from the action and which he wants to bring about. The difficulty is in deciding what consequences he may have seen as following upon his action, and which if any of these he may have desired. These difficulties are encountered, for instance, in determining whether Bismarck intended to provoke France to war by supporting the Hohenzollern candidate for the Spanish throne. Eyck, having confessed the difficulty of deciding whether he did, then adduces reasons for believing Bismarck might have seen war as a consequence of his policy, and evidence of his wanting such a consequence at the time. The data, however, does not establish either fact beyond doubt, so the question of Bismarck's intentions, in Eyck's eyes, remains a bit uncertain (Eyck, 1958, pp. 169–70). A. J. P. Taylor has argued to an opposite conclusion: 'Bismarck knew that there would be some French opposition; this is very far from saying that he expected it to provoke the French to war. His calculation seems to have been the opposite: by making the French anxious on their Spanish frontier, it would make them less ready to go to war for the sake of south Germany' (Taylor, 1954, p. 202). Taylor further suggested that there is no evidence that Bismarck at that time wanted war with France. So he concluded that such a war was not Bismarck's intention in supporting the Hohenzollern candidate.

There is seldom much difficulty in deciding the effects of an action, but where there is it is usually the result both of imprecision in the rule which sets out criteria for something being an effect for which an agent is responsible, and of uncertainties about the facts of the case. One may say that event A caused event B if A was necessary for B in the circumstances, and if A made B probable. The nature of causal relations will be discussed in later chapters. The point to note at present is the vagueness of 'made B probable'. How probable? Did the scientists who developed the atomic bomb in doing so bring about the destruction of Hiroshima and Nagasaki? Did Hitler kill the roughly six million Jews who died under his rule? One is inclined to answer the first question in the negative and the second in the affirmative, as the probability of the consequences is much greater in the second case than the first. But how probable the consequences should be, and how probable they actually were in each case, is very hard to say.

Historians' statements about people's intentions and about the effects of their actions are, therefore, often quite tentative. The degree to which there is reason to believe them true can be expressed in terms of a probability estimate. That being so, the conclusions of arguments in which they appear as premises must be probability statements as well.

The general structure of those arguments is as follows:

(1) If a person's movements were performed with a certain intention, they may be described in terms of that intention.
This person, in performing movements M, probably intended to
ϕ.
Therefore, this person in performing movements M was probably ϕ-ing.

(2) If a person's movements caused a certain event to take place,
then those movements may be described as bringing about
that effect.
This person, in performing movements M, probably caused an
event E to occur.
Therefore, this person in performing movements M was probably bringing about E.

The degree of probability in the conclusion is just the same as the degree
of probability of the minor premise, since the probability of the major
premise is regarded as one. The probability of the conclusion expresses
the degree to which it is rational to believe that its predicate correctly
describes the movements of the agent referred to.

The rationality of arguments from criteria

The difficulties of arriving at rationally justifiable conclusions to arguments from criteria have been mentioned already in defending the claim
that they should be regarded as probability statements. Simple classification is frequently made difficult by uncertainty about precisely what are
sufficient criteria for the uses of certain words. W. B. Gallie has argued
that some important concepts we use, like 'a religion', 'art', 'democracy'
and 'social justice', are what he calls 'essentially contested'. There are
strong differences of opinion about the criteria of their use which show no
signs of being resolved (Gallie, 1964, ch. 8). Jonathan Gorman has
pointed out that in the experience of lawyers there are almost always
borderline cases in the interpretation of descriptions, which are difficult
to decide: 'Thus in a standard example – where the law forbids vehicles in
a public park, is a pram, a bicycle, or a lorry on a plinth forbidden?'
(Gorman, 1982, p. 64). So the difficulties in finding a precise statement of
the criteria of a term can be severe. Historians can express their degree of
confidence in a statement of criteria in terms of a probability rating. But
have they a rational basis for that rating? How can they know how close
they are to the truth? What they usually go on is a personal impression of
the proportion of cases in which the criteria are satisfied and the related
description is or is not generally accepted. They usually have some data
upon which to judge this proportion, but seldom have they established
that that data is either exhaustive or representative of all cases. However,
an experienced historian might know a large range of cases – of medieval

charters, for example – and have good reason for believing he knows sufficient criteria for the application of the relevant term. Thus Bloch drew his analysis of feudal terms from charters containing them. 'The villein tenement, which the charters of the eleventh century, anticipating the jurists of the thirteenth, already expressly distinguished from the feif, was burdened with labour services as well as with rents in kind' (Bloch, 1965, vol. 1, p. 167).

The rule which expresses the relation between the descriptions of actions and the intentions with which they were done is not uncertain. But that which relates the descriptions of actions and their effects is imprecise, as the strength of the causal connection required in such cases is not clearly specified. Indeed one suspects that in these cases there is a further complication as well. For to say that A brought about E by doing M suggests not only that A's doing M was an important cause of E, but also that A was morally responsible for E's occurrence. If A gave an order for E to happen, then even if the chances of E's occurring as a result of the order were not great (let E be the destruction of an enemy's position, for example), if E did occur one would be inclined to say A had done it. Uncertainty over this point makes the rule relating action descriptions to effects even more uncertain. It is clear that moral responsibility is not required in all cases. If someone drives a car over a dog which unexpectedly ran under its wheels, then the driver killed the dog even though he was not morally responsible for doing so. It is just that moral responsibility might be enough (though what degree is enough is uncertain) to justify describing a person's movements in terms of their consequences in some cases.

These uncertainties in the rule about describing actions in terms of their consequences do not affect the argument if the effects being referred to are clearly ones which the agent made very probable or for which he was plainly morally responsible. It is only when the causal connection is weak or the degree of moral responsibility is slight that the appropriateness of describing an action in terms of its effects is uncertain too. The uncertainty about these borderline cases is adequately expressed by a probability estimate in the minor premises: 'probably A's doing M caused E' or 'probably A was responsible for E's occurrence'. Notice, though, that the uncertainty expressed in this way could be a compound of the uncertainty about what counts as a causal relation or as a case of moral responsibility in the present context, plus the uncertainty about the actual strength of the causal relation or the degree of moral responsibility in the specific instance. Can these degrees of uncertainty be rationally assessed? There are grounds for judging the strength of a causal relation and the degree of a person's responsibility, so that a rational assessment of these is theoretically possible. These grounds will be explained in Chapter 8. But how can one estimate the degree of uncertainty about whether a causal relation of such and such a strength or a degree of moral responsibility of such and such a magnitude is sufficient for the purposes of the rule governing action-descriptions? The only objective basis for such an estimate would be the frequency with which it has been accepted that people's movements having a causal relation to their effects of the same strength may be described in terms of those effects; or the frequency with which people who have had the same degree of moral responsibility for an outcome are accepted as having produced that outcome. Again a rational judgement is possible, though it is seldom made systematically.

The last cause of uncertainty about the conclusions of arguments from criteria which should be reiterated is the uncertainty historians frequently feel about attributing intentions to people in the past, which leads to uncertainty about any description of their actions in terms of that intention. The probability that an agent intends to bring about ϕ should be a product of the strength of his expectation that his movements will in result in ϕ and of his desire to bring about ϕ. If an agent is rational about the matter, this will provide a basis for estimating the strength of his intention, assuming the relevant information is available. The only other basis for such an estimate is knowledge of the frequency with which the agent pursues such goals in such circumstances. But this method presupposes a consistency of behaviour which is not always warranted. Because people are neither as rational nor as consistent as computers, these grounds for estimating strength of intention are not very reliable. They are therefore usually supplemented, when they are used at all, by an argument to the best explanation, or even by a statistical inference (perhaps from the agent's reported declaration of intention) to provide, if possible, additional support to the conclusion. It quite frequently is the case that people act for an intention which they do not hold very passionately, and one can only be certain of their intention in acting by showing that no other intention explains their behaviour nearly as well.

2 Arguments from analogy

Arguments from analogy resemble statistical syllogisms in one important respect: their conclusions are not always worthy of belief, but may be rationally accepted if certain conditions are satisfied. Like statistical syllogisms, taken alone they are incomplete, inadequate arguments.

The logical form of analogical arguments is simple enough. It may be represented thus:

> One thing (object, event, or state of affairs) has properties $p_1 \ldots p_n$ and p_{n+1}.
> Another thing has properties $p_1 \ldots p_n$.
> So the latter has property p_{n+1}.

The conclusion is credible only if the properties $p_1 \ldots p_n$ of something make it likely that it will also have property p_{n+1}. Clearly this is not always the case. Two people of the same sex, for example, might have literally hundreds of physical properties in common. But if one were, say, a lawyer by profession, those common features would not provide rational warrant for thinking the other was a lawyer too. Generally a person's physical properties provide no grounds for believing any particular statement about their occupation. This is frequently expressed by saying that a person's physical properties are generally not relevant to their occupation. Thus, arguments from analogy which conform to the simple model set out above do not always yield credible conclusions. They do so only if there are reasons for believing that the properties which two things are known to have in common make it likely that they will have the additional property in common as well.

The interesting question which arises now is what would constitute reasons of the required sort? What are the additional conditions which have to be satisfied for the conclusions of analogical arguments to be rationally credible? There are two equivalent conditions, either of which will do. Quite briefly, if it is generally true that some or all of the properties $p_1 \ldots p_n$ are sufficient to ensure the presence of p_{n+1} in something, then the conclusion of the analogical argument is warranted, and, to put it another way, if the occurrence of p_{n+1} is necessary for the occurrence of some or all of $p_1 \ldots p_n$ in something, then the conclusion is warranted too. These two conditions, though logically equivalent, are expressed differently to indicate the two strategies historians commonly adopt in appraising arguments by analogy. They either look to see whether a projectible generalization of the form '$p_1 \ldots p_n$ is sufficient for p_{n+1}' is warranted; or they check whether there are grounds for thinking that p_{n+1} was a necessary condition, or cause, of $p_1 \ldots p_n$. If either condition is satisfied, then the conclusion of the argument from analogy is accepted; but not otherwise. Each condition establishes the relevance p_{n+1} to $p_1 \ldots p_n$.

There are several different grounds for thinking that a generalization is projectible, that is that it is true of hitherto unexamined cases. The two most common are, first, the existence of a sufficient number and variety of instances of the generalization to warrant that belief; and, second, grounds for believing that the antecedent conditions will cause the consequent to occur, in accordance with some known process. These grounds will be discussed in the chapter on generalizations. It is interesting to see here how historians appeal to them in appraising arguments from analogy.

First, here is an example of an historian refusing to accept the conclusion of an argument from analogy because the relevant generalization did not hold. There are too many known exceptions to it for it to be true. The author is A. Momigliano, and he is here discussing an argument from analogy which might have been used by his teacher, G. de Sanctis, in support of the theory that the monarchy came to an end in Rome by a gradual process, in which 'little by little the king lost his political and military power and was relegated to a few and not very important religious functions' as *rex sacrorum*. Momigliano observes:

De Sanctis had been a historian of Athens before becoming a historian of Rome; and Athens offered the best analogy for the alleged progressive decline of the *rex* in Rome. The evidence, as far as we have it, seems to indicate that the Athenian king, the *basileus*, had been progressively stripped of his powers, had become an annual magistrate, and had been included in the college of the nine archons as the *archon basileus* – a man with religious prestige but no military powers. Yet the Greek world also offers examples of kings stripped of their powers and reduced to the position of harmless priests, not by evolution, but by revolution . . .

Thus the Greek analogies do not help us to decide whether in Rome the monarchy slowly declined or was replaced by revolution. (Momigliano, 1969, pp. 15–16)

The point of referring to kings being stripped of their powers by revolution was to show that it is by no means generally the case that kings in the ancient world lost their powers gradually. The Athenian analogy, which provides a case of progressive decline in royal power, is therefore not reliable as an analogy of the end of the monarchy in Rome.

The next example is of an historian arguing that because certain conditions in one country caused a certain effect, it is reasonable to suppose that similar causes in another country produced a similar effect. The passage is from R. G. Collingwood's *Roman Britain*, and is set in the midst of a discussion of the reasons why, in Collingwood's opinion, at the end of the fourth century a money economy in Britain was replaced by one based upon barter. Collingwood attributed this change to the impoverishment of the villas, largely itself caused by barbarians who plundered them and by robber gangs which disrupted their trade. But another cause of the decline of the villas, Collingwood believed, was the rebelliousness of the peasants who worked on them. These peasant rebels were called Bacaudae. Deprived of both wealth and security by the power and the rights of the great landowners, these peasants took advantage of the disruption caused by barbarian invasions to strike out for themselves. This is what had happened in Gaul, and Collingwood argued that it is reasonable to think that the same happened in Britain.

The same legal and administrative system, the same distinction between rich men in great villas and poor men in village huts, and the same barbarian invasions, were present towards the end of the fourth century in Britain. Causes being identical, it is hardly to be doubted that effects were identical too; and that the wandering bands which Theodosius saw in Britain included large numbers of Bacaudae. But every man who became a Bacauda ceased to be a productive labourer. Consequently the rich estates, in addition to suffering actual plunder and the deprivation of trade, suffered a diminution in their own productive powers. (Collingwood, 1937, p. 304)

Sometimes what interests an historian is not the effect but the cause of those properties which two things have in common. Analogies are not always reliable grounds for conclusions about causes, because although like causes generally produce like effects, the reverse is not always true. In history particularly, similar effects can be the result of a variety of causes. How many different causes, for example, have resulted in a change of government in a country! To argue from like effects to like causes, there-fore, an historian must show that the causes in question are universally necessary for the effects. There is some reason to think that this was the intention of Stanley M. Elkins when he compared the experiences of North American negro slaves with those of prisoners in Nazi concentra-tion camps, in his book *Slavery*. Elkins suggested that North American slaves had a type of personality which was unusual, and which needs to be explained.

One searches in vain through the literature of the Latin-American slave systems for the 'Sambo' of our tradition – the perpetual child incapable of maturity. How is this to be explained? If Sambo is not a product of race (that 'explanation' can be consigned to oblivion) and not simply a product of 'slavery' in the abstract (other societies have had slavery), then he must be related to our own peculiar variety of it.   (Elkins, 1968, pp. 84–5)

Elkins then put forward the hypothesis that the personality of North American slaves was the result of the closed, authoritarian society in which they lived. He went on:

Two kinds of material will be used in the effort to picture the mechanisms whereby this adjustment to absolute power – an adjustment whose end product included infantile features of behavior – may have been effected. One is drawn from the theoretical knowledge presently available in social psychology, and the other, in the form of an analogy, is derived from some of the data that have come out of the German concentration camps.   (p. 87)

In German concentration camps, Elkins observed, people from a variety of cultural backgrounds lost their old personalities and generally were 'reduced to a complete and childish dependence upon their masters' (p. 113). Psychologists have been able to identify the causes of such per-sonality changes – the detachment of an old personality by acts of degra-dation and cruelty, and the creation of a new, subservient one by making people totally dependent upon their masters. Using this analogy, Elkins claimed that the same sort of causes produced the same sort of effects in North American slaves. What makes the analogy compelling is the theo-retical support given to the analysis presented. The conditions which social psychologists have identified as necessary and sufficient for the development of infantile personalities were present in many plantations. The theory establishes that the connection is not accidental, but causally significant.

An additional point, about negative analogies, can be illustrated from Elkins' discussion. He repeatedly admitted that there were striking differ-ences between plantations and concentration camps.

Of slave system and concentration camp it may be, and has been, said that the basis of one was property, of the other, terror; that one was purposeful, the other purposeless. Morally the two existed on entirely different planes. The slaveholder boasted of 'responsibility'; the SS took pride in brutality.   (Ibid., p. 226, and see p. 104)

The differences, the negative analogies as they are sometimes called, do not matter so long as they do not diminish the probability of the property being investigated occurring whenever the properties which two things are known to have in common occur. The features mentioned by Elkins here do not include any which have been identified as necessary to the production of infantile dependence, nor do they include any which would significantly alter the effect of those causes, so they do not affect the force of Elkins' argument. In Latin America, however, there existed a disanalogy which did matter. There, slaves could relate to several people besides their master – to the priest, the magistrate, to wife and children and to others besides. Unlike North American slaves and the majority of people in concentration camps, they were not dependent upon one person for every aspect of their lives. This difference was crucial, in Elkins' opinion, in allowing Latin American slaves to retain adult personalities (pp. 134–7). (In response to critics, Elkins has agreed that prisons and asylums, what Erving Goffman has called 'total institutions', provide an even closer analogy to the plantation life of slaves than do concentration camps. See Elkins, 1971, pp. 353ff.)

Each of the conditions described so far which justify belief in the conclusion of an analogical inference is a condition which establishes a generalization which says that the properties which two things are known to have in common ($p_1 \ldots p_n$) are sufficient to make it likely that they will have an additional property in common (p_{n+1}) as well. This can be established by a sufficient number and variety of instances of the generalization, 'If anything has properties $p_1 \ldots p_n$, then it will also have property p_{n+1}'; it can be established by showing that the additional property was an extremely probable effect of the other properties; and it can be established by showing that the additional property was a necessary cause of them. In fact, in arguments from analogy, it is normally this generalization which justifies the conclusion, not the analogical case. The latter plays no part in the justification whatever. It has at most only the heuristic function of serving to remind the reader of the relevant general knowledge. For this reason it is proper to regard arguments from analogy which depend upon such a generalization for their justification as covert statistical syllogisms. Their true justification conditions, then, are those of statistical inferences, described in Chapter 3.

If an historian lacks the appropriate generalization to support an argument from analogy, then its conclusion is not worthy of belief – unless it can be defended by an argument to the best explanation. Analogies often suggest hypotheses to historians, possible explanations of events, which they can then test and assess further. If an explanation suggested by an analogy does turn out to be the best one, it will not be because of the analogy which inspired it, but because of what it explains and how well it explains it. Once again the analogical case plays no part at all in the justification of the conclusion.

For these reasons, arguments from analogy are not distinct forms of historical inference capable of justifying belief in their conclusions. The most they do is suggest hypotheses for further investigation.

5

Some common inferences in history

In the last three chapters, three basic kinds of historical inference have been identified and discussed: arguments to the best explanation, statistical inferences, and arguments from criteria. Hitherto these forms of inference have been examined in isolation, and it may be wondered whether they are in fact frequently employed in historical inquiry. Are these the arguments which historians use when dating their evidence, for example, or when deciding whether one document was derived from another? Are these the forms of argument used by historians when assessing the meaning of texts? Are these the ways in which historians justify their conclusions about other people's intentions, beliefs, wishes and other dispositions?

To illuminate the nature of these common kinds of historical inquiry, and to show the use made by historians of the forms of argument which have been described above, typical examples of each of those kinds of historical inquiry from the work of reputable historians will now be analysed in detail. Where relevant, previous philosophical analysis of the arguments used in these processes of inquiry will be discussed as well. Not being an expert in any of the historical fields discussed, I do not wish to endorse the conclusions drawn by the historians quoted here. It is difficult for a lay reader to know whether an historian has done justice to the evidence or not. The examples are intended only to illustrate the common, repeated use made by historians of the three basic forms of historical inference to singular descriptions of the past.

The examples to be studied show that historians generally justify their conclusions about the past on the basis of their beliefs about present observable evidence. This fact may dismay those who believe that the credibility of historical descriptions depends upon their coherence with other accepted beliefs about the past at least as much as upon whether or not they are implied by observable evidence. Such an assumption about the justification of historical descriptions misrepresents the importance of evidence to historians, however. It makes no allowance for differences in the strength of historians' beliefs. Historians normally hold strong beliefs about data which they can perceive, and are less confident about the truth of existing written history. If an historical description is irremediably inconsistent with what can be observed, then historians will usually doubt the historical description rather than their beliefs about what they can observe.

In interpreting historical evidence historians make use of general knowledge, and this is itself often justified by accepted historical beliefs. But this general knowledge, and the beliefs from which it is derived, are only accepted as credible if they are known to be consistent with, and in many cases implied by, observable facts. Thus observations impose a fundamental constraint upon historical beliefs. That is why well-justified historical descriptions are generally accepted as true descriptions of the world, and not as mere figments of historians' imaginations.

Although historians' justifications of their descriptions of the past rest upon their beliefs about perceptible evidence, it should not be thought that their actual inquiry always begins with evidence. Normally it begins with some questions about the past which the historians want answered. These direct their search for evidence, and also direct them to look for implications of the evidence of one kind rather than another.

In tracing causal chains back into the past from present data, historians are seldom willing to go further than three links, at least with much confidence. The three links are, first, the physical history of the piece of evidence, reaching back to the date of its creation; second, the state(s) of mind of the person(s) who created the evidence; and, third, the states of the world which caused those states of mind and to which the person who produced the evidence was usually responding. Each of these important stages of historical inquiry is fraught with its own difficulties, which professional historians have elaborated upon in books on historical method. Our interest, though, is in the justification of the conclusions which historians draw at each stage. In this chapter I shall describe some common ways in which historians are able to justify their conclusions at the first two of these three stages of inquiry.

1   The physical history of evidence

There are commonly three stages in discovering the physical history of present historical data. First, there is the dating of the evidence, discovering the date of its creation. Second, it is sometimes necessary to determine whether an object is an original or a copy and, if a copy, what its relation to the original might be. Almost always it is necessary to discover, thirdly, the identity of the author or creator of the evidence if one is to discover its interesting historical implications. Some documents and other artefacts are the work of more than one person, in which case the historian will want to know what the process or chain of events was which produced it: a chain of executives, or committees, or researchers might have been responsible for its final form, and the process of its creation must be understood if its significance is to be correctly appraised.

In historical research, these stages are often all accomplished at once. If an historian picks up a dated letter written in a familiar hand by someone whom he knows to be accurate, then he will conclude without further ado that it was probably written when dated, that it is an original, and that its author was the person who signed it, whose handwriting he has recognized. On the other hand, sometimes each stage is achieved only with great difficulty, if at all. The dating of documents which bear no dates depends upon identifying something in them or on them which can be dated. For instance, if an English deed contains the phrase *exceptis viris religiosis et Judeis* (with the exception of religious men and Jews), then it can be dated as written probably within the period 1279–90, since the exclusion of 'religious men' was the result of the Statute of Mortmain in 1279, and in 1290 the Jews were expelled by Edward I and so would not be mentioned after that date (Dymond, 1974, p. 63). The identification of copies is sometimes made easy by the presence of external evidence detailing the existence of the original and the circumstances under which the copy was made. Without such external evidence, the historian has simply to compare documents and use his general knowledge about the habits of copiers to decide which was the copy and which the original. If one document omits sections of the other, or if it makes mistakes which destroy the sense of sentences or which introduce historical absurdities, then it is probably a careless copy. The authorship of unsigned documents can also be difficult to establish if ready clues like handwriting are not available. The authorship is usually fixed, if at all, by deciding who could have known and said what is in the document being studied, just as Galbraith decided who wrote Asser's *Life of Alfred*.

Galbraith's discussion of who wrote Asser's *Life of Alfred*, which was studied in Chapter 3, adequately illustrates the way in which historians commonly decide the authorship of unsigned documents. In this section, therefore, we shall study only how evidence is dated and how copies are identified.

The dating of evidence

There are many ways of establishing the date of the creation of evidence. If archaeological evidence is included, some of the modern dating procedures are quite technical (see Fleming, 1976). Where direct evidence of the date of an object is not available, then almost always an historian will look for features of the object which indicate the date of its creation. The example now to be examined illustrates this procedure well. It is an essay by M. V. Clarke, entitled 'The Wilton Diptych', first published in 1931 (Clarke, 1931). The Wilton Diptych is a beautiful picture of the presentation of Richard II to the Virgin and Child. There is no known literary evidence of its origin. As Clarke explained: 'No reference to the diptych in chronicles or records has yet been traced and all attempts to explain it must depend upon the interpretation of internal evidence in the light of contemporary events and relevant documents' (p. 272). In 1882, G. Scharf wrote that the diptych was created in 1381, but Clarke argued for a different date, between 1396 and 1399.

There are five features of the picture which Clarke used to date it.

(1)   The man in the picture is identified as Richard II (how, Clarke did not say), and she concluded: 'It can hardly be doubted that the painting was executed either for Richard or in his honour and we may then adopt as limiting dates the years 1377 to 1399' (p. 273). These are the dates of Richard II's accession to the throne and of his deposition from it. Why did Clarke draw this conclusion? She clearly assumed that paintings which depict a king are usually painted during the reign of that king. This generalization is supported by two facts. First, it represents an observed relative frequency: most pictures of monarchs have been painted while the monarchs reigned. Second, it is implied by a causal generalization, namely that most pictures of monarchs are painted to honour a reigning king or queen. It seems that this generalization was in Clarke's mind. The possibility of an alternative reason for painting a monarch was not even considered by her. Her conclusion is justified by a simple statistical inference.

(2)   The picture does not include Richard II's first wife Anne of Bohemia, nor do her armorial or other devices appear in the picture. In Clarke's opinion

it is highly improbable that a painter would have omitted the imperial arms or her two collars – rosemary and ostrich – while she was queen . . . The chroniclers are agreed upon the king's devotion to his wife, and the omission of her arms and devices therefore suggests that the picture was painted either before their marriage in 1382 or after her death in 1394. (pp. 273, 274)

How can this argument be filled out? If the picture had been painted when Anne was queen, it seems that convention would have required some reference to her existence in a picture of the king. Presumably Clarke knows of this convention from other examples of royal portraits. She hints at a possible exception to this rule, namely that if a king did not like his queen, perhaps no reference would be made to her in a painting showing the king. But this exceptional condition did not apply here: King Richard was devoted to Queen Anne. So the lack of reference to her implies the painting was not painted while she was queen. (If a singular statement plus a generalization imply another singular statement, and the latter is false but the generalization is true, then the first singular statement is false.)

As it is presented, this looks like an argument from a certain negative feature of the painting – its lack of reference to Queen Anne. There are many things which the painting lacks, however. To explain why Clarke paid particular attention to this one, it is useful to see the argument as one of testing and qualifying the conclusion of the first argument, that the painting was executed during Richard II's reign, 1377–99. If it had been painted in the years 1382–94, then, for the reasons mentioned above, reference would have been made to Queen Anne in the picture. Since no such reference was made, it probably was not painted during those years of his reign.

(3)   The picture depicts a shield which bears the quartered arms of England and France impaled with those of Edward the Confessor (1042–66), that is the quartered arms of England and France are on one half of the shield and those of Edward the Confessor are on the other half. Clarke noted that 'the St Albans author of the *Annales Ricardi Secundi*' described the king publicly adopting these impaled arms, probably in the winter of 1397–8. There is also evidence of their use by the king's cousin, Edward, Earl of Rutland and Cork, in March 1396, so it is possible that the king had used them earlier than 1397. From this discussion the reader is left to conclude that the picture was probably painted in the period 1397–9, though possibly earlier.

The argument here clearly depends upon a generalization that painters depicting arms in a picture would only depict those in use at the time of painting. Indeed Clarke prefaced her discussion of the significance of heraldic evidence with a paragraph justifying belief in this generalization. She asserted that 'an artist would not have dared to employ heraldic devices merely as fanciful ornament' but 'knew that each detail must be used to convey a definite meaning. For this reason,' she wrote, 'the heraldry of the diptych may be taken as valid evidence' (pp. 272–3). The argument is from the customs of painters at the time, which customs themselves were probably inferred from instances of them. If an artist would only depict arms in use at the time of painting, and if the impaled arms were not in use until say 1395, then the fact that they appear on the painting implies that it was painted after 1395.

The argument is an elaboration of a statistical inference. From the generalization that artists only depicted arms in use at the time of painting it follows that if a picture included a coat of arms, then it was probably painted when those arms were in use. This picture contains certain impaled arms; so it was probably painted when they were in use. From evidence available, it seems they were certainly in use by 1397–8, and possibly in use after 1395. So the painting was probably produced after 1397, though it could possibly have been painted after 1395.

(4)   King Richard and eleven angels in the picture wear a badge of a white hart with crown and chain. Clarke reported that according to the Monk of Evesham, the king first gave this badge to someone at the Smithfield tournament in October 1390. For reasons similar to those

set out in (3), Clarke concluded that the painting must have been executed after 1390.

(5)　Richard and the eleven angels wear collars of broom cods. Clarke stated that 'there is ample documentary evidence that the broom was the emblem of Charles VI [of France] and that the collar of cods was his livery' (p. 280). She found the story that Charles gave Richard gifts of his livery collars on the occasion of his marriage to Charles' daughter, Isabelle of France, 'confirmed by the account for the wedding expenses of 1396, presented by Charles Poupart, *argentier du Roy*' (p. 281). She remarked: 'The occasion cannot be earlier than the opening of marriage negotiations after Richard's return from Ireland in May 1395' (p. 282). In this case, the hypothesis that the collars were a gift to Richard from the King of France best accounts for all that is known about them, and is to some degree made probable by the extract from Charles Poupart. To this point the argument is an argument to the best explanation. Accepting that hypothesis as true, then, it follows for the reasons stated in (3) that the painting was not created before 1395.

In the light of arguments (3) and (5) Clarke concluded that the diptych could not have been painted before 1395, and that it was probably executed between 1397 and 1399 (arguments (3) and (1)). Arguments (4) and (2), when taken together, also imply that the painting was not painted before 1395.

Next Clarke considered the evidence which is inconsistent with this conclusion. If the painting had been created about 1397, then Richard's face would have resembled that of the copper effigy on his tomb, executed 1395–9, which looked cunning and had a double beard. The double beard appears in other portraits of him at this time too. But the face in the diptych is 'boyish' and without a double beard, and Richard is there depicted as 'slightly built' (p. 285). These features of the painting would, of course, support the view that it was painted at an earlier date. 'Yet the evidence, drawn from a variety of sources, runs so flatly counter to an early date that we must conclude that the artist deliberately idealized his portrait of Richard, substituting a look of sensitiveness and hope for the sly cynicism of the effigy' (p. 285). Clarke appears to have done two things here. First she compared the amount and variety of evidence in favour of one hypothesis with that in support of the other, and decided that her own hypothesis was much better supported than the other. It is interesting to note that she did not compare the probability of each. That was, perhaps, fairly close, as the youthful features of the kind in the picture do make it probable that the picture was painted at an early date, given that painters usually depict monarchs as they appear at the time of painting. Allowing that the probability of the two hypotheses is roughly even, the question then arises as to which one would best explain the available data. As there are more facts inconsistent with the early-date-hypothesis than with the late-date-hypothesis, the latter was deemed superior. But if the latter is adopted, can the evidence in support of the early-date-hypothesis be accommodated? Clarke invented an *ad hoc* hypothesis to do that. She suggested that the artist had deliberately idealized Richard's features.

To strengthen her case, Clarke then looked for support for this *ad hoc* hypothesis about the intention of the artist which would explain why he might have idealized Richard's features. Clarke had already made the point that once the date of a document is known, it then becomes possible to discuss the intention with which it was produced (p. 273). Having reached a conclusion about when the Wilton diptych had been created, Clarke felt better able to investigate the purpose of the painter.

The first hypothesis she considered was that the diptych was intended as a wedding gift for the eight-year-old Princess Isabelle. That would explain the youthful portrait of the king, and the 'emphatic treatment of the French collar'. Clarke dismissed this hypothesis, however, because three of its implications were false: the diptych is not mentioned in the carefully compiled schedule of Isabelle's wedding presents; the picture makes no reference to the bride herself; and the picture is clearly of religious rather than secular significance, in which 'the English royal saints and St John the Baptist present or dedicate the king to the Virgin and Child' (p. 285).

The second hypothesis about the intention of the painter which Clarke put forward is that the diptych was painted as part of a propaganda exercise by members of the Order of the Passion, founded and promoted by the Frenchman Philippe de Mézières, to recruit Christians to restore and govern the kingdom of Jerusalem. In the diptych, the Child points to a banner, bearing a red cross on a white ground, which is a crusading flag associated with St George. 'If it be admitted that the picture has a crusading significance we have at once an explanation of the idealization of Richard, of the offering of the banner, and of the general feeling of movement and expectation in the heavenly host round the Virgin and Child' (p. 286).

In defence of the suggestion that propagandists for the Order of the Passion would produce pictures having the features of the diptych, Clarke refers to other pictures known to have been produced for the Order. They, like the diptych, include a variety of white banners with red crosses, the lamb, a crown of thorns, and, most significantly, Richard 'painted as young and beardless and this at a time when he certainly wore a double-pointed beard and was certainly not less than twenty-eight years of age' (p. 291). Clarke concluded: 'This coincidence of detail can hardly be accidental when considered in relation to the theme of the diptych. A crusading picture with the liveries of England and France united and executed between 1396 and 1399 cannot be traced to any other origin than de Mézière's propaganda for the Order of the Passion' (pp. 291–2).

The hypothesis that the picture was created as part of the propaganda for the Order of the Passion explains so many, and such a variety, of the features of the diptych, that there is little chance of its having another source. The argument is from manifold circumstantial evidence. It is reinforced, one suspects, by Clarke's knowledge of the period. When she asserted that the painting 'cannot be traced to any other origin', one suspects that one of her reasons for saying this is that were there another likely source of the picture, she would have known of it.

The detection of copies

An interesting example of how historians decide between two documents, as to which was a copy and which an original is provided by David Knowles's review of the debate about the relation between the *Rule of St Benedict* (RB) and the *Rule of the Master* (RM), both written, it seems, early in the sixth century (Knowles, 1963). St Benedict's *Rule* has been followed by the Benedictine order of monks, and until the 1930s it was generally assumed to have been entirely the work of St Benedict, the abbot of the monastary at Monte Cassino in Italy. The Prologue and first seven chapters of his *Rule* closely resemble the opening of the *Rule of the Master*, but it was assumed the latter had been copied from the former. Now, however, there is reason to think that RB was copied from RM.

Knowles paid particular attention to five kinds of evidence in his summary of the debate.
(1)   First, Knowles referred to arguments from theories of textual criticism.

Which text, according to the approved rules of this technique, now several centuries old, is the original and which the copy? Unfortunately, after more than twenty years, and despite the efforts and assertions of numerous well-qualified scholars, the verdict of an outsider must be: *non liquet.* (p. 173)

In this case, arguments from theories of textual criticism are made uncertain because the manuscripts of the Rules available to historians are not the originals. We do not know, therefore, precisely which manuscript each author might have been copying, nor precisely what alterations he, as opposed to subsequent scribes, may have made to it. Setting aside this serious cause of uncertainty, however, Knowles said

I feel that those who seek to demonstrate the dependence of RB upon RM win heavily on points, but that there are undoubtedly several passages in which, when they are considered in isolation, the textual dependence may well seem to be the other way round, and in consequence no way exists, within this particular technique, of resolving or eliminating these obdurate contradictions. (p. 174)

The arguments from theories of textual criticism are not stated by Knowles, but the rules to which he referred are probably those such as appear in Paul Maas's well-known little book *Textual Criticism* (1958). A much more comprehensive statement of those rules, however, has been presented by L. D. Reynolds and N. G. Wilson in *Scribes and Scholars: A Guide to the Transmission of Greek and Latin Literature* (1968). Some of the rules they mention are as follows:

If one of the available readings is more difficult to understand, it is more likely to be the correct reading. The justification of this maxim is that scribes tended . . . to remove from the texts the rare or archaic linguistic forms that were no longer readily understood, or to simplify a complex process of thought that they could not master. (p. 150)

Since the best manuscript is that which gives the greatest number of correct readings in passages where there are rational grounds for decision, it is more likely than the others to give the correct reading in passages where no such grounds exist. It is this argument from probability which justifies the appeal to the best manuscript in the circumstances indicated. (*viz.*, 'where there is a variety of readings among manuscripts and there are no grounds for preferring one of those readings to another.') (p. 146)

In many textual traditions investigation will show that the oldest manuscript is the best. But there are some exceptions which serve to show that the generalization must not be carelessly applied. (p. 146)

If these generalizations were to be accepted, it is clear that they could be used as bases of statistical inferences about which of several manuscripts, or passages in manuscripts, is most likely to be original. It is interesting to note, though, that not all the principles used by textual critics are generalizations of this sort. Many are generalizations about likely causes of error through copying, and these can guide historians in forming hypotheses to explain anomalies in manuscripts. The authors list, and illustrate, no fewer than eight kinds of situation which typically have caused mistakes in the transmission of texts. The first, for example, are mistakes arising from some feature of ancient or medieval handwriting.

Typical causes of error within this class are (i) the lack of division between words in many manuscripts, (ii) a close similarity of certain letters in a script which results in their being confused, (iii) the mis-reading of an abbreviation . . . (p. 151)

This information helps historians think what the original may have been like, when they strike an anomaly in a text. But the hypothesis which an historian forms will be constrained by other facts besides these causal generalizations. It will also have to fit the context of the text, and be historically plausible. If another, parallel text is available, it may contain a variant of the passage which is entirely satisfactory, so that the historian can confidently assert that it is more likely to be the original, incorrectly transcribed in the first text he had examined.

It is clear, then, that historians can use both statistical inferences and arguments to the best explanation in deciding which text was original (or an unchanged copy of the original) and which was a copy (or changed copy of the original).

In the case David Knowles was studying, it appears that although there were many instances in which it was reasonable to conclude that *RB* had been copied from *RM*, there were some places where the reverse could be argued. To decide the issue Knowles therefore turned to evidence of other kinds.

(2)   Perhaps the most telling evidence in favour of the hypothesis that *RB* was copied from *RM* is concerned with the use of certain words in the two texts. If one designates the chapter which *RB* and *RM* have in common as *BM*, one can say that what is peculiar to *RB* is *RB* − *BM*; and what is peculiar to *RM* is *RM* − *BM*. On examination it has been found that the material peculiar to each document has strikingly different patterns of verbal usage from the other, and that repeatedly the verbal usage in the common sections (*BM*) resembles that in *RM* rather than that in *RB*. The implication is that the common section probably was originally written by the author of *RM*. Knowles designated the material peculiar to *RM* as '*M*' and that peculiar to *RB* as '*B*'.

BM throughout shows solidarity with *M* and differs sharply from *B*. Thus the word *scriptura* is used more than forty times in *M* to introduce a quotation, whereas there is not a single instance in *B*, where the word only occurs twice, in both cases in quite different contexts. Similarly, *M* uses parts of the word *dicere* some two hundred times when introducing a quotation, whereas *B* has the verb in this way only six times. (p. 176)

Knowles concluded:

The cumulative weight of these and similar examples of verbal usage is very great. Unlike the purely textual arguments it reflects the author's settled and subconscious bent of mind, not the isolated idiosyncrasy or mechanical reaction of a copyist. It is indeed possible to bring arguments against this or that instance, but the number of words and phrases that have been adduced is large and the reiterated force of the proof is great. No traditionalist has succeeded or even attempted to adduce contrary evidence . . . The conclusion that *RB* is following *RM* would therefore seem to impose itself beyond question. (pp. 177–8)

What Knowles seems to be arguing here is that the best explanation of the observed patterns of verbal usage common to *BM* and *M* is that they reflect 'the author's settled and subconscious bent of mind', and that although alternative explanations for individual cases of verbal discrepancy between *BM* and *B* might be available, again and again there is none other than that just mentioned, namely that the common chapters (*BM*) were first written by the author of *RM*, and were copied by the author of *RB*. There is no evidence to think this explanatory hypothesis false, so it must be accepted as the best explanation of the data.

(3)   Next Knowles considered the liturgical usages set out in the two documents. Those in *RB*, he said, provide 'a clearer and more integrated

scheme' than those in *RM*, setting out much more precisely than *RM* the liturgy to be followed each day and each season. Having given several examples of their differences in this regard, Knowles concluded:

Indeed, the liturgical evidence of greater antiquity in *RM* is overwhelming, and although this does not necessarily or even probably imply priority in date of composition or use, it is hard to believe that the compiler of such a liturgical directory could have seen and appropriated a great part of a Rule such as *RB*, where clarity and order reign with such evidence, without modifying his own liturgical practice at least in some respects. (pp. 179–80)

There are two parts of Knowles's argument here. First he denies that the liturgically simpler of two Rules will always be the older. The two might be contemporaneous, and merely represent two different traditions. His second point is that, nevertheless, if a member of a tradition with a simple liturgy were adopting a Rule from a tradition with a highly developed liturgy, he would probably take the opportunity to improve the 'clarity and order' of his own tradition in the light of what he read. So, if *RM* had been copied from *RB*, as had been traditionally believed, it is likely that it would include a much more precise set of liturgical requirements than it does. In effect, Knowles has argued that the traditional theory has an implication which is in fact false. If his argument is acceptable, it provides a reason for doubting the truth of the traditional hypothesis.

(4)   Knowles next drew attention to arguments from the sources used by the two Rules. *RM* uses sources which *RB* scarcely ever does, namely 'the apocryphal Acts and Passions of the apostles and martyrs that circulated in the fifth and early sixth centuries'. *RB* quotes from such sources only twice, both times in chapter 7, which is common to both Rules. It looks therefore as though the common section was originally composed by *RM*, this being the best explanation of the occurrence of those two quotations there, in the common chapter, but nowhere else in *RB*.

More significant is the treatment of the work of Cassian. He is quoted frequently by both *RM* and *RB*, and occurs repeatedly in *BM*, but there is a general agree-ment, such as is rare in this controversy, particularly on a textual point, that the quotations in *BM* are derived from *RM*, which is consistently nearer to the text of Cassian than is *RB*. (p. 180)

Presumably what Knowles meant was that in the section of *RM* peculiar to that Rule, that is in *M*, the quotations from Cassian were nearer to the text than in the section of *RB* peculiar to that Rule, that is in *B*; and since, like the quotations in *M*, those in the common section *BM* were also close to the text, it is more likely to have originated in *RM* than in *BM*. This hypothesis explains these facts more easily than the traditional one does.

(5)   Finally Knowles noted what each Rule had to say about monastic discipline and observance. The rigid authoritarianism of the *RM* con-trasts at many points with the more respectful and even democratic features of the *RB*. Knowles's argument here is similar to that which he

used when discussing liturgy: if *RM* had been copied from *RB*, it would surely have included many more of *RB*'s sensible rules than it did.

It is very difficult to suppose in this field also, that any reasonably intelligent legislator would have failed to accept some, at least, of these same, simple and practical directions. (p. 183)

Clearly the five arguments presented by Knowles all contribute to an argument to the best explanation. The hypothesis that *RB* was derived from *RM* accounts for the verbal similarities between *M* and *BM*, and for the similar use of sources made by *M* and *BM*, which would otherwise be virtually inexplicable, given the striking differences in these respects between *B* and *BM* (arguments 2 and 4). The traditional hypothesis that *RM* was derived from *RB* not only fails to explain those facts as well, but is rendered even more dubious by the absence in *RM* of very sensible features of the *RB*'s rules about monastic liturgy and discipline (arguments 3 and 5). The purely textual evidence favours the new hypothesis too (argument 1).

At the end of his article, Knowles briefly considered some other hypotheses about the relation between *RM* and *RB*, besides the two which have been discussed so far. The hypothesis that both were the work of the same author he discounted, saying that

the proved literary and what might be called 'doctrinal' and 'liturgical' differences are so great and so well defined as to preclude any theory of single authorship even over a period of twenty years. (p. 186)

The argument alluded to here could be one in which the hypothesis is discredited by seeing that one of its implications is false – if both Rules had been written by the same person they would not contain such great differences; or it could be a statistical inference, along the lines that documents containing such striking differences as these were probably written by different authors. Indeed Knowles might well have been hinting at both these arguments.

As to the hypothesis that what *RB* and *RM* have in common belonged to a third document from which each borrowed independently, Knowles regarded this as unnecessarily complex and hardly superior in explanatory value to the simpler hypothesis that *RB* copied from *RM*. If the third document contained only the common material, it would be but a fragment of a rule. If it were said to include all the material which was to some extent similar in *RB* and *RM*, then it would include almost all of those documents. There is no known evidence of the existence of a third document, and no adequate reason for postulating one.

The consideration of alternative hypotheses, however implausible, at the end of the article is, of course, essential to Knowles's argument. For to establish the credibility of an explanatory hypothesis, all the remotely plausible alternatives have to be shown to be inadequate, not just the alternative which has been traditionally held.

2 Justifying beliefs about the meaning of texts

To draw inferences from texts, historians almost always need to know their meaning. Physical features of paper or handwriting sometimes suffice to indicate the date of composition and the author of a document, but even this information an historian would normally want to confirm by reference to the meaning of the text.

A comprehensive account of the nature of meaning and of the understanding of meaning will not be presented here, as the purpose of this chapter is just to illustrate the forms of inference previously described. Certain difficulties in relating those forms of inference to the justification of beliefs about the meaning of texts will be discussed, however. Two of these difficulties relate to the understanding of languages with which the historian is quite familiar, and two are about the justification of translations from languages which are not known beforehand. The problems can be stated briefly as follows:

(1) Understanding the meaning of texts in a familiar language does not involve any process of inference, but is immediate. How, then, can a person's understanding be rationally justified?

(2) Some, such as J. G. A. Pocock, have stressed the importance of knowing the meaning generally given to words by an author in interpreting his writing; whereas others, such as Quentin Skinner, believe it most important to know the author's intentions in writing in order to understand his work. What role do these play in the justification of beliefs about the meaning of texts?

(3) Since it is theoretically possible to give more than one adequate interpretation of an unfamiliar language, can one possibly show that belief in one is rationally justified?

(4) Since it is impossible to interpret an unfamiliar language without making several assumptions about the people and their use of language, is an interpretation of its meaning really capable of rational justification?

Discussions of each of these questions will illustrate the use made of the forms of inference previously described in justifying conclusions about the meaning of texts. At the same time, it is hoped that some worries about the nature, indeed about the possibility, of justifications of this sort will be disposed of.

Understanding without inference

It is true that we grasp the meaning of familiar languages without having to infer it by reference to dictionaries or rules of grammar. We simply read or hear the words, and their meaning is at once apparent to us. How, then, can an historian justify his understanding of words in a familiar language?

First let us make clear exactly what has to be justified. The words an historian reads produce ideas which the historian identifies as the meaning of those words and which he can often express in different words, whose meaning is equivalent to the words he first read. An historian's understanding of the meaning of words can thus be expressed, and what requires to be justified is the claim that the meaning of the words which the historian expresses is the same as the conventional meaning of the words he originally read or heard. Another way of demonstrating one's understanding of sentences in a language is by stating their implications. If this method is adopted, then what has to be justified is the claim that what an historian says are implications of a sentence really are its conventional implications. Both these methods are used by historians expounding the meaning of texts, as will be seen.

The fact that historians do not reach an understanding of the meaning of texts in a familiar language by means of any inference, does not exclude the possibility of their providing a rational justification of their beliefs about their meaning just the same. It is pretty clear that an historian's understanding of a text is in fact a product of his beliefs about the meaning of its words and the significance of its grammatical forms. It is to these beliefs that he can and does appeal to justify any element of his interpretation of a text which has been or might be disputed.

The rules about the meaning of words and the significance of surface grammatical forms to which an historian appeals, however, by no means exhaust all the rules which relate sentences to their meanings. Linguistic analysis of the rules of generative grammar has shown them to be subtle, complex and difficult to state. It was Noam Chomsky's opinion that 'a person is not generally aware of the rules that govern sentence-interpretation in the language that he knows; nor, in fact, is there any reason to suppose that the rules can be brought to consciousness' (Chomsky, 1966, p. 7). Without knowledge of these rules, historians cannot demonstrate the correctness of their understanding of the meaning of texts.

What reason could there be, then, for believing that their understanding is correct? All the historian can appeal to is the opinion of others expert in the language of the text being interpreted. In any sophisticated language such as English, there are numerous specialist areas – the language of diplomats, of economists, of working-class people, for example – where nuances of meaning can be correctly caught only by people who have read and perhaps used the language a lot. If such experts agree with an historian's interpretation of a text in their own field, then there is good reason to suppose that that interpretation is correct.

Normally, however, although an historian could justify his beliefs about the meaning of a text by an appeal to experts, he does not do so. Rather he regards the reader as an expert, able to assess the correctness of the interpretation – except at points where the usage of the author of the text is different from normal, everyday usage at the time the historian is writing. Then the historian will justify the unexpected reading of the text by displaying the grounds he had for adopting his interpretation of it.

The roles of habits and intentions, of rules and contexts in the justification of beliefs about the meaning of texts

The justification of an historian's understanding of the meaning of texts in a familiar language is restricted to justifying interpretations, usually of just words or phrases, which general readers in the historian's own day would find surprising. The basic form of these justifications is fairly simple. First the historian produces evidence that the suggested meaning of a phrase is in fact the one which best fits many other contexts in which the author used it, suggesting that this was the meaning which he habitually expressed by means of that phrase. That might be justification enough, unless the author can be seen to use the phrase in more than one way, according to the context. In that case, the appeal to the author's habits would yield a small range of possible meanings, and to justify the adoption of one of those meanings, the historian has to demonstrate that it fits best in the given context.

In appealing to the linguistic habits of his author, the historian is justifying his interpretation by means of a statistical inference. The author's habit of expressing a certain idea by a certain phrase can be expressed as a generalization, and this generalization can be used to warrant appropriate interpretations of that phrase in future. For example, if we found a letter signed 'your loving friend', we would assume a close relationship between the author and the person addressed in the letter. But that phrase was not used by Thomas Cromwell to express such a relationship. His habit was to use it rather as we would use 'yours sincerely', as a formality. As G. R. Elton observed: 'Thomas Cromwell almost invariably signed himself as his correspondent's "loving friend"; it would be extraordinarily rash to base any deductions as to relationship or personal feelings on that phrase, though something might quite possibly be inferred from its absence' (Elton, 1967, p.78).

Discovering what people normally meant by the words they used can be a very difficult task, especially when their conceptual framework is not very familiar. Gordon Rupp remarked upon this difficulty in his study of Luther.

Some words may be likened to single notes in music: they have one clear and distinct definition . . . But there are other words which are more like chords of music, rich complexities. Many of the great Biblical notions are of this kind, and for Luther 'Righteousness', 'Word', 'Faith' are such master words. Luther fills them with meaning almost to the point of overloading. (Rupp, 1953, p. 255, n.1)

Rupp's account of what Luther meant by 'faith' illustrates his point well.

We have watched the growth of 'Faith' into a great master Word: magnetically attracting to itself a rich complex of meaning. For Faith comes to embody for Luther that double movement involved in the doctrine of Justification. On the one hand, Law – judgement – 'accusatio sui' – humiliatio – humilitas: for there can be no living faith, until a man turns from himself, and is stripped of his own self-righteousness. On the other hand, there is the dynamism of Justification itself, by which the eschatology, the perfect Righteousness of Christ is appropriated by the believer in time; the movement 'semper peccator, semper penitens, semper justus', 'grace' and 'the gift' – 'justificetur adhuc' – 'magis et magis' – until the new day of resurrection. (p. 255)

It is clearly important that an historian know what a person normally meant by words if he is to understand his use of those words aright. J. G. A. Pocock has developed this point in his essays on the way historians should study political thought. To understand all the connotations of the words as used by past political theorists, he said, the historian should become familiar with the functions those words served in political theories, or 'paradigms', at the time. 'The historian's first problem then, is to identify the "language" or "vocabulary" with and within which the author operated, and to show how it functioned paradigmatically to prescribe what he might say and how he might say it' (Pocock, 1972, p. 25). For example, in his essay 'Machiavelli, Harrington and English Eighteenth Century Ideologies', Pocock first described a political theory which he said appeared in the works of Polybius, Machiavelli, Harrington, the first Earl of Shaftesbury and Andrew Marvell, and then pointed out how it was presented, in a slightly modified form, in the writing of Country pamphleteers in eighteenth-century England. In terms of this theory, Pocock was able to explain what those pamphleteers meant when they wrote of 'corruption' by the Crown:

It is important to realize that the word 'corruption' in the eighteenth century is very often being used in its Machiavellian sense, as well as in the vulgar sense of bribery. That is, it is used to denote a disturbance of the balance of the constitution [between the power of the Crown and that of Parliament], with the demoralization of individuals and the public that is supposed to go with it. (Pocock, 1972, p. 131; and see pp. 138–40)

If an historian can point to a well-established generalization of this sort in support of his interpretation of a word, and if such an interpretation fits the context both in a linguistic sense, so that the sentences in which the word appears make sense given that interpretation, and in a logical and historical sense, so that no obvious absurdities or inconsistencies are introduced by using the word in that sense, then the interpretation warranted by the generalization is justified. The argument is a form of statistical inference. If the interpretation suggested by a rule does not fit in any one of the senses just mentioned, however, then the historian must form a hypothesis about the author's usage of the word which does seem to fit the contexts in which it occurs. Eventually he will defend such a hypothesis by means of an argument to the best explanation. It is in this way that historians' knowledge of unusual meanings is normally built up. Similarly, if a rule yields more than one meaning for a word, the historian must judge which best fits the context, and then argue that if the author intended the word to have that meaning, that would best explain his usage of it. These methods of justifying an interpretation of a word are similar to those used by historians defending an interpretation of a word in a totally unfamiliar language. Those methods will be illustrated shortly.

Clearly, the context in which a word is used helps to determine its meaning, especially if it is a word which can have several quite different meanings, such as the word 'point', in English. However there is another way in which the context of a statement can determine its meaning as well, a way which has been described and discussed at some length by Quentin Skinner. To appreciate Skinner's point one must note that statements often have two kinds of meanings. They often have a literal meaning, according to linguistic conventions, but they may also have a further meaning, namely what the speaker meant to do in uttering them, or what the utterance as a whole meant to contemporaries. This further meaning of utterances is often called their 'illocutionary force', following J. L. Austin's use of that term in *How To Do Things With Words* (1962). Thus, discussing More's *Utopia*, Skinner described it as embodying 'by far the most radical critique of humanism written by a humanist' (Skinner, 1978, Vol. I, p. 256), and he defended this description by showing how More denied that true nobility was to be found in the life style of aristocrats, as most humanists had supposed, and how More argued that true nobility could only exist when pride and injustice had been eliminated by the prohibition of private property. To say More meant *Utopia* to be a critique of the humanism of his time is to describe what Skinner, following Austin, called its 'illocutionary force'.

The concept of illocutionary force has proved far from clear. It is ambiguous in at least two important respects. First, there are often several distinct levels of illocutionary force which may be ascribed to a statement. A passage in More's *Utopia*, for example, might be correctly described as an imaginative description, and as a piece of political irony, as well as a critique of prevailing humanism. Second, it is not clear whether the illocutionary force of a passage is what its author intended it to mean, or what its readers at the time were entitled to take it to mean. These are often the same thing, but not always.

Quentin Skinner's discussion of the illocutionary force of texts of political theory has been very illuminating, but there is a mistake in his theory which needs to be corrected. The mistake has been Skinner's assumption that the conventional significance of an utterance is identical to the significance which the speaker intended it to have. In his essay '"Social Meaning" and the Explanation of Social Action', for example, Skinner slipped from talking of 'what the act of issuing an utterance with that meaning might itself have meant in the given circumstances', to 'how he intended his utterance to be taken', without noticing that these can be different (Skinner, 1972a, p. 116). By waving to a friend at an auction one can in fact bid without ever intending to. In another essay Skinner has admitted that the conventional illocutionary force of a speech act corresponds to the speaker's intention only if the speaker 'both knew of . . . [the] convention and intended to follow it in the given case' (Skinner, 1971, p. 14). But he still insisted that a speaker could not intend to communicate with an illocutionary force which was not conventionally recognizable. His reason for believing this seems to have been his conviction that unless a person communicated his intentions by conventional means, he could not be understood. For example, he has drawn attention to

many types of social action in which . . . the recovery of the agent's intentions must be secondary to recovering the meaning of the action itself, since the agent can only mean by his action what the action already means, and will be in danger of meaning nothing at all unless he expresses himself through the medium of the action's conventional significance. (Hollis and Skinner, 1978, p. 58. Cf. Skinner, 1972b, p. 406)

If it can be shown that a writer's illocutionary intentions can be grasped when they are unique and not at all conventional, then no reason will remain for holding that the intended illocutionary force of an utterance must correspond to a conventional force.

Skinner has said that an author's intentions can be understood only if they are expressed by means of conventions.

Any intention capable of being correctly understood by A as the intention intended by S to be understood by A must always be a socially conventional intention – must fall, that is, within a given and established range of acts which can be conventionally grasped as being cases of that intention. It must follow that one of the necessary conditions for understanding in any situation what it is that S in uttering utterance x must be doing to A must be some understanding of what it is that people in general, when behaving in a conventional manner, are usually doing in that society and in that situation in uttering such utterances. (Skinner, 1970, p. 133)

J. L. Austin had said the same (1962, pp. 103, 114, 118, 120–1, 127), though his view has been criticized by P. F. Strawson (1964, esp. 26–7) and by S. R. Schiffer (1972, p. 91). There certainly are occasions on which the illocutionary force of verbal behaviour is specified by a convention. In saying the words of a wedding service in a church before a minister and witnesses, a man and a woman marry each other, according to convention. Normally that is their intention in saying those words, as well. Most utterances studied by historians, however, have no regular conventional significance, but have a unique significance which it is the historian's task to discover.

It is much more instructive to examine Skinner's practice in uncovering the illocutionary force of political texts, than to study his theory about how this is done. In practice Skinner constructs hypotheses about authors' intentions in writing on political matters, hypotheses which he is at pains to show are consistent with the substance of their writing and with their known political interests. When two incompatible hypotheses seem equally plausible, he scouts further afield for evidence which will help decide between them. The works of Hobbes and Bayle, for instance, can be interpreted quite literally as works of religious men extolling the laws of God, or as ironic, written to destroy prevailing religious orthodoxies. Skinner argued for the latter interpretation by pointing out that this is how all their contemporaries understood them, and that, in later editions of their works, Hobbes and Bayle made no attempt to correct that interpretation of their work (Skinner, 1969, pp. 33–5). Clearly the hypothesis that the author's intentions were ironic and destructive better explains these facts than the hypothesis that they were pious. Skinner virtually never infers an author's intention simply by reference to a convention, but almost always constructs a hypothesis about it, and defends it by means of an argument to the best explanation.

Once it is admitted that the illocutionary force of an utterance is not always conventional, the historian can allow his imagination to roam more freely to suggest hypotheses about what it might have been. He will also be driven to pay especial attention to the contexts in which statements are uttered, for the contexts often provide the best clues about the statements' point. Peter Gay, for example, has pointed out that many of Voltaire's writings had a meaning, an illocutionary force, which the reader fails to grasp if he does not know the political contexts in which they were written, and, we might add, if he does not know Voltaire's political sympathies.

With few exceptions Voltaire's political pamphlets grew out of controversies. The pamphlets rarely unveil their true nature to the twentieth-century reader, for they are nearly always elliptical: Voltaire seldom alludes directly to his opponent or to the point of contention. In *La Voix du sage et du peuple* (1750), to take one prominent example, he advocates undivided sovereignty and secular supremacy over all public affairs, including ecclesiastical matters. His language throughout is general: he appears to be stating principles of universal validity and of no specific application. There is not a word about the *vingtième* tax, which the French government was at this time trying to impose upon all orders of society; not a word about *chancelier* Machault, who had originated the tax and whose policy Voltaire supported with enthusiasm; not a word about the rebellious Assembly of the Clergy of 1750, which was resisting the government's claim that the state had a right to tax the church. Yet *La Voix du sage et du peuple*, although silent on the *vingtième*, Machault, and the Assembly, is precisely about these three. His contemporaries knew it, the Kehl editors knew it, and the modern student of his political ideas must once again learn it. Voltaire's universal pronouncements may have universal import, but we can comprehend it only when we understand the environment in which they originated. (Gay, 1971, pp. 60–1)

The immediate context of an utterance is usually relevant to its conventional significance. The fact that Voltaire had his pamphlets published shows that he intended them to be public statements and not just private literary exercises. To appreciate their further point, however, the historian must view them in a wider context, in this case the context of a political debate in which Voltaire was supporting one side against another.

The most important role for conventions in determining the illocutionary force(s) of texts is that of suggesting, and to some extent delimiting, the range of possibilities. The conventions of political writing make it possible that a political text was intended to be read literally, ironically or allegorically. However, a particular ironic or allegorical intention cannot be discovered from conventions; it must be discovered by close investigation of the dispositions of the author and of the political context in which he wrote. A knowledge of the political traditions known to members of a society might further delimit the range of political programmes which a pamphleteer might have had in mind, though an historian must always allow for the possibility of novel programmes emerging. Thus an historian's general knowledge can often assist in suggesting the intended illocutionary force of a text; but hypotheses about their illocutionary force are usually justified by means of arguments to the best explanation.

Skinner believed that unless the illocutionary force of an utterance or text could be conveyed in accordance with a convention, people who heard the utterance or read the text would not understand it. In practice, however, as Gay remarked, contemporaries, familiar with the background and context of an utterance, are themselves able to see what its point must be even though they have no clear conventions to guide them. Presumably they do what historians have to do to see the point of a text, namely consider what interpretation of it fits best with the circumstances of its production.

In texts which are meant to be taken literally, the purpose of the author is often plainly stated in the text itself – well at least some of his purposes are stated there. Thus John Locke declared in his Preface to his *Two Treatises of Government* that together they were intended

to establish the Throne of our Great Restorer, Our present King *William*; to make good his Title, in the Consent of the People, . . . and to justify to the world, the people of England, whose love of their just and natural rights, with their resolution to preserve them, saved the nation when it was on the very brink of slavery and sin. (Locke, 1690)

Some historians have been wary of accepting this as a true declaration of Locke's intent, however. Charles D. Tarlton believes that it does not accord with the Treatises' 'particular structure and specific internal developments' (Tarlton, 1978, p. 44). Peter Laslett has argued that although Locke's declaration might honestly state his intentions in publishing the *Two Treatises*, they were probably written before the Glorious Revolution of 1688, 'to be a demand for a revolution to be brought about, not the rationalization of a revolution in need of defence' (Locke, 1690, p. 47). Clearly the context of the composition of the work is vital in determining its author's intentions in writing it. An author's declaration of intent often gives a reliable indication of his actual intention in writing, but not always.

Justifying an interpretation of an unfamiliar script

It is fascinating to see how historians decipher unknown scripts, whose rules of interpretation are a mystery. Generalizations and analogies are used to suggest hypotheses, but the ultimate justification of the successful hypothesis is an argument to the best explanation.

Take, for example, John Chadwick's account of *The Decipherment of Linear B* (1967). Arthur Evans identified what he said were three phases in Minoan writing, in Crete. The first was of pictorial signs, which he called hieroglyphic, dated roughly 2000–1650 B.C.; the second was a script in which the pictorial signs were reduced to mere outlines, and this Evans called 'Linear A', dated roughly 1750–1450 B.C.; the third was a variation of Linear A, which Evans called 'Linear B', used until 1400 B.C. and perhaps later. Between three and four thousand clay tablets in Linear B have been found at Knossos. Evans did not succeed in deciphering the script, however. That was the achievement of Michael Ventris, in the 1950s, with some assistance from John Chadwick.

The story of the decipherment of Linear B is well told by John Chadwick. Here we shall simply note some of the arguments which, he said, played an important part in Ventris's success. First there are three arguments based upon generalizations about the nature of written language:

(1) 'There are only three basic ways of committing language to writing, and all known graphic systems use one or a combination of these.' These methods are 'ideographic', in which a picture represents a word; 'syllabic', in which a symbol represents a syllable; and 'alphabetic', in which a symbol represents a letter. Ideographic languages, like Chinese, use thousands of signs; alphabetical use about thirty (English, twenty-six; modern Russian, thirty-two); simple syllabic scripts, like Japanese and Cypriot use about fifty signs.

The number of signs used in Linear B is about eighty-nine. 'It is far too small for a wholly ideographic system, and it is much too large for an alphabet. It must therefore be syllabic.' . . . 'This elementary

deduction was neglected by many of the would-be deci-
pherers.' (pp. 41–3)

(2)   In the Linear B script there occurred quite regularly sign-groups, or
      words, followed by an ideogram, a little picture. 'If a word is
      regularly associated with a particular ideogram, it is likely to be the
      name of the object denoted by that ideogram; but if there are several
      varying words associated with the same ideogram, then there may
      be epithets denoting the various types.' By means of this generaliz-
      ation, it was possible to identify words meaning man, woman,
      horse, pig, tripod, cup, amphora, sword, spear, arrow, chariot and
      wheel. (pp. 45–6)

(3)   'If words are written in a syllabary which has signs only for pure
      vowels and for consonants followed by vowels . . . [then] no matter
      what the language is; if it is written in this way, the analysis of the
      use of the signs will show a characteristic pattern of distribution:
      the plain vowels occur rarely in the middle of a word (like *a* in
      individual), but frequently at the beginning, because every word
      beginning with a vowel must begin with a [pure] vowel sign.'
      Using this generalization, two and possibly three signs were
      identified as pure vowels. (pp. 52–3)

These generalizations lent substantial support to the conclusions drawn
from them. Another source of useful hypotheses were analogies, though
the support they provided was, of course, much less. In the end, however,
they yielded the most fruitful hypothesis of all.

(4)   Evans nearly identified a number of strokes as representing
      numbers, 'much as in Roman numerals'. (p. 44)

(5)   Another analogy with Latin usage helped interpret a sign which was
      frequently attached to the end of words. 'Ventris deduced that [it]
      was a conjunction, probably meaning "and" and attached to the end
      of the word it served to connect (like -*que* in Latin).' (p. 53)

(6)   Other suffixes Ventris tried to interpret on analogy with Etruscan,
      but he noticed that some functioned like Greek suffixes. (p. 60)

(7)   From an analogy with other ancient lists like those in Linear B,
      Ventris assumed some sign-groups must have represented towns. He
      let different signs stand for Cypriot syllables, and tried constructing
      local place names from them. In this he was successful, spelling
      Knossos, the nearby harbour town of Amnisos, and another town,
      Tulissos. (pp. 62–3)

This was the turning point. Ventris was to find that Linear B represented
the language of archaic Greek. 'As he transcribed more and more texts, so
the Greek words began to emerge in greater numbers; new signs could
now be identified by recognizing a word in which one sign only was a
blank, and this value could then be tested elsewhere' (p. 67).

Particularly impressive was the confirmation provided by words for ideograms. 'The odds against getting this astonishing agreement purely by accident are astronomical' (p. 82). Indeed, as Chadwick admits, the probabilities cannot be calculated. 'What are the chances that two series of equine heads will be introduced by words exactly corresponding to the Greek for horses and asses? Such probabilities are beyond mathematical analysis; we can only have recourse to the guidance of common sense' (p. 86). What Chadwick needed to say was that if one compares the hypothesis that Linear B was intended to express archaic Greek and the hypothesis that its correspondence with archaic Greek in these cases is by chance, then the former makes the correspondence much more likely, and so explains it much better, than does the latter. The slight anomalies which occur on the basis of the former hypothesis Ventris was able to explain away as the result of scribal error (p. 83).

Theoretically, philosophers have shown, there are many ways in which a language could correspond to things in the world. Is there any good reason to suppose that Ventris's interpretation of Linear B in terms of archaic Greek is correct? We have noted that his interpretation can be defended by an argument to the best explanation. The logical point is that there could be many other interpretations of the language, so what reason is there for believing Ventris's to be true? This is really a challenge to the rationality of arguments to the best explanation. For any fact which an historian tries to explain, there could be many different explanations. This is the main reason why arguments to the best explanation can never yield conclusions which are necessarily true.

Murray G. Murphey has carefully explained and discussed the problem of the indeterminacy of translation as it was enunciated by W. V. Quine (Murphey, 1973, pp. 33–56). He has pointed out how anthropologists, and to a lesser extent historians, are able to construct hypotheses about the meaning of unknown words and phrases and to test them until they are convinced that only one interpretation of them is adequate. There are two respects, however, in which his discussion is unsatisfactory. First, he asserts that 'where the historian confronts an entirely unknown language and has not even a partial translation to start with . . . any interpretation which he places upon its symbols will be purely speculative' (pp. 55–6). In saying this, Murphey underestimates the ingenuity of historians, for as has just been seen in the case of Linear B, a quite credible interpretation of an unknown language can be produced by historians.

The second point is more serious. Murphey shows quite convincingly that in many cases an interpretation of a language can be so well supported that it would appear to be entirely reasonable to accept that interpretation as accurate. He even shows how one could tell whether a native meant by 'gavagai' rabbits, temporal-slices of rabbits, or rabbits as a mass term (pp. 50–1). What Murphey establishes is that from a practical point of view translations need not be as indeterminate as Quine had suggested. That is true. But what Murphey does not address is the theoretical question. The fact that an historian can think of only one adequate interpretation of a language does not mean that others are not possible. Since others are possible, at least logically possible, how can an historian ever justify the claim that the interpretation he judges to be the only adequate one is in fact true?

When this question was discussed before (see pp. 38–40), it was pointed out that one cannot prove the conclusions of good arguments to the best explanation true in a correspondence sense. That is, one cannot demonstrate a correspondence between a description's possible truth conditions and the world. The fact that a·statement is very well supported, and an excellent explanation, does not entail its truth. False statements could be well supported, but not known to be false because evidence showing them to be false was not available. The conclusions of arguments to the best explanation cannot be demonstrated to be true in a correspondence sense. They can, however, be believed true, and generally are believed so. Ultimately the only justification for such belief is pragmatic, as was argued in Chapter 1, sect. 1. It is natural to interpret our perceptions realistically, and it is both natural and useful to interpret our historical explanations of what we can perceive realistically as well.

The function of assumptions in translating unfamiliar languages

Historians make many assumptions in order to arrive at plausible hypotheses for testing. Evans and Ventris assumed that Linear B was like Latin at some points, and then like archaic Greek at others. It is interesting to compare the methods used by J. Eric S. Thompson in *Maya Hieroglyphic Writing* (1960). Thompson assumed that both the language of the Mayas and the ideas expressed in their hieroglyphic writing to some extent resembled those of their descendants in Middle America (pp. 16, 35). More particularly, when he tried to discover the original Maya word and its meaning for each of the twenty days of the Maya calander, for which hieroglyphic representations have been identified, he compared the name given to each day in each of the known Maya dialects and considered what word and concept would best account for them all. He also took into account the known auguries for each day, which normally relate to the kind of god whose name was given to the day and who was believed to govern it. Finally, he tried to reach a hypothesis compatible, not only with the Maya glyphic representation for each day, but with the Mexican glyphs as well, which he believed to have had the same ancestors as the Mayan ones. 'As previous students have done, we shall make the assumption, for which there is ample support, that Maya and Mexican glyphs have the same ancestors, and that, therefore, a Maya day is probably related in meaning to the Aztec day in the corresponding position in the series' (p. 69). Thompson used his historical knowledge to draw conclusions about the content of Maya thought and the nature of Maya language. His assumptions were not arbitrary, but reasonable. These assumptions put constraints upon the hypotheses he could consider – indeed they sometimes yielded specific hypotheses to be considered. The constraints are not always narrow, however, for there is considerable diversity among the views of the Maya's descendants. As Thompson admits:

There is too much danger of finding what one seeks, for many opposed ideas exist in the religious concepts of the peoples of Middle America, and one is free to pick and choose. To take an extreme instance, I have built a structure, the walls of which are assumptions with a light bonding of fact, to explain the religious significance of the day Cib . . . Is this a well-reasoned reconstruction of the Maya ideas behind that day, or have I built on sand? I take confidence from the realization of how the same religious ideas pervade the Maya area in particular and Middle America in general. (p. 35)

Thompson at times displays considerable ingenuity in relating his interpretation of a glyph to known Maya and Mexican words and beliefs, so that although the explanatory force of some of his hypotheses is not great, their explanatory scope is large.

The role of Thompson's assumption, that the Mayans who made the glyphs used a language and held beliefs akin to those of inhabitants of Middle America, is crucial to his argument. For if that is not true, there is no point in demonstrating that his hypotheses explain known languages and beliefs well. Indeed, if Thompson is to defend his conclusions rationally, he must provide a rational defence for that assumption. For its role is not merely that of suggesting an explanatory hypothesis which can then be defended independently of it, as the analogies assumed by Ventris did. Thompson does not argue: let us discover the language and beliefs of the forbears of the inhabitants of Middle America, use those to suggest an interpretation of the Maya glyphs and then defend the interpretation merely on the grounds of its internal cogency. Their internal cogency alone would not have made Thompson's interpretation of the glyphs credible, for they are very bizarre. For example, Thompson interprets a carving of a man carrying a bundle on his back as a particular God, whose name is a number, carrying a period of time (pp. 59–61). Such an interpretation would be hard to believe on grounds of cogency alone, as it is so unusual. It only becomes credible in the light of literary evidence of such beliefs in the books of Chilam Balam, books written in Yucatec with European characters by Maya in the colonial period, to preserve a knowledge of their old culture (pp. 60, 34). Thompson was quite careful to defend his assumption that the Mayans who produced the glyphs were ancestors of the authors of the books of Chilam Balam.

The inventors of the Maya hieroglyphs almost surely spoke a lowland language, because Maya hieroglyphic texts occur only in the area covered by peoples of the lowland group, and because the hieroglyphic writing presumably developed after the lowland and highland groups began to diverge.

I am convinced that the inventors of the hieroglyphic writing spoke a language which was very close to modern Yucatec and to Chol-Chorti-Mopan. Unless there have been unsuspected shifts in population, a view which is contradicted by the gradual transitions from one contiguous group to another, the glyphs probably originated among the ancestors of the people who spoke Yucatec, Chol, or Chorti at the time of the Spanish conquest. (p. 16)

The argument rests upon a generalization about the cultural continuity of stable populations over centuries. The Maya glyphs were mostly produced in what Thompson calls the Classical Period of Maya culture, A.D. 320–909 (pp. 5–6). The Spanish conquest was not accomplished until the sixteenth century. As the population had not shifted much between those periods, Thompson concluded that their cultures would have had much in common.

Thompson's assumption that the language and beliefs of some sixteenth- and seventeenth-century Middle American people had descended from the Mayas of the Classical Period, is in fact typical of assumptions historians frequently make in determining the relevance of data to an explanatory hypothesis. On a small scale, if an historian is seeking evidence of a person's state of mind at a certain time, he might take certain letters as evidence of that state of mind – assuming that the letters were indeed the product of the person being investigated. Often historians have good reasons for such assumptions, just as Thompson had for his. The evidence of handwriting, for example, might make it certain that a letter was written by the person in question. But, even so, the assumption does play a part in the justification of the final explanation. It is deemed a virtue of an explanation that it help to account for data which the historian assumes to be causally related to it. But precisely what part does the historian's belief in the relevance of certain data to an explanatory hypothesis play in the justification of that hypothesis?

It seems that in the end the assumption becomes embedded in the explanatory story which the historian decides to tell. Thompson not only accounted for the glyphs he was studying, but also suggested the causal antecedents of many later Mayan ideas. The credibility of his hypotheses is largely dependent upon their success in explaining the later, recorded beliefs. The fact that there is independent evidence in support of a causal connection between early Mayan beliefs and later ones is not at all inconsistent with viewing that connection as part of the historian's explanatory hypothesis. There often is independent support for elements in an historian's explanatory story.

The suggestion that the assumptions historians make prior to constructing explanatory hypotheses may be viewed as part of those hypotheses, helps to overcome another worry about the justification of interpretation of strange languages. In several articles Steven Lukes (1967) and Martin Hollis (1967a, 1967b) have argued that anthropologists have to assume that the people they study are in certain respects rational, if they are to interpret their language and rituals. Anthropologists assume, for example, that the people they study distinguish the real from the imaginary, that they respect rules of identity and non-contradiction, have some rules of inference, and even that they have similar perceptions to ourselves in many cases. The question which arises is, if such assumptions have to be made prior to an explanatory hypothesis being constructed, how can an explanatory hypothesis be justified? Would not the assumptions of rationality have to be justified first? And how can that be done?

The assumptions might be justified independently by means of a generalization that they are true of all men whose language is understood. There are difficulties establishing this, however, for when the Nuer people seriously assert that a human twin is a bird, and that a cucumber is an ox, it seems that they do not share even the minimum conditions of rationality mentioned above. As Ernest Gellner said: 'This kind of statement appears to be in conflict with the principle of identity or non-contradiction, or with common sense, or with manifest observable fact: human twins are *not* birds, and vice versa' (Gellner, 1962, p. 34).

An assumption of rationality does not have to be justified independently, however, for a hypothesis based upon it to be capable of rational justification. The assumption upon which the hypothesis was constructed finally becomes a feature of the hypothesis itself, and is supported by whatever supports the hypothesis as a whole. This is particularly well illustrated in Robin Horton's essay 'African Traditional Thought and Western Science' (1970), in which Horton drew attention to general patterns of thought which he assumed true of Africans and which he has illustrated in his reconstruction of their religious beliefs. These patterns of thought, he said, in many ways resemble those of Western scientists. His assumptions about the rationality of African thought are embedded in his exposition of it, and when his account of their thought is criticized, so too are the assumptions of rationality upon which it is structured. J. H. M. Beattie, for example, has pointed out a weakness in Horton's hypothesis, and suggested another hypothesis, based upon different assumptions, as superior.

Ingenious though Horton's analogy between traditional African religion and modern scientific thought is, it is perfectly possible to make sense of traditional (or for that matter non-traditional) religious and magical acts and beliefs without regarding them as being in any significant respect 'like' science. Indeed it seems to me that Horton's analogy, if pressed, is likely to obscure rather than to advance understanding. The 'bizarre and senseless features' of such beliefs do not become immediately comprehensible, to me at any rate, when they are seen as the produce of a model-building process comparable with that of modern science. If they were this, their presence and persistence would indeed be inexplicable. On the contrary, they make sense when they are regarded very differently, that is, as symbolizing certain important aspects of the physical and socio-cultural environment. (Beattie, 1970, p. 263)

The rationality of African thought is being discussed here in the context of a specific interpretation of African beliefs.

3   Inferences about past people's state of mind

There are two common reasons why historians investigate past people's state of mind. They usually want to know either how reliable their testimony is of events which they have described, or what reasons they had for acting as they did. Such information is clearly vital for our knowledge and understanding of past events, but it is often very difficult to acquire. Generally speaking statements about other people's mental states are the hardest for historians to justify.

Consider first of all the possibility of inferring statements about them by means of statistical inference. Here are three generalizations which an historian can use as the basis of statistical inferences about other minds.

(a)   If a literate author is writing honestly, then his statements expressing his perceptions, beliefs, desires and intentions will probably be accurate.

(b)   People generally intend to act in a way which they believe will bring about what they strongly wish for as efficiently as possible, so long as the action has no likely consequences which they would dislike.

(c)   People usually wish for at least one of the consequences they could predict as following from an action they intend to do.

These generalizations have in fact been used successfully by historians, as will shortly be seen. What limits their use, however, is the fact that none can be used unless quite a lot of information has already been acquired about the person whose mind is being investigated, and this information is not always available.

The first generalization, for example, can be used only when it is known that the author is honestly expressing his beliefs. In the absence of evidence to the contrary, historians usually assume that people write honestly. But there are all sorts of reasons why people may not be speaking honestly. They may be speaking in the hope of gaining political advantage. This fact makes it impossible to be sure that politicians really believe what they say, especially when historians have no other data about their beliefs to go on. As Maurice Cowling said:

In asking whether politicians believed the opinions they explored, one is reaching for the limits of explanation . . . Accumulation of material will not tell us whether conservative leaders *believed* there was a threat to the social order in 1867, 1885, 1910 or 1921. It will not tell us in what sense Bright, Gladstone, Joseph Chamberlain or Lloyd George *believed* in the attacks Conservatives may have believed they were making. Belief in these, and in all other cases, must be imputed not to an affirmation of the heart, but to public conduct, the tip of an iceberg we assume emerged from real humanity by courses too random and obscure to yield to the historical conventions. (Cowling, 1971, p. 9)

In practice, though, it is often only when the taking of a person's words at their face value generates inconsistencies, that historians explore the possibility that the words were not honest expressions of belief. An interesting example of this is Gene Wise's reassessment of a sermon by John Winthrop. This sermon, delivered on a ship bringing new settlers to Boston in 1630, was interpreted by Winthrop's biographer, Darrett Rutman, as an honest expression of Winthrop's hopes. Winthrop had expressed the hope that Boston would be a God-fearing city, quite unlike the cities of the Old World being left behind. In fact Boston did not live up to Winthrop's expectations, yet, Rutman noted, Winthrop did not, in his old age, seem to be very disappointed. This inconsistency is removed, Wise suggests, if we view Winthrop's sermon, not as a frank expression of his expectations, but as meant to encourage the people to a holiness which he feared they might not, perhaps even which he believed they would not, achieve (Wise, 1973, pp. 160–5).

Inconsistencies between historical evidence and accepted historical facts can indeed be removed by imputing to the authors of the inconvenient texts motives other than those of honest assertion. But such imputations are rather *ad hoc*, and are not convincing without independent supporting evidence. Here is an example in which an historian's reasons for not taking a description as accurate are quite well defended. It is a discussion by F. Barlow of an account given by William, Archdeacon of Poitiers, of an embassy by Harold, Earl of East Anglia and subsequently successor to the throne of England, from King Edward the Confessor to William, Duke of Normandy, in 1064 or 1065. According to William of Poitiers, Harold came to confirm Edward's will that the kingdom of England should pass to William on Edward's death, and to swear vassalage to William. In this way, writing in 1073, William of Poitiers helped to justify William's invasion of England and the killing of Harold who took arms against him in 1066, after Edward's death. But Barlow comments:

We can put little trust in the chronicler's unsupported statements. He was writing a panegyric of the duke and a justification of the conquest of England and the killing of Harold, making use of everything that came to hand in a completely biased way. His theme was that William never fought an unjust war. He was not, apparently, very well-informed about events, and, since he was not writing history, was probably not interested in historical truth. Where his detail can be checked it is often found to be incorrect, and usually, it seems, he was not an eye-witness of the events he describes. He makes it clear that he was not present when Harold took his oath. (Barlow, 1970, p. 225)

Barlow was unwilling to accept William of Poitiers' account of Harold's embassy, and he has produced good reasons for believing that William of Poitiers did not intend to tell the truth but to provide an account of the embassy which would justify the Duke of Normandy's later seizure of the throne of England from Harold. Throughout the account, William of Poitiers justified the actions of William of Normandy quite uncritically; and he took little care over historical detail, often getting it wrong. These are independent reasons for thinking he might not have described Harold's embassy correctly. The fact that he was not present at the events he describes rules out the possibility that he was, on this occasion, recording his memories of the events.

There is almost no limit to the number of purposes for which people might write other than a desire to record their beliefs, wishes and intentions honestly. It is hard for historians to be sure that, in a given case, no alternative purpose was involved. Knowledge of the context in which evidence was recorded is clearly of great importance in assessing its significance. Sometimes statements which historians have later mis-takenly assumed to be true, have been made merely to satisfy legal or administrative requirements. G. R. Elton, for example, has frequently pointed out the ways in which the writing and behaviour of Tudor officials were determined by regulations, and he has emphasized the importance of recognizing this fact if one is to interpret correctly the significance of what they said and did. Often what was said was not believed but was only said *pro forma*. For example: 'In the Tudor Star Chamber, complainants invariably charged the opposing party with a violent or riotous act; but since this was requisite if the court was to have jurisdiction, it may be no more than a matter of form' (Elton, 1967, p. 78). In another place Elton has given a different example of how knowledge of rules and regulations can help an historian distinguish which statements express their author's beliefs and which do not. When reporting on the state of monasteries, ecclesiastical visitors in late medieval Britain customarily recorded charges of misconduct among the clergy, but they had to leave the investigation of these charges to courts of law. Their reports of clerical offences, therefore, do not reflect their beliefs about them; many charges were doubtless malicious and subse-quently not proven.

But historians considering the moral or intellectual standards of, say, the late-medieval clergy have very commonly accepted the allegations of a visitation as equal to the truth, and there cannot be much doubt that in consequence they have produced badly distorted descriptions which in turn have been used to form the very insecure foundation for general analyses of the 'causes' of the Reforma-tion and similar things. (Elton, 1970, pp. 90–1)

One of the most famous debates about whether a declaration of intention was honest or not is that about Hitler's statement of his intentions recorded in the Hossbach Memorandum. The Memorandum is an account of a long speech which Hitler made to his War Minister, the Commanders in Chief of the German Army, the Navy and the Air Force, and his Foreign Minister, on 5 November 1937. In his speech, according to the Memorandum, Hitler described how he intended to acquire extra territory, *Lebensraum* (literally 'living room'), for Germany. The first stage would be the occupation of Austria and Czechoslovakia. That might involve war with Britain and France, but there was a chance that it would not. Most historians have taken the Hossbach Memorandum as an honest report of an honest declaration by Hitler of his intentions. For example, Alan Bullock wrote of it as 'documentary confirmation' of Hitler's intentions at the time (Bullock, 1955, p. 338). A. J. P. Taylor, however, asserted that 'he did not reveal his inmost thoughts' to his ministers on this occasion. Rather, he said, Hitler was just setting out possibilities in order 'to win them for a programme of increased armaments. His geopolitical exposition had no other purpose' (Taylor, 1964, p. 170). T. W. Mason has shown that this account of Hitler's purpose is improbable (Mason, 1964, pp. 112–14) and, in the light of his argument, Taylor has admitted he was 'quite wrong' (Taylor, 1965, p. 136). Still, he has refused to accord Hitler's speech any significance, seeing it as an occasion on which Hitler evaded a decision over a dispute between Blomberg and Goering 'by ranting in his usual fashion' (*ibid*). Was Hitler sincere or not? Because the evidence that he was is not great, historians have looked for independent support for the supposition that he was. Bullock has found it in Hitler's subsequent actions. If he was speaking honestly, and did intend to occupy Austria and Czechoslovakia when he could, one would expect him to act accordingly. Since he did act as he had said, Bullock has argued that his statement was honest.

To brush the Hossbach meeting aside and say that this was just Hitler talking for effect and not to be taken seriously seems to me equally wide of the mark . . . When Hitler spoke of his determination to overthrow Czechoslovakia and Austria, as early as 1938 if an opportunity offered, and when both countries *were* overthrown within less than eighteen months, it is stretching incredulity rather far to ignore the fact that he had stated this as his immediate programme in November 1937. (Bullock, 1967, p. 202)

The hypothesis that Hitler did intend to act as he was reported to have said in 1937 explains both his speech to his ministers and his subsequent actions. It is of greater explanatory scope than the hypothesis that he was merely 'ranting' in 1937, and so is more credible, other things being equal.

The second of the three generalizations stated at the beginning of this section is another which can only be used when an historian already knows a lot about the mental state of his subject. The generalization was that people generally intend to act in a way which they believe will bring about what they strongly wish for as efficiently as possible, so long as the action has no likely consequences which they would dislike. It can be used to infer a person's intentions, so long as one already knows much about that person's aspirations, fears, and beliefs.

A good example of an historian drawing an inference by means of this generalization is provided by R. G. Collingwood's inferences as to Caesar's intentions in invading Britain in 54 B.C. Unfortunately in his writing Caesar did not declare the purpose of his invasion, so the historian has had to infer it from other things which there is evidence that Caesar knew. Collingwood did not actually state the generalization being discussed, but his arguments clearly assume it. To begin with he used it to infer Caesar's general purpose with respect to Britain. He referred to a passage in *The Gallic Wars*, where Caesar mentioned that contingents from Britain had been fighting on the side of his enemies; and then Collingwood pointed out that in his *Commentaries* Caesar showed himself to be 'preoccupied with the problem of keeping the peace' in Gaul, which he had invaded between 58 and 55 B.C., but over which his control was tenuous. In the knowledge of this belief and this desire, Collingwood concluded that Caesar probably wanted to prevent opposition to his rule from developing in Britain, this being the most efficient means of securing the peace he had fought for.

Then Collingwood considered what Caesar's particular intentions might have been in invading Britain. He first turned, by way of an analogy, to Caesar's expedition across the Rhine just before his invasion of Britain. That expedition had been to punish the Germans for disturbing Gaul, so Collingwood considered whether the invasion of Britain had been intended as a short punitive measure as well. He dismissed this possibility with the argument that one of its implications was false: had this been Caesar's intention, he would have said so in his *Commentaries*, but he did not, so it could not have been.

Then, in search of another hypothesis, Collingwood once again drew an inference from what he knew of Caesar's desires and beliefs. He wrote:

... in estimating his intentions at the beginning of his British campaign [in 55 B.C.] we must be guided by the situation as it then appeared, and by his record of achievement in Gaul as it must have stood in his own eyes at that time. He knew the size of Britain with a fair degree of accuracy; he knew that its inhabitants were less civilized and less highly organized both in politics and in war than the Gauls; he meant in the following year to invade the country with five legions and to keep them there for the winter; and when all these facts are considered at once, it can hardly be doubted that his plan was to conquer the whole island.

Given the size of Britain, the loose organization of its forces, and Caesar's desire to keep five legions there securely over a winter, the only reasonable way of preventing rebellion and securing the country, in Caesar's eyes, must have been by conquering the whole island (Collingwood, 1937, pp. 32–4).

In his autobiography Collingwood forgot that he had inferred Caesar's intentions thus from his desires and beliefs, and instead briefly represented his argument as an argument to the best explanation. The hypothesis that Caesar intended to conquer Britain explains both his silence about his intentions in the *Commentaries*, because his plan failed, and the size of the force he took in 54 B.C., which was comparable to that used by Claudius to conquer the island nearly a century later. Neither of these facts is compatible with the hypothesis that his intention was merely punitive, as it had been in Germany (Collingwood, 1939, p. 131). This was not the form of argument used in *Roman Britain*, however, as the quotation from that text shows.

To illustrate the use made of the third generalization, that people usually wish for at least one of the consequences they could predict as following from an action they intend to do, we must return to the discussion of the origins of the Second World War. This generalization is often invoked by historians when trying to assess responsibility for an event. If someone could predict an event as being a likely consequence of their free action, then they are normally held responsible for its occurrence. P. A. Reynolds has argued that Hitler was responsible for the Second World War, with the following remarks:

In law, and in common sense, the consequence of an action is presumed to have been intended if a reasonable man would suppose that the particular consequence would follow from the action in question. . . .
The actions that he [Hitler] said he would perform, and that he did perform, were such as any sane man would expect eventually to lead to war.

Consequently, Hitler can be said to have intended war, and so can be held responsible for it (Reynolds, 1961, p. 217).

It is sometimes said that because Nazi policies were likely to produce an economic recovery from the depression, and indeed did so remarkably successfully in 1933 and 1934, it could be the case that supporters of Nazism were motivated by a desire for that recovery and not by a desire for war. The possibility that this was so arises because of the generalization at present being discussed: economic recovery was a predictable consequence of Nazi policies, so perhaps that was what Nazi supporters wished for. Bullock raises this possibility but rejects it with these words: 'Whatever truth there may be in this so far as it is a question of the rank and file of the movement, so far as Hitler and the Nazi leadership are concerned, this is a view contradicted by the evidence' (Bullock, 1955, p. 326). Indeed the Minister of Economics, Dr Schacht finally resigned objecting to Hitler's refusal to take even elementary economic precautions in building up his military machine. 'Anyone who visited Germany in 1936–1937 needed to be singularly blind not to see the ends to which all this vast activity was directed' (*ibid.*, p. 327). Nevertheless it is hard to be sure what the German people thought would be the consequences of their support of the Nazi party. Consequently, it is difficult to know what they wished for by supporting it. (The complexity of their aspirations is revealed in David Schoenbaum's *Hitler's Social Revolution, Class and Status in Nazi Germany 1933–1939*, 1967.)

Although some inferences about other people's mental states are statistical, mediated by one of the generalizations stated above, most are arguments to the best explanation. This is because historians often lack sufficient information to make use of those generalizations. Even when they can use them, historians often find that they yield more than one probability, so that their argument must be completed by deciding which of the likely implications best explains the available data. Such arguments are of a hybrid form, partly statistical and partly an argument to the best explanation. From what we know of Caesar's beliefs, he might have intended to repress the Britains by a short punitive invasion or by conquest. To decide between the two, Collingwood was assisted by noticing that the first possibility involved inconsistencies which the second did not.

When evidence is sparse, arguments to the best explanation are often no more able to establish one hypothesis as beyond doubt than are statistical inferences. The difficulty of establishing the intentions of politicians has been clearly exposed by Maurice Cowling.

In the Epilogue to his book on the 1867 Reform Bill, Cowling drew attention to the many places at which the evidence of politicians' intentions is ambiguous. In April 1867, for instance, Gladstone argued that Disraeli's quite liberal franchise bill was not liberal enough, and urged him to make even more concessions than he had (Cowling, 1967, pp. 220–1). Cowling was of the opinion that Gladstone's intention in saying these things was not to ensure the passage of a more liberal bill, but to unite the Liberal party in an attack on Disraeli's government which would bring about its defeat in the House of Commons, leaving the way open for himself to take office. One piece of evidence in support of this interpretation of his intentions is Sir William Heathcote's report that Gladstone had told him he was opposed to household suffrage pure and simple. But Cowling admitted that Gladstone's remarks to Heathcote could be interpreted as 'a party politician fishing for support', not just 'one earnest churchman' talking to another; and that Gladstone might really have wanted to get Disraeli to pass a very liberal reform bill so that he would not have to propose one to satisfy the radical wing of his party when it came to office (*ibid.*, pp. 332–3). Because Cowling could not tell whether Gladstone's declaration to Heathcote was honest or not, he was not sure what Gladstone really intended at the time. Cowling adopted the interpretation he did because it seemed more consistent with Gladstone's previous attitude to reform, and because he believed that in April Gladstone could not have anticipated the possibility of Disraeli's getting a very liberal bill through the House, as he finally did in May 1867. These facts render Cowling's interpretation a little more probable than the alternative.

Generalizations (b) and (c) can be used by historians to discover people's intentions and desires. There is another generalization, which enables historians to discover people's beliefs, namely (d): that people usually have beliefs which imply that the actions they intend to do to bring about their wishes will probably be effective. This generalization cannot be used to mediate a statistical inference, however, since the beliefs in question cannot be directly inferred from a person's intentions and wishes. Rather it guides historians in constructing hypotheses about people's beliefs, which can be used to explain their behaviour. Alison Hanham used it to prove that William, Lord Hastings, was not executed by Richard III on 13 June 1483, as has frequently been reported, because she found evidence which shows that members of the London mercers' company believed him to be alive on 15 June.

The case does not . . . rest on conjecture. There is firm contemporary evidence that Hastings did indeed die not on 13 June but on 20 June. I first began a serious examination of the basis for the received opinion to the contrary when I noticed the implications of an entry in the records of the London mercers' company. This makes it clear that whenever the arrests of Hastings, Morton and Rotherham took place, it was after 15 June. On Sunday 15 June 1438 an assembly of the mercers' company was summoned and told about an important conversation that a servant of Lord Hastings had overheard between his master (the lord chamberlain), Bishop Russell (the chancellor) and Dr Morton, bishop of Ely . . . These three high officials had remarked on the efficiency with which foreigners in London promoted their own interests, and expressed surprise that they received no similar lobbying from English merchants. The mercers took the hint immediately and resolved to send that same afternoon to the bishop of Ely to test the truth of the report and sound him out on the desirability of appointing a delegation . . . Clearly the arrests and execution had not yet taken place . . . The minutes of the mercers' company prove that Hastings was still alive and at liberty on 15 June. (Hanham, 1972, pp. 236, 240)

Clearly the mercers' company wanted to promote their own interests, and resolved on 15 June to inquire of Dr Morton, Bishop of Ely, about the desirability of sending a delegation to himself, Lord Hastings and Bishop Russell. Equally clearly they must have believed those people to have been alive and free at that time, or their behaviour was irrational.

There are in fact many different kinds of mental states which historians can infer by means of arguments to the best explanation, not just intentions and beliefs but other purposes, habits, values, principles and dispositions. There is no point in illustrating them all. There are also other generalizations which historians can use to draw statistical inferences about other minds, generalizations which form part of psychoanalytic theories. Robert G. L. Waite, for example, explained Hitler's intense hatred of the

Jews in terms of his self-hatred: 'If psychoanalytic theory is correct, such massive hatred of the Jews must have been caused in part by a truly massive amount of self-hatred and self-loathing which he projected onto the Jews' (Waite, 1971, p. 207). Clearly Waite is here appealing to a generalization which attributes a person's hatred of others to hatred of himself. There are doubtless many such generalizations in psychoanalytic theory, which need not be enumerated here.

Of more interest to us are the difficulties historians encounter in justifying conclusions about other minds, either by means of statistical inference or by arguments to the best explanation. There is one particular difficulty which should be mentioned. The knowledge an historian draws upon in reaching a conclusion about other minds is often particularly difficult to state. There are two things about it which are hard to articulate. First, it is often hard to state all the causes of an action which an historian judges to be possible in a certain situation, or all the implications of a mental state which he thinks likely in a certain case. Second, inferences about mental states depend to a large extent upon judgements about the relative strength of beliefs, desires, intentions, habits and so on, and an historian's estimate of these degrees of strength is often difficult to formulate.

These difficulties can be illustrated by referring again to Cowling's discussion of Gladstone's intentions in attacking Disraeli's franchise bill. What analogies or general knowledge did Cowling draw upon to arrive at the hypothesis that Gladstone might have urged Disraeli to make his franchise bill even more liberal in the hope of having it defeated in the Commons? He would probably find it hard to say. And precisely how much franchise reform did Cowling think Gladstone favoured? If only a little, then probably Gladstone did not want a very liberal bill passed by Disraeli's party, and he probably was speaking honestly to Heathcote in declaring his opposition to household suffrage pure and simple. If, on the other hand, he favoured much more reform, then both these judgements would be wrong. And how strong did Cowling think Gladstone's belief that Disraeli would be unable to get a very liberal franchise bill through the House of Commons? If he strongly believed that, then his attempts to make the bill even more liberal were probably designed to ensure the defeat of Disraeli's government: but if he did not believe it strongly, then this was less likely to have been his purpose. Clearly Cowling's judgement of Gladstone's intentions rested decisively upon his estimate of the strength of Gladstone's desires and beliefs. Precisely what that estimate was, and what other facts about Gladstone's life it was based upon, Cowling would probably find it hard to say.

When historians draw upon knowledge which they find themselves unable to articulate, they are said to think intuitively. It is little wonder that many judgements about other minds are intuitive. As Cowling said about the politicians he was studying:

From what one finds them writing and from what others wrote about them, and from the context in which they wrote, one intuits their intentions. Even with material so extensive, and apparently as categorical, however, intentions can seldom be established certainly. Yet the historian has to judge, and to work with the judgement he has made. (Cowling, 1967, p. 6)

Often historians who draw a conclusion intuitively are able to remember all the evidence upon which it was based and to construct a reasonable defence of it. Sometimes, however, the evidence admits of different interpretations, each of them plausible, and in the light of that evidence there is no way of conclusively demonstrating any interpretation true or false.

A case in which different historians have different intuitions about the significance of the evidence and there is no decisive reason for preferring one to the other is the debate about whether or not Nero played his lyre as Rome burned. Michael Grant thinks he probably did, judging Nero's love of drama to have been so great as to have driven him to it. 'It is all too probable that Nero did give such a display. A man of his artistic tastes and emotions, offered a background of such superlative fireworks, would have found the temptation irresistible' (Grant, 1970, p. 152). Gerald Walter on the other hand, from a careful reconstruction of Nero's feelings that night, believes he would not have played and sung as the fire burned, since it was not an occasion he would have wished to celebrate, particularly at short notice in the middle of the night. Walter pictures Nero receiving news of the fire at his residence in Antium, about twenty-seven miles from Rome, and rushing off on horseback to the scene of the fire, arriving, as we know he did, before the break of day. 'Nero was asleep. They woke him with the news that the fire was about to destroy the palace which contained his treasures, his art collections and the magnificent wardrobe he possessed as a prince, a citharist and a tragedian' (Walter, 1957, p. 154). Suetonius said that he sang on the terrace of the garden of Maecenas. It would have provided a good observation post, and Walter believes Nero might well have gone there to contemplate the ruins of his palace. 'But did Nero really sing, dressed as a citharist and accompanying himself on a lyre? Did he have the forethought, when setting out from Antium, to take with him his costume and instrument? For, after all, he could scarcely have gone to look for the accessories for this exhibition among the ruins of the palace' (*ibid.*, p. 155). The issue hinges on the historian's assessment of the strength of Nero's passion for drama. Grant thinks he would have seen the fire as a dramatic setting for his own dramatic performance. Walter's Nero is much more prosaic: saddened by the destruction of his palace and its contents, and rushed by the course of events, Walter thinks Nero would have had neither the desire nor the opportunity to mount such a dramatic performance. These historians offer no evidence which clearly establishes the superiority of either interpretation.

The arguments considered in this section justifying statements about other minds have been either statistical, arguments to the best explanation, or combinations of the two. There are also arguments from criteria. These are commonly used to justify statements about personality traits, rather than for drawing inferences about beliefs, desires or intentions. Chapter 7 of Alan Bullock's biography of Hitler (1955), for instance, provides many descriptions of his character, some of which are justified by arguments from criteria. He wrote, for example: 'Hitler enjoyed and was at home in the company of women' (p. 357). 'While Hitler's attitude towards liberalism was one of contempt, towards Marxism he showed an implacable hostility' (p. 369). These statements he justifies by drawing attention to Hitler's words and deeds which satisfy criteria for 'enjoying the company of women', 'being contemptuous of liberalism', and 'being implacably hostile towards Marxism'.

Psychiatrists sometimes formulate the criteria of personality traits explicitly. Thus when Erich Fromm described Hitler's personality he wrote:

Hitler's personality, his teaching, and the Nazi system express an extreme form of the character structure which we have called 'authoritarian' . . . The essence of the authoritarian character is the simultaneous presence of sadistic and masochistic drives. Sadism is understood as aiming at unrestricted power over another person more or less mixed with destructiveness; masochism as aiming at dissolving oneself in an overwhelmingly strong power and participating in its strength and glory. (Fromm, 1941, p. 25)

Fromm then systematically illustrated the presence of these characteristics in Hitler and his party.

The *sadistic craving for power* finds manifold expression in *Mein Kampf*. It is characteristic of Hitler's relationship to the German masses whom he despises and 'loves' in the typically sadistic manner, as well as to his political enemies towards whom he evidences those destructive elements that are an important component of his sadism.

. . . [The] masochistic side of the Nazi ideology and practice is most obvious with respect to the masses. They are told again and again: the individual is nothing and does not count . . . But this masochistic longing is also to be found in Hitler himself. For him the superior power to which he submits is God, Fate, Necessity, History, Nature. Actually all these terms have about the same meaning to him, that of symbols of an overwhelmingly strong power. (Ibid., pp. 25–6, 28)

There are many other examples of the use of statistical inferences, arguments to the best explanation and arguments from criteria which could be given. But perhaps enough have been provided to show how commonly, and effectively, they are used by historians to justify belief in their singular descriptions of the past.

◁ 6 ▷
Historical generalizations

German philosophers of history in the nineteenth and early twentieth centuries were fond of distinguishing historical knowledge from scientific knowledge, or more generally history from science. (George G. Iggers has presented an excellent account of their ideas in *The German Conception of History*, 1968.) Some thought that history differed from science in its subject matter, history being about human actions, science being about physical events; some thought that historians understood their subject matter in a way which contrasted markedly with scientific understanding, for while historians explain actions by the particular thoughts which gave rise to them, scientists explain physical events by general laws and abstract theories. Wilhelm Windelband disputed these grounds for distinguishing history and science, for some scientists, psychologists and linguists for example, study human behaviour, and historians often have to refer to general laws to explain historical events. In his inaugural address as rector of the University of Strassburg in 1894, entitled 'History and Natural Science', Windelband distinguished history from science instead in terms of the kinds of knowledge at which they aim. Natural scientists, he said, proceed by quantification and abstraction to formulate, as precisely as they can, general laws of nature, true of many individual sequences of events. Historians, on the other hand, are forever seeking a richer, more detailed knowledge of events which takes cognizance of their particularity and uniqueness. Windelband called the natural sciences 'nomothetic' (lawgiving) and the historical disciplines 'idiographic' (describing the separate, distinct, individual) (Iggers, 1968, pp. 147–9).

Windelband's characterization of history as concerned with the unique rather than with the general has been widely accepted. (Its acceptance has been particularly common among critics of covering-law models of historical explanations. See, for example, Gardiner, 1952, pp. 40–6; Dray, 1957, pp. 44–50; Donagan, 1959, p. 429.) While this contrast between history and science is essentially sound, Windelband's characterization of history as concerned only with the particular and the unique is misleading in two important ways. Certainly historians are interested in the particular and the unique, but their interest is in what is unique, not only to certain single individuals or events, but also to certain groups and societies over certain periods, and indeed to certain groups *of* societies over certain periods. And in order to ascertain what is true of certain groups of people and groups of societies, one thing historians do is formulate and test generalizations about them, or rather about things in them. Thus historians' interest in the unique does not preclude them from forming generalizations, albeit of a spatio-temporally restricted sort. If they are to describe what life was like for groups of people in the past, they must generalize. Consequently, books on social and economic history, and to a lesser extent on cultural history, abound in generalizations.

Windelband's description of history as concerned only with the unique is misleading in a second way. It overlooks the historian's need to know the conventions of a society if he is to understand documents relating to it, and many of the deeds done within it. Historians must know the general significance within a society of certain words and actions if they are to make sense of the evidence they have of that society, and of the deeds to which that evidence relates. So in order to construct an intelligible story about the particular course of any segment of history, an historian requires general historical knowledge of the period in question.

1 The general nature of historical generalizations

To judge whether historians can rationally justify belief in the truth of historical generalizations, one has to know what such generalizations are like, what their distinctive characteristics are. Although there are several different varieties of historical generalization, all have some features in common, and it will be useful to begin by stating those.

Historical generalizations normally state that a certain proportion of things which are members of one class (the reference class) are also members of another (the attribute class), and sometimes the generalizations also indicate how this proportion changed over a certain period of time. This general description accommodates generalizations of several different forms. The description of the attribute class may refer to a quality of a certain proportion of the things which are members of the reference class; or to some kind of thing which occurs in association with a certain proportion of the members of the reference class; or to a kind of cause or effect of a certain proportion of the members of the reference class. (Occasionally historians are also interested in the mean value of a variable within a population, usually for comparative purposes. The calculation and use of such means is well described by Floud, 1973.)

The grammatical form of historical statements is not always a reliable guide as to whether they are singular or plural. Often their subject is fairly obviously a general term referring to some members of the class of things. An example is contained in this extract from a book by Phyllis Deane:

There is no doubt of the importance of the harvests in eighteenth-century England. Most eighteenth century industries depended directly on agriculture for their raw materials. The output of spirits, starch, malt and beer, for example, clearly tended to fluctuate with the output of particular cereals; the output of leather and tallow industries fluctuated with the progress of the livestock industry; even the major textile industry was dependent on the price of wool. (Deane, 1965, p. 229)

The second sentence contains a generalization whose subject is 'eighteenth century [English] industries' (the reference class), and its predicate 'depended directly on agriculture for their raw materials' (the attribute class) is asserted to be true of most instances of the subject. Some of those instances are mentioned in the sentences which follow.

Occasionally, however, a sentence having a general term as its subject predicates properties of the subject, the reference class, as a whole. When that happens, the sentence is really a singular description, about the single reference class as a whole, and not a generalization true of members of the reference class. Thus, when Deane wrote 'Until the 1850s . . . the labour force in agriculture was still expanding, the population in the rural areas was still growing' (p. 270), she clearly did not intend to attribute the predicates to individual members of the labour force or of the population in the rural areas, for to read it in this way would be absurd. This statement therefore is not a generalization, but a singular statement describing a particular labour force and a particular population as a whole. On the other hand, when she wrote 'Most of the middle class was literate' in 1850 (p. 265), she obviously meant most members of the middle class were literate. So this statement is a generalization, even though it is singular in grammatical form.

Finally, sometimes the subject of a generalization appears to be an individual. Consider the following:

Huskisson was concerned not so much to abolish protection as to rationalize the tariff system. He did away with import prohibitions and prohibitive duties and export bounties, none of which were yielding any revenue. He reduced to nominal levels some of the rates which fell on the raw materials of British industry and thus inflated manufacturers' costs . . . (Ibid., p. 187)

The first sentence is about an individual, William Huskisson, but it is a generalization nevertheless as it describes a disposition of his which was manifest on every appropriate occasion, namely the disposition 'to rationalize the tariff system'. Some of the instances on which he manifested this disposition are mentioned in the sentences which follow – indeed Deane's list is much longer than that quoted here. Because Huskisson's concern to rationalize the tariff system on appropriate occasions was instantiated several times, that disposition can be regarded as logically equivalent to the generalization, 'Whenever the opportunity of doing so presented itself, Huskisson acted to rationalize the tariff system'. (Gilbert Ryle presented this analysis of dispositions in *The Concept of Mind*, 1949, e.g. at p. 119.) Statements of this sort are sometimes called 'singular hypotheticals' (see Donagan, 1964, pp. 137–8) because they are about an individual. Their scope is indeed restricted to one individual, so that they lack the universality often attributed to general laws. They are generalizations, however, for they describe a kind of behaviour which could be instantiated on more than one occasion by the subject.

Some statements which predicate a general term of an individual, then, are properly regarded as generalizations, namely those in which the general term designates a disposition to behave in a certain way on certain occasions. But those in which the general term does not designate such a disposition cannot be construed as generalizations. Thus 'Napoleon was dictatorial' is a generalization, whereas 'Napoleon was short' is not. The latter is merely a classificatory statement; it states that the subject is a member of the class named by the general term. It does not state something which could have been repeatedly instantiated in the world, as Napoleon's disposition to behave in a dictatorial manner was. So it is not a general statement but a singular one. Some have written misleadingly of an act of classification as an act of generalization. (This was done by several contributors to Gottschalk, 1963, notably by M. I. Finley, on page 21; Arthur F. Wright, on page 36; Louis Gottschalk, on pages 124–5; and by David M. Potter, on pages 187–8.) Many colligatory statements describe particular groups of events by means of general terms, and so are classificatory. When G. R. Elton called Thomas Cromwell's administration under Henry VIII 'a revolution in government', he was classifying it, not making a general statement (Elton, 1955, ch. 7; and Elton, 1962; see McCullagh, 1978).

Accidental generalizations, laws and law-like generalizations

When discussing the justification of historical generalizations, it is important to distinguish between accidental and law-like generalizations. The most fundamental distinction is between those generalizations which are only accidentally true and those which are law-like. Some generalizations are known to be true of an actual set of instances of their subject term, and so warrant a corresponding indicative conditional: If something was a member of that set, it probably had the characteristic specified. Other generalizations are believed true, not merely of an actual set of instances, but of any instance of the subject term which could have existed, whether it did or not. These warrant a corresponding subjunctive conditional: If something had been a member of that set, it probably would have had the characteristic specified. Generalizations of the first kind can be called 'accidental', and those of the second kind 'law-like'. The difference between these two kinds of generalizations does not lie in their logical form – both are just general statements of a relative frequency. Rather it lies in the kind of justification available for them, which determines what implications one may draw from them.

Laws are those generalizations which are true of all instances of the reference class without exception, at any place or time. Furthermore, they cannot be derived from other laws. The chief difference between laws and law-like generalizations is that the latter are only conditionally true, whereas the former are true categorically. If a generalization is true of only a limited time and space, then it is probably true in that period because of certain things which exist at that time and not at others. It is true while those conditions exist, but not in their absence. Thus, to use J. S. Mill's example, the generalization that day follows night is only law-like, as it is true only so long as our solar system remains undisturbed. Should another sun enter it, we might have perpetual daylight; should our own sun be extinguished we might have perpetual night. Sometimes we know that a generalization is non-accidental, and true of only a limited period, without knowing the laws and conditions upon which it depends. Nevertheless, because it is not true of all times and places, it is assumed to be conditional and so merely law-like.

Mill pointed out that sometimes generalizations which have been taken to be universal and categorical are found to be derivable from still more general laws. Thus, he said, the generalization that 'terrestrial bodies tend towards the earth' was found to be derivable from a more general law of gravitation, namely that bodies of positive mass attract one another (Mill, 1872, Bk III, ch. 7, sect. 5). Mill was inclined to deny that generalizations which can be derived from more general laws are really laws of nature. Instead he called them 'empirical laws' and 'derivative uniformities' (ibid, Bk III chs. 4, 16, 19). His reason was probably that these are only conditionally true. Terrestrial bodies only tend towards the earth while no stronger source of gravitation is influencing them. So they are law-like generalizations, rather than pure laws.

If we accept Mill's account of laws of nature, then it follows that historians discover no laws of nature. All their generalizations are either accidental or law-like. Some law-like generalizations they derive from laws of nature, and although these may happen to be true of every time and place, they are conditional just the same. For example, even if Marx's statement 'At a certain stage in their development, the material forces of production in society come into conflict with the existing relations of production' were true of all societies, it would be true only because of certain laws of nature from which it can be derived and from the presence of certain relevant circumstances (see below, pp. 156–9).

Whether statistical generalizations are ever laws is an interesting question. If, as Mill assumed, laws state uniform and unconditional relations, then they cannot be, for they allow that the relations they describe are not uniform, but occur in only a proportion of cases of the reference class. Most historical generalizations are statistical because they are conditional and because the conditions which are necessary for them to be exemplified are not always present. They are clearly not laws, on Mill's account. However, a case might be made for thinking that statistical generalizations about physical events are genuine laws of nature when they are not conditional, that is when they cannot be derived from more general laws, for the frequencies they describe might be quite regular. For example, the generalization that the probability of an alpha particle penetrating the nucleus of a uranium atom is 10^{-38} is perhaps a law of nature.

Are historical generalizations universal?

Before examining the justification of historical generalizations, it might be of interest to inquire more closely whether any historical generalizations are universal. A generalization is universal if it is true without exception. Because the spatio-temporal scope of generalizations can be written into their formulations, it is possible for some historical generalizations to be universal, literally without exception, even though their reference class is circumscribed in time and space, as well as limited by reference to the properties of its members. Thus it might have been true that all the nobility in England in 1650 owned ten or more manors, in which case this is a true universal generalization of an accidental kind. All laws of nature are universal, are true without exception, but it is possible that there are universal generalizations which are not laws.

Can law-like historical generalizations be universal? Some certainly are, but most of those used by historians are not. There are many negative law-like generalizations which are universal, stating what attributes certain classes of things lacked in the past. No one in Europe in the Middle Ages had an aeroplane or radio. This is a law-like generalization because, given the state of science and technology in that period, it was virtually impossible for anyone to have produced them. Negative generalizations can be useful to historians in ruling out some possible explanations of data.

There are some positive law-like generalizations used by historians which are universal, namely some derived from laws of nature. These derived generalizations are held to be universally true because the conditions under which they are true are believed to be invariable. Most universal law-like generalizations used by historians are very familiar, for example that people whose heads are chopped off die. This can be derived from laws of physics and biology, and the conditions which make it true, such as the absence of an adequate alternative supply of blood to the head, are held to be invariable.

Most of the law-like generalizations used by historians, however, are about human behaviour, and none of these is universal, except perhaps some very vague and trivial ones. Generalizations about human behaviour are not derived from any well-established laws of nature, as many generalizations in physics and biology are. Sometimes they are inferred from a theory of human nature or from a theory of social or economic change, but such theories are acknowledged not to be universally true. Usually such law-like generalizations are inferred inductively from instances of them, and none has been found to have been exemplified universally.

Alan Donagan has presented a well-known *a priori* argument against the possibility of any historical generalizations being universal. Historical generalizations describe patterns of human behaviour in the past, and Donagan said they cannot be universal because human behaviour is not determined. Rather, people are free to varying extents to act as they choose. Most historians, he said, would be sceptical of any suggestion

that all agents of the same psychological type, or in the same sociological position, when confronted with a situation of the same kind, will act in a certain kind of way . . . They take account of the possibility that, in the same situation, a man may act differently from other men of the same emotional dispositions, habits, character, psychological type, or sociological situation or status; and that he himself may act differently at different times. This methodological scepticism may be formulated as what I shall call 'the presupposition of individual choice'. (Donagan, 1964, pp. 148, 149)

Whether or not people's actions are determined has been debated for years, and the debate still goes on. Good examples of it can be found in the August Comte Memorial Trust Lectures of Isaiah Berlin (1954) and A. J. Ayer (1964). Berlin argued the existence of indeterminism and free will as a condition of people's moral responsibility. Ayer questioned whether the sense of freedom required for moral responsibility was incompatible with determinism, and argued that motives and beliefs could determine human actions. There is no sign yet of a final solution to this cluster of problems.

Interestingly enough, Donagan believes there is a universal law relating people's intentions with their corresponding actions. The law is, roughly: If a person intends to ϕ at time t, then he will ϕ at t so long as he does not change his mind and is able to ϕ at t. At first Donagan thought this was an analytic truth, but he has since, in the face of arguments like Carnap's and Hempel's, agreed that the conditional statements entailed by dispositional statements are only contingently, and not necessarily, entailed by them (see Hempel, 1962, pp. 119–20 and Hempel, 1965, pp. 459–63, and pp. 473–4). Donagan has admitted in conversation that it is not possible at present to specify all that is meant by 'is able to ϕ', but assuming this is at least theoretically possible, he has maintained that this generalization is truly universal. Whether he is right, is hard to say. The generalization seems to be true as a (contingent) rule of language, stating what we currently agree is meant by 'intending to ϕ'. In that case it is tautological, universally true but not very informative. On the other hand, if intentions are distinct mental events or states, the generalization might be a law of human nature, and could be universal. Until it can be stated more precisely, however, it is not of much use, for one cannot tell to which circumstances it applies and to which it does not.

Reverting to Donagan's original point, if people have freedom of choice in the libertarian sense, then it is not surprising that historical generalizations about human behaviour are not universally true. It is quite compatible with freedom of the will, however, for there to be generalizations of a statistical sort, stating how most people behave in certain circumstances.

An *a posteriori* argument against the existence of universal historical generalizations has been offered by W. H. Dray. For a universal historical generalization to be true, Dray has said, it must either be so vague and trivial as to be useless, or so heavily qualified as to apply to only one instance. Consider Dray's point about vagueness and triviality first. It has been said that the Dust Bowl farmers in the United States migrated to California to avoid repeated droughts and sandstorms, and all that they entailed. What true generalization, Dray asked, could justify this causal explanation? Not 'Farmers will always leave dryland when damper areas are accessible', since this is not true (Dray, 1957, p. 28). C. G. Hempel, when considering this example, suggested the following: 'Populations will tend to migrate to regions which offer better living conditions.' But even this could be false in many instances. So to arrive at a true generalization, Dray concluded, the historian will 'have to soar to still greater heights of generality' (ibid.). Dray probably had in mind something like 'People try to improve their lot if they can.' Generalizations such as this, although perhaps true, are trivial because they do not provide interesting information about the reasons for events like the farmers' migration which they are invoked to explain; and they are very vague, because their terms refer to wide and inprecise classes of things, so that their application is uncertain. What activities are instances of 'trying to improve one's lot', and what circumstances are circumstances 'when they can'? (This problem is discussed at length by Danto, 1965, pp. 222–32; and by Murphey, 1973, pp. 73–86.)

The triviality and vagueness of universal laws of history is quite well illustrated by those which appear in Arnold J. Toynbee's *A Study of History*, the first six volumes of which are devoted to the discovery of laws governing the growth and decay of civilizations. It is doubtful whether any of the laws Toynbee arrives at would be accepted by historians as true. Pieter Geyl (1946) has demonstrated how Toynbee usually ignores historical examples which run counter to his theories, and distorts the examples which he does use to make them exemplify the law they have been adduced to support. The vagueness of the terms in which the laws are couched assists him in doing this and, in an effort to bring them closer to the truth, Toynbee modifies them to the point of banality. The following extract from a chapter entitled 'The Golden Mean' is typical:

We have ascertained that civilizations come to birth in environments that are unusually difficult and not unusually easy, and this has led us on to inquire whether or not this is an instance of some social law which may be expressed in the formula: 'the greater the challenge, the greater the stimulus' . . . We have still, however, to determine whether its validity is absolute. If we increase the severity of the challenge *ad infinitum*, do we thereby ensure an infinite intensification of the stimulus and an infinite increase in the response when the challenge is successfully met? Or do we reach a point beyond which increasing severity produces diminishing returns? And, if we go beyond this point, do we reach a further point at which the challenge becomes so severe that the possibility of responding to it successfully disappears? In that case the law would be that 'the most stimulating challenge is to be found in a mean between a deficiency of severity and an excess of it'. (Toynbee, 1960, vol. 1, p. 140)

Commenting on this 'law', Geyl objected to its utter imprecision: 'Is it not essential to define what is too much and what too little, to stipulate where the golden mean lies? As to that, the 'law' has nothing to say. That has to be defined anew each time by observation' (p. 124; and see p. 141; see also Dray, 1964, ch. 7, especially pp. 93–6). The trouble with Toynbee's law is that its terms are so vague, so imprecise, as to be both uninformative and difficult to use. Without knowing what constitutes a moderate challenge to a society, one cannot tell when the law, predicting the growth of a civilization from such a challenge, is meant to apply. The advantage of such imprecision is that the law is difficult to falsify – it can be interpreted to include or exclude difficult cases at will. But its great imprecision makes it virtually useless.

Interesting and useful historical generalizations admit of exceptions. But could they not be made universal by means of qualifications which by narrowing the reference class might prevent them from being applicable to exceptional cases? Specific reference to the group or society of which they are true might be one way of doing this. This was the solution recommended by Murphey (1973). He wrote: 'Once it is seen that reference to particulars in no way compromises the law-like character of a generalization, this entire problem vanishes' (p. 81). Certainly such qualifications can protect a generalization from many counter-instances, but it is doubtful whether they can be protected in this way from them all. Even Murphey wrote of them as stating 'high probabilities', rather than universal truths (p. 79), and admitted that 'no generalizations about human behaviour . . . hold with absolute generality' (p. 88). Dray's argument has not been refuted, that to qualify an interesting historical generalization sufficiently to exclude all exceptions to it, an historian would have to make it applicable to only one case. Dray considered generalizations which might be used to explain the unpopularity of Louis XIV. Having shown that 'Rulers who pursue policies detrimental to their subjects' interests become unpopular' is not universally true, and how various qualifications made to it fail to eliminate all exceptions, Dray suggested that the only true generalization would be 'Any ruler pursuing policies and in circumstances exactly like those of Louis XIV would become unpopular' (Dray, 1957, pp. 33–9). But probably this could only be applied to the case of Louis XIV, because he was almost certainly the only ruler who satisfied the conditions it states.

Positive, law-like generalizations about human actions and attitudes, which are both interesting and true, it seems, must admit of exceptions. They must, in other words, be statistical in form, no matter how qualified they may be. They state that certain characteristics were true of only a certain proportion of things of a certain kind, in a specific society over a specific period of time. For the purposes of inference and explanation historians would prefer generalizations which are universal. As it is, they must often make do with, at best, statements which predicate certain characteristics of a very high proportion of things of a certain kind.

Occasionally, especially in economic history, historians use law-like generalizations to draw inferences or explain events, and these generalizations are universal in form. For example, when considering whether the industrial revolution in Britain in the late eighteenth and early nineteenth centuries brought about an increase in the general standard of living, Deane made the following remark:

It might be expected that the process of industrial revolution, bringing with it, as it does, a great lowering in costs of production both in agriculture and industry, a perceptible reduction in the amount of human effort required to produce a given unit of output and consequent increase in the flow of goods and services available for consumption would automatically involve a corresponding rise in the standard of living of the working man. (Deane, 1965, p. 237)

The generalization appealed to here, roughly that whenever the costs of production are lowered there will be an increase in the goods and services available for consumption, is derived from simple economic theory. The universal generalizations presented in such theories are intended to describe ideal types of economy which differ from actual economies in being much simpler and closed against outside interference. In their simple universal form they are not intended to be descriptions of the real world. When applying them, as Deane did, to increase our understanding of the real world, scholars are aware that they are only true so long as a number of conditions are satisfied, namely that the actual economy exemplifies the ideal type sufficiently in the relevant respects, those being the respects which according to the theory are relevant for the truth of the generalization, and also that nothing in the economy is likely to interfere with the process of events described by the generalization. The theory from which the generalization is inferred will often indicate circumstances capable of preventing its being true. Thus Deane continued:

Whether or not it [the industrial revolution] does have these consequences, however, depends on a variety of circumstances, not least of which is the rate of population growth . . . It is only too easy for the number of mouths to be fed to multiply more rapidly than productivity per person in active employment, and hence for the average standard of consumption to fall . . . Moreover, if there are important discontinuities in the development process such that the growth of new kinds of industry requires substantial initial expenditure on new capital assets (buildings, harbours, roads, canals, railway-lines, ships and vehicles, plant and machinery) before incomes begin to rise, current consumption may actually have to be reduced so that funds can be diverted to these capital expenditures. (pp. 237–8)

Scholars can never be quite sure that they have identified all the possible circumstances which could falsify the universal generalizations of their theories. An unexpected event, like the outbreak of war, can easily impede many normal economic processes, and occasionally less dramatic developments do too. It is impossible, therefore, to list all the circumstances which can falsify these universal generalizations. They can only be declared true *ceteris paribus*, other things being equal, that is in the absence of any conditions which would make them false. In this sense, universal generalizations are just trivially true; they could not possibly be false.

Without the saving *ceteris paribus* clause, the generalizations derived from theories describing an ideal type of economy or society are not true without exception, are not universally true. At best they are true only in a high proportion of cases. Indeed if they are stated without any qualification at all, the proportion of cases of which they are true might not be very high at all. As interesting general descriptions of the real world, such generalizations must be interpreted as statistical, true in only a proportion of cases. Sometimes the fact that a theoretical generalization is not always true of events in the world is conveyed by stating it as a tendency statement, as Quentin Gibson has pointed out. Thus 'instead of saying that tariffs usually lead to inefficiency in home production, we can say that they invariably tend to do so' (Gibson, 1960, p. 141). Tendency statements, Gibson says, imply that the exceptions to the generalization can be accounted for, rather as we noted Deane accounted for exceptions to the generalization about the effects of an industrial revolution. However, whether scholars can account for all the exceptions to a generalization or not, while the exceptional conditions remain unspecified, the generalization is not universally true. It is true only in a proportion of cases.

2 The justification of accidental generalizations in history

There are two reliable ways in which an historian can justify belief in the truth of accidental generalizations. If the subject of the generalization designates a set with relatively few members, the historian might be able to examine each member of that set to discover the proportion of them of which the predicate of the generalization is true. In ideal circumstances, this is an extremely reliable form of justification. If the members of the reference set are too numerous or inaccessible to be examined individually, then an historian may justify a generalization about them by studying a representative sample of them. There is always room for error in extrapolating from a sample to the whole population from which it was drawn, though there are procedures for minimizing the likelihood of error sufficiently to make the sampling method fairly reliable. Each of these methods of justifying historical generalizations will now be examined in more detail.

Justification by exhaustive examination of the reference class

A generalization which an historian can justify with information about every member of its reference class will be entirely credible so long as every member of the reference class has been correctly identified and adequately examined, and so long as reliable indicators have been found for the attributes being studied (i.e. for class membership).

Many interesting historical generalizations have been established this way. For instance, the occasional elevation of businessmen to the peerage in nineteenth-century Britain gave some contemporaries the impression that feudalism had surrendered to industry. But when Ralph E. Pumphrey examined all the new peerages created that century in Britain, he found that it was not until the 1880s that 'new' families, from neither the nobility nor the gentry were being elevated to the peerage in appreciable numbers.

The first Salisbury ministry in 1885–1886 appears to have been the turning point so far as the introduction of persons with commercial and industrial connections into the peerage is concerned. For the first time, and always thereafter, 20 per cent or more of all recipients had such connections. Furthermore, at least 16 per cent always came thereafter from backgrounds other than the nobility and gentry, a hitherto unprecedented percentage. (Pumphrey, 1959, p. 172)

The study of parliamentary parties provides most of the historical generalizations checked by exhaustive examination of instances. Many are arrived at by the use of quite sophisticated statistical techniques. (A useful (non-technical) explanatory survey of these has been provided by Bogue, 1974, pp. 110–15.) One of the most interesting is the Guttman scaling technique, which can reveal political groupings not immediately apparent to observers. A striking, and clearly explained, application of this technique, leading to the discovery of ideologically coherent political groups in the British House of Commons in the 1840s which had not been detected before, has been described by William O. Aydelotte (1963). (The ideological basis of these groups has been hard to discover, as Aydelotte there explained. See also his further study of parties during this period: Aydelotte, 1972. Another clearly explained example of the Guttman scaling technique is Bogue, 1967.)

It is easy to see that generalizations arrived at by examining every instance, though usually very accurate, are accidental rather than law-like, and might well not be true of populations other than those to which they specifically refer, which have been thoroughly examined. We know that after 1885, the chance of a new peer in Britain being connected with commerce or industry has not been less than 20%. But the statistical information upon which that conclusion is based does not warrant our saying that if *anyone* were made a peer after that date there was not less than 20% chance of his being connected with commerce or industry. No reason has been given for thinking that the generalization is law-like. The percentage could have fallen below 20% had, for example, a very conservative party come to power.

Statistical methods of justification

The most useful advance in historical method this century had been in the verification of historical generalizations. (Precursors of this development are mentioned in Clark, 1967; pp. 176–8.) This development has accompanied increasing interest among historians in the conditions, opinions and behaviour of those large sections of society which received scant attention in the political and diplomatic histories, and in the histories of cultures, which dominated nineteenth-century historiography. It has also accompanied the development of sociology, and in particular the application of statistical techniques to the verification of sociological generalizations. It was not really until the middle of this century that historians widely recognized the importance of those techniques in their own discipline. Textbooks on historical method as late as 1950 (Louis Gottschalk, *Understanding History*) and 1957 (Jacques Barzun and Henry F. Graff, *The Modern Researcher*, rev. edn 1970) pay little heed to their use in establishing historical generalizations. The spate of books on the subject in more recent years, however, some of which are referred to in what follows, indicates a general awakening to their importance.

There can be no disputing that the use of statistical techniques has put new rigour into the formulation and justification of historical generalizations. Prior to their use, historians often based their general knowledge of past societies on a few instances with which they were acquainted and which they took to be typical, though in fact they were often not so; or upon the observations of contemporaries, that is of people living in the society at the time to which the generalization referred, though their remarks were often mistaken too. One has only to see how frequently generalizations based upon either of these two kinds of evidence have been completely disproved by statistical methods, to be convinced of the value of those methods. G. Kitson Clark has used them in his book *The Making of Victorian England* to correct many misconceptions. For example, the people of Victorian England thought their society was a religious one; yet the religious census of March 1851 revealed that less than half the population went to church on Sunday (Clark 1962, pp. 148–9). In American history, a number of beliefs about Jacksonian democracy have been corrected by statistical methods. For instance, historians had long thought that the late 1820s and 1830s saw a 'mighty democratic uprising' in the United States, with a new interest in participation in elections, and that it was this which swept Andrew Jackson to the presidency in 1828. But when Richard P. McCormick (1960) exmined the number of votes cast on that occasion compared with the number cast in previous elections, he found that in only six of the twenty-two states involved did a higher percentage vote in the 1828 election than had voted in previous elections. 'Instead of a "mighty democratic uprising" there was in 1828 a voter turnout that approached – but in only a few instances matched or exceeded – the maximum levels that had been attained before the Jackson era' (McCormick, 1960, p. 377).

The general impressions of a society expressed by those who were members of it, if not systematically arrived at, are no more reliable than those of an historian writing years later who bases his generalizations upon acquaintance with two or three instances. Both tend to exaggerate the significance of their inadequate sample. Lawrence Stone has explained how this is true of contemporary impressions of social mobility in seventeenth-century England.

The evidence [of social mobility] is twofold, contemporary comment and statistics. The former is unreliable, firstly because what seems like great social mobility to contemporaries may appear very small to us; secondly because, when dealing with a small élite class, a numerically very small opening into it may seem gigantic to the élite but insignificant to the outsiders; and lastly because the individual example, which may be quite exceptional, cannot be used to prove a generalization. Finally, myth may not correspond to reality. The rags-to-riches legend of Dick Whittington may bear little relation to the actual life-prospects of an apprentice, although the fact that the legend first appears in 1605 may indicate growing aspirations for upward mobility. (Stone, 1966, pp. 243–4)

For another example of the unreliability of contemporary impressions, let us turn again to the Jacksonian era. Contemporaries of Andrew Jackson believed his claim that he was replacing old Federalists in his administration with plebeian Democrats, taking government out of the hands of the privileged few and putting it in the hands of the people. A systematic study of the higher civil servants in his administration by Sidney Aronson, however, has revealed that the overwhelming majority of them came from the socio-economic élite. (*Status and Kinship in the Higher Civil Service.* This result is mentioned in Lipset, 1968, pp. 30–1.)

Indicators of variables

It might be thought, since statistics have been compiled on so few of the general features of past societies which interest historians, that statistical methods of establishing historical generalizations could very seldom be used. But as Stephan Thernstrom pointed out when considering this comment, in fact there is much more quantifiable data of use to historians than is commonly supposed.

In my own field of specialization, for instance, American urban history, there are literally tons and tons of untapped material in manuscript census schedules, local tax returns, city directories, school attendance records and similar sources. The problem has been not a lack of sources, but either ignorance of the existence of these sources or a lack of knowledge of what to do with them. (Thernstrom, 1968, p. 61)

(For another indication of the range of material available, see W. O. Aydelotte, 'A Data Archive for Modern British Political History', in his *Quantification in History*, 1971, ch. 4. A massive collection of quantifiable data relating to American political history has been assembled by the Inter-University Consortium for Political Research at Ann Arbor, Michigan.)

It is not only in such official lists that historians find indicators of the variables they want to measure. They can find them in other evidence of what people have said or done. The problem of finding reliable indicators of the variables which interest them is familiar enough to sociologists who have designed surveys. They have to frame questions which will elicit information, for instance about a person's attitude, without asking for that information directly. (See P. F. Lazarsfeld and M. Rosenberg, 1955, sect. I; and P. F. Lazarsfeld, A. K. Pasanella and M. Rosenberg, 1972, sect. I.) Historians cannot, of course, ask questions of past people, but they can detect in what people have already said or done indications of the attitudes or states of affairs under scrutiny.

The examination of people's writing for indications of their verbal behaviour and personal attitudes is called 'content analysis'. (See Swierenga, 1970, pp. 77–80, for a bibliography of works related to content analysis.) The best-known example of its application in history is Richard L. Merritt's essay 'The Emergence of American Nationalism: A Quantitative Approach' (1965). The findings of this essay were incorporated into a book by Merritt entitled *Symbols of American Community, 1735–1775* (New Haven, 1966). Merritt studied the words used in American newspapers when referring to America between 1735 and 1775, phrases such as 'British North America', 'His Majesty's colonies', 'our colonies in America', 'the American colonies', 'America', and took these to be symbols of the author's identification of the country and people either with the British people, or their King, or with the American people, or with their land. He found that before 1755 the number of such symbols identifying their country and people with the British was greater than the number identifying them with America, but that after that date the reverse was the case. 1755 was therefore a turning point in the emergence of American nationalism (Merritt, 1965, p. 154). Symbols identifying just the land as American 'crossed the 50 per cent threshold in 1762'; symbols identifying just the colonists as American crossed the same line in 1770 for the last time (i.e. they remained above it thereafter), 'thus suggesting that the perception of the land as being a part of an American rather than a British community clearly preceded a similar perception of the inhabitants of that land'. (Ibid., pp. 154–5. For further discussion and examples of content analysis, see Fred I. Greenstein's inquiry into whether or not achievement values in

American children changed between the 1890s and the 1940s, 'New Light on Changing American Values: A Forgotten Body of Survey Data', 1964.)

People's responses to questions, and their writing, are by no means the only indicators of facts about them. The variety of indicators which an historian can use is illustrated by those which Stephan Thernstrom employed in analysing the occupational mobility of different religious groups in Boston. In only two of the six samples he studied was the religion of the people specified. So, to discover the religious affiliations of those in the other groups, he took as indicators the type of wedding they had (one sample was of marriage licence applications), their nationality, itself indicated sometimes by their name, and even the religious affiliation of the hospital where their children were born. On checking the reliability of these indicators when applied to those whose religion was known, he found them correct in 'roughly nine out of ten cases' (Thernstrom, 1972).

Establishing the representativeness of a sample

As has been said, historical generalizations state that a certain proportion of things which were members of one class, the reference class, were also members of another, the attribute class. The distinguishing property of the reference class is 'the independent variable' and that of the attribute class 'the dependent variable'. Historical generalizations have, basically, the form '$r\%$ of things which were A, were also B'. The argument from a sample which an historian can use to justify such a generalization, has the following form:

(1) This sample accurately represents the proportion of all things which were A, which were also B.

(2) In this sample, $r\%$ of things which were A were also B.

(3) Therefore, $r\%$ of all the things which were A, were also B.

The truth of the conclusion follows necessarily from the truth of the premises, so that the credibility of the conclusion is simply a function of the credibility of the premises. Let me therefore examine each of the premises in turn, and see how they may be justified.

One of the most important and difficult tasks of an historian using a sampling technique is to ensure that his sample accurately represents the relevant features of the population from which it is drawn. So long as the sample is representative of the whole in these respects, it does not matter if it is unrepresentative of the whole in others. Lee Benson, for example, defended his generalizations about the groups which supported the Democratic and Whig parties in Jacksonian America by arguing that a large number of the wards, towns and counties included in his sample from the state of New York were typical of those throughout the northern states in the relevant respects, even though the state as a whole was peculiarly heterogeneous.

Although it may be argued that New York during the Jacksonian period was so heterogeneous that it must be considered unique, few specialists would deny that it contained many towns, wards, and counties that more or less resembled towns, wards, and counties in other northern states. Since my data have been collected on the local as well as the state level, generalizations based upon them probably do not apply uniquely to New York. (Benson, 1961, p. viii)

Even if the sample is known not to be typical, its bias can sometimes be allowed for easily. This is Stephen Thernstrom's opinion in the following passage, where he argues that by studying the occupational mobility of Catholics in Boston between 1880 and 1963, one can get a fair impression of their mobility in the country at large, even though Boston is not 'America writ small'.

Boston, of course, is but a single city, and some critics would argue that it is a far from representative one. I certainly would not claim that Boston is America writ small and that all the findings of this essay may be generalized to the society as a whole without qualification. But it is an inescapable if cruel fact that the task of piecing together the evidence necessary for a systematic analysis of social mobility in the American past is so formidable that the investigator customarily must confine himself to a single city. Given that necessity, and acknowledging the need for similar research in other communities in the future, there are grounds for believing that Boston is a quite satisfactory choice for inquiry into the question at hand. It was – and is – one of the greatest centers of Catholic strength in the United States. If it could be shown that even there Catholics suffered from distinctive career disabilities, as was in fact the case, it would be reasonable to assume that they confronted similar, if not greater, disabilities in places where the Church's position was more precarious. (Thernstrom, 1972, p. 126)

(For further discussion about ways of using biased samples, see Murphey, 1973, pp. 170–5.)

Over the last few decades, statisticians have developed increasingly sophisticated ways of ensuring that samples represent those aspects of a population which the researcher wants to measure, to whatever degree of precision and accuracy is required. The 'precision' of a sample is the degree of similarity between the results of the sample and the results which would have been obtained had the whole identified population been examined in precisely the same manner as the sample. The 'accuracy' of a sample is the degree to which it represents the true state of the population from which it is drawn, in the relevant respects. If the method of determining the characteristics of a sample is entirely accurate, then the precision of a sample will be the same as its accuracy. But if they are not, then these will diverge: even a sample which is very precise will not then be very accurate. (For a full explanation of recent sampling theory see Taro Yamane, *Elementary Sampling Theory*, 1967.) Without launching into technical details, it is possible to explain the reasons why samples are sometimes not representative, and so not reliable grounds for generalizations about the population from which they have been drawn, and the approaches which have been devised to avoid these distorting influences.

The problems all arise from lack of homogeneity of the population (or 'universe' as it is sometimes called) being studied, with respect to the dependent variables being considered. If every member of that population was precisely the same as every other, with respect to the relevant variable, then a sample of one member would be large enough to indicate the state of the whole population, no matter how large it was. But the variables which interest historians are never so uniformly distributed. They do not inquire, for instance, whether all Americans at a certain period had heads, but whether they all felt patriotic. Levels of patriotic feeling in the eighteenth century might have differed considerably among the members of the population, and to get an accurate indication of either the mean level of patriotism at any one time, or of the proportion of people who felt patriotic as compared with the number who still felt attached to Britain, quite a large sample would probably be needed. Generally, the larger the degree of variation in the variable being measured among a population, the larger the sample size must be, if it is to be truly representative of the whole. If the population is small and the differences between its members, in respect of a certain variable, very large, then it could be that no sample would be representative, but that all members of the population should be examined. A formula has been devised for determining the size a random sample should be, given the degree of precision and accuracy required, and the degree to which it is thought the dependent variable is likely to vary among the population (Blalock, 1972, pp. 213–5).

But now another problem has to be faced. The sample one takes from a population might be biased in some way, so that although the sample taken is large enough, it is not representative. If a researcher examining the wealth of farm owners in a certain country at a certain time confines his sample to those working in a prosperous industry, say cereal production, ignoring large numbers working in less prosperous sectors, then his sample will hardly be representative. How can such biased sampling be avoided? Three methods of avoiding it are commonly used, random sampling, stratified random sampling and cluster sampling. Let us briefly explain each in turn.

Sampling methods

If the variations in a variable are fairly evenly distributed throughout the population, then random sampling of the population may be used. This involves roughly the following procedure. Each member of the population is numbered, and from a sequence of random numbers (printed in books) members of the population are selected until the sample has reached the required size. Suppose there are 500 members of the population, and a sample of 50 is required. One notes the first 50 numbers less than 501 in a list of random numbers, and selects the items in the population corresponding to those numbers for inclusion in the sample. This ensures that each member of the population has an equal chance of being selected.

Sometimes, however, the variations in a variable are not at all evenly distributed throughout a population, so that there is a greater probability than there would otherwise be that random sampling would, by chance, produce a biased sample, unrepresentative of the whole. This is particularly worrying for historians who are trying to establish the mean value of a dependent variable in a population. Suppose that in New York City there was a small group of extremely wealthy people, millionaires, living in one area, who might well be unrepresented in a random sample of people living in the city, so that such a sample would give a misleading impression of the average wealth of the citizens there. To ensure that minority groups in which the occurrence of a variable is far from the mean for the whole population are adequately represented in a sample, a method called 'stratified random sampling' may be used. This requires the population to be divided into groups, or 'strata', each of which is fairly internally homogeneous with respect to the variable being considered, though the size of the variable, say wealth, should differ from group to group. A random sample is then taken from each group, or 'stratum', the size of each sample being proportional to the size of the stratum relative to the whole population from which it is taken. In this way the investigator can ensure that each group is fairly represented in his sample.

When very large populations are being studied, it might be impractical to adopt either the method of random sampling or that of stratified random sampling. For both require that all members of the population be numbered, so that a random sample can be taken, in the one case from the population as a whole, in the other from the strata into which it has been divided. If the population is large, it might be prohibitively costly, in time and money, or even impossible, for want of enough detailed data, to tabulate all members of the population and then to examine a widely scattered random sample of them. In these situations the method of 'cluster sampling' may be used. It involves dividing the population into groups or 'clusters', which are as internally heterogeneous as possible, with respect to the variable being considered, but each cluster resembling the others in the distribution of different sizes of the variable within it. Then a random sample is taken from among the clusters, and members of the clusters which have been drawn into the sample are examined. It may be that all members of each cluster are examined; or, more frequently, a random sample of them is examined. The success of this method of cluster sampling depends chiefly upon the degree to which each cluster fairly represents the whole population. (For a fuller, non-technical discussion of the reliability of these and other sampling methods, see Blalock, 1972, Part 5.)

If methods such as these are not adopted to ensure that a sample fairly represents the whole population from which it is drawn, with respect to the variables under consideration, then even a large sample can be useless as the basis of a statistical generalization. C. Vann Woodward has pointed out, for example, that the sixteen volumes of interviews prepared by the Federal Writers Project (FWP) in 1936–8 do not provide a representative sample of the opinions of all ex-slaves at the time, because they did not give due proportional consideration to the experiences of slaves in different states, nor were those interviewed selected at random, to ensure that all relevant categories were sampled.

The claim of 'a high degree of representativeness and inclusiveness' that has been made in behalf of the FWP narratives is clouded by evidence of skewed sampling of several kinds. For example, the states included are very disproportionately represented. Arkansas, which never had more than 3.5 per cent of the slave population, furnished about 33 per cent of the ex-slaves interviewed, while Mississippi, which in 1860 contained more than 10 per cent of the slaves, is represented by little more than 1 per cent of those interviewed. The border states are skimpily sampled; Louisiana did not participate, and Virginia diverted all but a small portion of her collection to another publication. While the number interviewed has been estimated to be approximately 2 per cent of the total ex-slave population surviving at the time the interviews were taken, it cannot be assumed that this was a random sample. There is too much evidence of chance or self-selection to assure randomness. Among categories of the population represented by larger than their proportional numbers are urban residents, males, and former house servants, with a consequent under-representation of rural population, females, and former field hands. (Woodward, 1974, p. 472)

The chances of a sample being biased, if it is not controlled by one of the three sample methods just outlined, are considerable, and the presence of distorting facts is not always immediately detected. This is illustrated in Stephan Thernstrom's description of previous attempts to measure the influence of religion upon occupational mobility.

Lipset and Bendix found no differences in the occupational mobility of Catholics and Protestants in a 1952 national sample of the U.S. population, but as Gerhard Lenski points out, they ignored the fact that a much larger fraction of the Catholics in the sample had been reared in big cities and should for that reason have fared better occupationally than Protestants, more of whom were of rural or small-town origins. In an analysis of career patterns in Detroit in the mid-1950s Lenski found substantial differences of the kind predicted by Weber [who thought that 'the Protestant ethic' would drive Protestants to greater achievements in commerce and industry than Catholics], and subsequent research in Detroit points in the same direction. It has been argued, however, that Lenski confounded religion and ethnicity, that Detroit Catholics happen to have come from such low-ranking ethnic groups as the Poles more often than American Catholics in general. (Thernstrom, 1972, pp. 124–5)

Lipset and Bendix's sample was biased in one direction by the disproportionate number of Catholic urban dwellers in it; and Lenski's was biased in the other direction by containing a disproportionate number of Catholic Poles.

Because it is so difficult to eliminate bias from a sample, historians often check the representativeness of a sample they have made by comparing its characteristics with those of another sample drawn in a similar manner from the same data: 'If the variation between the two independent samples is not statistically significant, then either could be used within certain limits of probability in analyzing the data. If the variation is significant, then a large sample, or perhaps one stratified differently, must be used.' Richard L. Merritt goes on: 'In my own work on changes in symbol usage in the colonial press, I have found that a random sample of four issues per year of a newspaper is ninetenths as good as an independently-chosen random sample of twelve issues per year' (Merritt, 1965, pp. 147–8). When Thernstrom became anxious that the samples he was using to measure the social mobility of religious groups in Boston were too small to be accurate, he took comfort from the fact that several separate and independent samples yielded the same results.

The argument of the paper does not rest upon the pattern observed in any one sample, but rather upon the recurrence of patterns through several separate and independent samples. A finding based on such small numbers that it might be due to mere chance in one of five instances could be attributed to chance less than 1 per cent of the time if it recurred in three separate samples ($1/5 \times 1/5 \times 1/5$). It is the consistency of findings between samples, not the high level of statistical significance of any one finding, that gives me confidence in the analysis which follows. (Thernstrom, 1972, pp. 129–30)

To sum up, an historian is justified in believing a sample to be representative of a whole population in relevant respects so long as (i) it is of adequate size, (ii) it has been selected in accordance with one of the three methods, either by random, stratified random or cluster sampling, and (iii) its information is not significantly different from that obtained by other samples of the same size, selected from the same population in the same way. Under these conditions a sample may not be perfectly representative of the whole population, but it will be very nearly as accurate as the historian planned it to be when calculating the sample's size.

The reliability of indicators

The second premise of the argument from a sample, it will be recalled, stated what proportion of the members of the reference class in the sample were also members of the attribute class. It has the logical form: 'In this sample, $r\%$ of the things which were A, were also B.' Normally the variables are not ones which an historian can immediately perceive by studying members of the sample, but are inferred by him from what he judges to be reliable indicators of their presence. In such cases, the historian in effect draws the following inference:

(a)   *F*s are good indicators of *A*s and *G*s are good indicators of *B*s.
(b)   In this sample, *r*% of things which were *F*s were also *G*s.
(c)   Therefore, in this sample, *r*% of things which were *A*s were also *B*s.

Demonstrating the reliability of a chosen indicator can at times be very difficult. Sometimes it is found that the variables about which information is being sought have been so imprecisely defined that it is impossible to tell what would be accurate indicators of them, and what would not. And sometimes it is discovered that what was taken to be an accurate indicator of one variable in fact is not an indicator of it at all, but of something else. Let us elaborate these points a little.

The need to clarify concepts in order to identify and observe instances of them has caused major improvements in the precision of social and political generalizations. Indeed Aydelotte has said many believe this to be the most important impact of 'the behavioral revolution', as the recent widespread adoption of statistical methods is called (Aydelotte, 1971, p. 19). Examples of such improvements abound, but one impressive for its degree of sophistication is Lee Benson's discussion of the nature of a political system, political power, and a political élite, and of indicators of these (in Benson, 1974, pp. 281–310). A better-known example is his discussion of the nature of 'public opinion' and ways of detecting it in 'An Approach to the Scientific Study of Past Public Opinion' (1967). The following quotation mentions some of the issues Benson faced:

What is meant by 'opinion'? When is 'opinion' simply the product of habit rather than thought? When is it a 'real opinion' instead of a 'mere prejudice or meaningless impression'? About what subjects is the 'public' capable of having opinions worth consideration by public officials? What degree of coercion by government, or by other agencies or agents, makes it invalid to speak of the existence of public opinion? Under what conditions, and in respect to what type of issue, should a minority submit to majority opinion?

The last question suggests another possible source of conceptual confusion. 'Public opinion' sometimes is equated with consensus. Does 'public opinion' imply unanimity, near-unanimity, or numerical majority? Does it refer to the 'effective' rather than the numerical majority? Differences on these and similar questions have confused the concept and provoked heated but unilluminating controversies. (Benson, 1967, pp. 106–7)

In trying to discover precisely what the variables in a generalization mean, historians look for descriptions of them which relate them to what they can observe. Another way of putting this is to say that they seek operational definitions of the variables they are studying in the hope that they will yield reliable indicators of them.

Some popular concepts have proved so vague that they would be better abandoned. As Kitson Clark has explained, the term 'middle class' as applied to nineteenth-century Britain refers to a wide range of social and occupational groups which are ill-defined at the boundaries, it being difficult to distinguish members of the middle class clearly from landed gentry and nobility on the one hand and operatives and labourers on the other. Not only did the term fail to distinguish usually important differences between the groups to which it referred, but being so imprecise it was sometimes hard to tell which people it included and which it did not (Clark, 1967, pp. 153–4). Similarly the word 'literate' could refer to such a wide range of skills, from the ability to write ungrammatical, misspelt sentences to the possession of sophisticated stylistic skills, that E. P. Thompson considered the word too vague to be used in an historical generalization (1963, pp. 783–4).

A good illustration of how the search for indicators drives investigators to clarify their concepts further is provided by Russell Middleton's inquiry into 'Alienation, Race, and Education' (1963). He begins by acknowledging that the concept of 'alienation' needs clarification, and refers to a study by Melvin Seeman which had untangled five different meanings of the word: 'powerlessness, meaninglessness, normlessness, isolation, and self-estrangement'. He then had to design statements for each sense of alienation, assent to which would indicate that the respondent suffered that kind of alienation. It was then found that one or two of these five senses of alienation were themselves ambiguous. Different research workers have interpreted 'normlessness' or 'anomia' in different ways. Some have used indicators which measure a combination of cynicism and pessimism, or despair. Middleton commented: 'Although pessimism and cynicism or despair may ordinarily accompany anomia, they do not in themselves constitute it.' He preferred to relate it to 'the expectation that illegitimate means must be employed to realize culturally prescribed goals'. The notion of 'isolation', Middleton pointed out, can be broken down to 'cultural estrangement', an awareness of not enjoying popular culture, and 'social estrangement', social isolation. But the concept of 'social estrangement' is itself ambiguous. It could refer to the fact of a person having few contacts with his or her family and the local community; or it could refer to a feeling of loneliness, which could be felt even by people having normal social contacts. Middleton decided that he was more interested in people's sense of alienation rather than the fact of alienation, so devised an indicator of their feeling of loneliness (p. 36).

An indicator is only reliable if its occurrences are highly correlated with occurrences of precisely that variable which an historian wants to study. To be confident of that high correlation, historians will normally use indicators which are in some way causally related to the variable, either its regular cause, effect or symptom (when the indicator and the variable have a common cause). Even so, indicators and variables are seldom, if ever, perfectly correlated. Paul F. Lazarsfeld and Wagner Thielens Jr. (1958) have emphasized that 'indicators are only related to an intended underlying classification with a certain probability' (p. 63). (See Lazarsfeld's interesting discussion contrasting 'predictive' and 'expressive' indicators of personality traits, 1959, pp. 17–24.) Sociologists sometimes use sets of indicators to get more accurate measurements of the presence of a variable, a set of indicators being called an 'index' of the variable (though 'index' is sometimes also used of single indicators (see ibid., pp. 11–13)).

Inadequate care in ensuring that indicators are indeed reliable has caused some striking mistakes in historical generalization. Two examples will suffice to illustrate this. The first is a short example in which historians interpreted children's replies to a question as indicating an attitude which, it transpired, they did not. It was discovered that George Washington was respected by almost 30% of American children as their greatest hero in 1902, but by little over 3% in 1958. What did this indicate? It was taken by some to indicate a strong aspiration towards political achievement among the youth of 1902, and a corresponding lack of political aspiration in 1958. In assessing this interpretation, however, Fred I. Greenstein has examined the reasons actually given by many of the children in 1902 for their admiration of Washington, and these reveal that Washington's political achievement was not what they admired most in him. Most admired his moral qualities, some his fame, some his wealth and some even his physical appearance. Their admiration of Washington was not, therefore, an indication of their political aspiration, as previous historians had thought (Greenstein, 1964, p. 304).

Probably the best-known example of an historian having a generalization rejected because of unreliable indicators is that of R. H. Tawney and his generalization that the gentry in Britain increased in wealth at the expense of the nobility between 1561 and 1640. Tawney put forward his argument in 1941, and since then it has been much discussed and criticized, notably by H. R. Trevor-Roper (1953), J. P. Cooper (1956) and J. H. Hexter (1958), from whose writing the following criticisms are drawn. Whether the criticisms are entirely justified or not does not concern us. Tawney (1954) thought several were not. The point rather is that they provide clear examples of historians rejecting a generalization because the indicators used by the investigator were unreliable.

Tawney justified his generalization that the wealth of the gentry in Britain increased at the expense of the nobility between 1561 and 1640 by providing evidence from a sample of 6 1/3 counties. Tawney took a person's manors in those counties to be a reliable indicator of his wealth, and his wealth to be a reliable indicator of his class status. Those who held four or fewer manors in those counties he identified as 'gentry' and those who held ten or more he regarded as 'nobility'. Tawney observed that over the period in question, the number of people holding ten or more manors diminished, whereas the number holding fewer manors increased. He concluded, therefore, that the gentry were prospering at the expense of the nobility. His argument was, of course, much more detailed and complex than this, but this expresses the basis of it, which critics were quick to attack.

Tawney had not suggested that the possession of manors in those counties he examined was a very reliable indicator of the wealth of their owners, but his critics argued that it was entirely unreliable. H. R. Trevor-Roper explained that a manor 'is not a unit of wealth but a definition of rights. The number of tenants holding of it, the payments and services due from them, the value and extent of the demesne land – all these are subject to the widest variations' (1953, p. 19; and see Hexter, 1958, p. 36). The Sidney family, for example, in disposing of 60% of their total manors between 1575 and 1600, lost only 28% of their total assets (Cooper, 1956, p. 377). Furthermore, an increase in the number of manors did not necessarily indicate an increase in real wealth; for the increase in income from rents might well have been offset by the devaluation of the currency which occurred during this period (Trevor-Roper, 1953, p. 22). Finally, possession of four or fewer manors in the 6 1/3 counties Tawney examined did not mean the owner was relatively poor, for he might well have owned many other manors in the remaining 33 2/3 counties of England, Wales and Ireland. Indeed many are known to have done so (Cooper, 1956, pp. 383–4; Hexter, 1958, pp. 34–5).

Tawney was also criticized for supposing that possession of wealth, even just of landed wealth, was a reliable indicator of class status. Many of the gentry at that time were very wealthy, and like members of the nobility, enjoyed the life of a large landowner. The gentry could be distinguished from the nobility on legal grounds – the nobility had titles whereas the gentry did not – but hardly on economic ones (Trevor-Roper, 1953, pp. 20–1; Cooper, 1956, p. 381; Hexter, 1958, p. 36). What Tawney was really interested in, as his discussion makes clear, was not the fortunes of the gentry but those of the poorer sections of the landed gentry, and the businessmen and lawyers who acquired land, whom he called 'middle class' and '*bourgeois*'.

The conditions under which an historian can justify the truth of a generalization on the basis of a sample have now been explained. The sample must be large enough and unbiased enough to warrant the claim that it accurately represents the proportion of members of one class of thing which are also members of another class in the whole population. Furthermore, the features of the sample which the historian observes must be reliable indicators of the variables he wishes to investigate. Clearly neither the representativeness of the sample nor the reliability of the indicators can be established beyond all possibility of error. So the conclusions justified by means of a sample may be accepted as true only within a certain margin of error. What that margin is, in any particular case, is quite hard to determine precisely. But often there is reason to think it is small.

Notice, by the way, that historians do not or at least should not, nowadays defend accidental statistical generalizations by straight enumerative induction, without any concern about the representativeness of the sample they have observed. They no longer argue that just because several *As* have been observed to be *Bs*, most or all *As* are *Bs*. There is no denying that each observation of an *A* which is *B* provides support for the generalization that most *As* are *Bs*. This is referred to as 'Nicod's criterion of confirmation', for discussion of which see C. G. Hempel (1965, pp. 10–13). Historians are now aware that the sample they observe has to be representative of the whole, before they are entitled to argue from it to a general conclusion.

Non-statistical justification of accidental generalizations

For large areas of history, there is not enough information to justify generalizations by either of the two reliable methods described above – by examination of every instance of the generalization, or by examination of a representative sample of all its instances. In such circumstances historians can often justify generalizations about the conventions and habits of a society by non-statistical means, as will be seen soon, but purely accidental generalizations, which are not at all law-like, can scarcely be justified in such circumstances at all. Historians are tempted, then, to adopt the old uncritical methods of impressionistic generalization, generalizing from whatever impressions they have gained from the sources they happen to have consulted. Such methods have rightly been denounced by critics (Kitson Clark, 1967, ch. 12; W. O. Aydelotte, 1971, passim; Robert P. Swierenga, 1970, p. 79).

Here is an example of the sort of predicament an historian finds himself in when he has no reliable statistics. It is from a work by G. M. Trevelyan, whom Kitson Clark chided for forming impressionistic generalizations 'without any attempt at quantification' (1967, pp. 178–9). If one examines the first chapter of Trevelyan's *England Under Queen Anne: Blenheim,* one finds him painting a picture of England at the beginning of the eighteenth century drawn very largely from the descriptions of a contemporary, Daniel Defoe, whose accuracy he respects. The picture which emerges is of a society that is idyllic in some respects and barbaric in others. Trevelyan goes on:

Confirmation of both these pictures emerges from a study of the period. But which picture contains the greater and more important body of truth it is hazardous to pronounce, partly because the dispute is about intangible values – we cannot put ourselves back into the minds of our ancestors, and if we could we should still be puzzled; partly also because even where statistics would help, statistics are not to be had. It is true that, a dozen years before Queen Anne's accession, the able publicist Gregory King made a calculation from the hearth tax and other data of the probable numbers in various classes of the community. The figures he gave represent a shrewd guess, no more. They will indeed serve negatively as a check on the enthusiasm of the *laudator temporis acti*, by recalling the fact that, even before the great enclosures and the industrial revolution, the number of farmers and yeomen was relatively small, and the numbers of the agricultural proletariat large. (Trevelyan, 1930, p. 17.)

Even this latter remark is suspect in the absence of reliable statistics, that is, without knowing that the cases observed constitute a representative sample of the reference class. Without this knowledge, no accidental generalization can be justified.

3   The justification of law-like generalizations in history

Whereas accidental generalizations can only be justified, ultimately at least, by facts about the actual instances of them, law-like generalizations can be justified in other ways besides. Law-like generalizations, it will be recalled, are meant to refer to all possible instances of them, whether actual or not. There are four ways in which historians can justify the claim that a generalization deserves to be taken as law-like. First, if a generalization can be shown to be derivable from a law of nature, it may be taken as referring to all possible instances. Second, if a generalization already known to be at least accidentally true of a society, exemplifies an acceptable general theory about man and society, it may be regarded as law-like. Third, if a generalization is known to have been true of many societies at different times, it may be accepted as true of all possible instances. And finally, if a generalization is implied by a credible statement about a community's conventions or about a person's habits or state of mind, it may be taken as law-like. Let us consider each of these ways of justifying law-like generalizations in turn.

Generalizations implied by laws of nature

When Olaf Helmer and Nicholas Rescher wanted to give an example of a law-like historical generalization, as opposed to an accidental one, they offered the following: 'In the seafights of sailing vessels in the period 1653–1803, large formations were too cumbersome for effectual control as single units.' They commented:

On first view, this statement might seem to be a mere descriptive list of characteristics of certain particular engagements: a shorthand version of a long conjunction of statements about large-scale engagements during the century and a half from Texel (1653) to Trafalgar (1803). This view is incorrect, however, because the statement in question is more than an assertion regarding characteristics of certain actual engagements. Unlike mere descriptions, it can serve to explain developments in cases to which it makes no reference. Furthermore, the statement has counterfactual force. It asserts that in literally any large-scale fleet action fought under the conditions in question (sailing vessels of certain types, with particular modes of armament, and with contemporaneous communications methods) effectual control of a great battle line is hopeless. (Helmer and Rescher, 1959, p. 183)

Although Helmer and Rescher did not explain why they believed this generalization to be law-like rather than accidental, Robert Brown, when assessing their claim about it, did. He said that it is law-like because it 'is derivable from (1) a very large set of physical and physiological laws taken in conjunction with (2) a set of statements that describe the initial conditions of the period 1653–1803, including the relevant tactics and strategies. Like all technological statements, this one depends for its explanatory force on the laws from which it is derived' (Brown, 1973, p. 102).

Generalizations implied by laws about man and society

History books do not contain many generalizations derived from natural laws. However, many do contain generalizations which instantiate a general theory of the nature of man and society, and consequently are accepted as law-like. The general theories employed in these cases may be distinguished from natural laws in that they have seldom been justified as rigorously as laws in the natural sciences. The most famous example of historical generalizations receiving support from a theory of man and society in this way, are the historical generalizations of Karl Marx. But many others have appealed to economic and political theories, and to theories of social and cultural change, to endorse historical generalizations as well.

The epistemological status of Marx's theory and of other theories about the general nature of man and society, is tricky to determine. The theory is clearly designed to render intelligible a large collection of historical generalizations, each of which exemplifies some part of it. On the other hand, the theory also receives some support, it seems, from some fundamental assumptions about the nature of man and society. Before amplifying these points, it might be useful to quote part of Marx's own summary of his theory.

The general conclusion at which I arrived and which, once reached, continued to serve as the guiding thread in my studies, may be formulated briefly as follows: In the social production which men carry on they enter into definite relations that are indispensable and independent of their will; these relations of production correspond to a definite state of development of their material powers of production. The totality of these relations of production constitutes the economic structure of society – the real foundation, on which legal and political superstructures arise and to which definite forms of social consciousness correspond. The mode of production of material life determines the general character of the social, political and spiritual processes of life. It is not the consciousness of men that determines their being, but, on the contrary their social being determines their consciousness. At a certain stage of their development, the material forces of production in society come in conflict with the existing relations of production, or – what is but a legal expression for the same thing – with the property relations within which they had been at work before. From forms of development of the forces of production these relations turn into their fetters. Then occurs a period of social revolution. With the change of the economic foundation the entire immense superstructure is more or less rapidly transformed. (Marx, 1859, p. 131)

What precedes and follows this passage in the Preface makes it clear that Marx regarded this general theory as an explanation of social, political, and cultural events he had studied. The opening sentence of the Preface shows that Marx developed his theory to explain his observations of history. 'I was led by my studies to the conclusion that legal relations as well as forms of State could neither be understood by themselves, nor explained by the so-called general progress of the human mind, but that they are rooted in the material conditions of life . . .' (p. 131). The range of cases Marx had in mind as relevant to his theory is indicated by a sentence near the end of the Preface: 'In broad outline we can designate the Asiatic, the ancient, the feudal, and the modern bourgeois modes of production as progressive epochs on the economic formation of society' (p. 132).

There are also passages in Marx's writings in which he suggests that his general theory of economics and politics can be derived, to some extent at least, from assumptions about the nature of man. Marx wrote that man is born into a natural environment in which he must be productive to survive. Man's productive activity determines his experience of life. Naturally, therefore, people try to work in ways which are rewarding to them in every sense, aesthetically and personally as well as financially. Marx assumed that the desire for rewarding work will predominate over all other desires, even over desires for justice, so that people will exploit others to improve their life style if they can. This view of human nature, set forth in *The German Ideology*, makes the general theory quoted above rationally plausible. This seems to have been Marx's view, as the following extracts show:

The first premise of all human history is, of course, the existence of living human individuals. The first fact to be established, therefore, is the physical constitution of these individuals and their consequent relation to the rest of Nature . . .

Men can be distinguished from animals by consciousness, by religion, or by anything one likes. They themselves begin to distinguish themselves from animals as soon as they began to produce their means of subsistence, a step which is determined by their physical constitution. In producing their means of subsistence men indirectly produce their actual material life.

The way in which men produce their means of subsistence depends in the first place on the nature of the existing means which they have to reproduce. This mode of production should not be regarded simply as the reproduction of the physical existence of individuals. It is already a definite form of activity of these individuals, a definite way of expressing their life, a definite mode of life. As individuals express their life, so they are. What they are, therefore, coincides with their production, with what they produce and with how they produce it. What individuals are, therefore, depends on the material conditions of their production . . .

This conception of history, therefore, rests on the exposition of the real process of production, starting out from the simple material production of life, and on the comprehension of the form of intercourse connected with and created by this mode of production, i.e. of civil society in its various stages as the basis of all history, and also in its action as the State. From this starting point, it explains all the different theoretical productions and forms of consciousness, religion, philosophy, ethics, etc., and traces their origins and growth, by which means the matter can of course be displayed as a whole (and consequently, also the reciprocal action of these various sides on one another). (Marx, 1845–6, pp. 126–7)

It is interesting to notice that when G. A. Cohen attempted to defend one of Marx's theoretical statements, he showed both how it might be derived from prior assumptions about human nature, and how it is justified by the many cases which exemplify it (Cohen, 1978, pp. 150–4). The prior assumptions about human nature are generalizations which are taken to be laws of nature, though Marx did not call them that. Cohen made particularly useful points when considering exceptions to Marx's sweeping generalizations. First, he said the generalizations should be taken as representing tendencies, not exceptionless truths. Thus the thesis that 'the productive forces tend to develop throughout history' allows that occasionally circumstances might prevent that development for a while (Cohen, 1978, pp. 134–5). At another point he suggested that they should be understood as statements of what 'normally' happens, when there is no undue interference in the social process. The suggestion here seems to be that the generalizations are true of an artificially isolated system, and true of actual societies if they approximate to that system in relevant respects. Thus, productive forces deteriorated during the decline of the Roman Empire because it did not resemble a normal social system in the relevant respects. Cohen allowed that it is very difficult to say what makes a system normal or abnormal (pp. 156–7).

The appropriate interpretation of Marx's general theory is not of immediate concern, however. What is important here is to see that historical generalizations not only support, but are supported by such a theory, which justifies regarding them as law-like. General theories of man and society such as Marx's are couched in terms too vague to permit detailed predictions, but not so vague as to prevent one from seeing certain historical generalizations as exemplifications of them. For example, this sentence from Marx's general theory, quoted above, is fairly imprecise: 'At a certain stage of their development, the material forces of production in society come in conflict with the existing relations of production.' But in the context of the theory, it is precise enough to enable one to see that it is exemplified by the following historical generalization, drawn from Marx and Engels's *Manifesto of the Communist Party*: 'The bourgeoisie, wherever it has got the upper hand, has put an end to all feudal, patriarchal, idyllic relations.' (Marx and Engels, 1888, p. 48.) Certainly the latter generalization provides independent support for the former. But the former, embedded in Marx's general theory, is supported by many other facts as well – some, other historical generalizations, such as those describing the conflict between bourgeoisie and proletariat (Marx and Engels, 1888, p. 58); others, general beliefs about the basic nature of man and society, such as those set out in *The German Ideology*, mentioned above. Although the explanatory power of the general theory is not great, its explanatory scope and its plausibility are considerable, which are reasons for thinking it true. (The frequency with which it has been falsified, of course, provides reason for thinking it false.) If, after careful inquiry, it was shown that Marx's general theory deserved to be believed true, then the historical generalizations which exemplified parts of it would also deserve to be believed true for that reason alone. In fact, among those who doubt the truth of Marx's general theory, the historical generalizations to which he appeals are believed true, if at all, on the basis of the number and variety of particular instances of them in history.

Marx is not the only author to support historical generalizations both by a general theory of socio-economic change and by an appeal to a wide variety of specific instances. W. W. Rostow, for example, did the same in *The Stages of Economic Growth* (1960). In this book, Rostow offered general descriptions of what he saw as five stages of economic growth. They were, in order, 'the traditional society, the preconditions for take-off, the take-off, the drive to maturity, and the age of high mass-consumption' (p. 4). All societies, he said, are in one of these five categories (p. 4), and throughout the book Rostow gave numerous historical illustrations of his general descriptions of each stage. But he also remarked: 'These stages are not merely descriptive. They are not merely a way of generalizing certain factual observations about the sequence of development in modern societies. They have an inner logic and continuity. They have an analytic bone-structure, rooted in a dynamic theory of production' (pp. 12–13). Rostow, like Marx, sought support for his historical generalizations both in particular historical events and in a general economic theory. (The theory is outlined on pp. 13–16.) He did not, however, attempt to ground the latter in a general theory of human nature.

Sometimes the implications of an historical generalization inferred from a general theory of man and society are found to be contradicted by observations. In that case the generalization is usually abandoned, as historians rightly have more faith in observations, or in inferences well supported by observations, than in their general theories of man and society, which are often imprecise and inaccurate. Thus, for example, on the basis of Malthus's theory that the population will naturally increase while people have no difficulty acquiring food for their children, the Poor Law Commissioners in Britain in 1834 assumed that a system which supplemented labourers' wages in proportion to the price of bread and the size of their families would inevitably lead to an increase in the labouring population and a corresponding decrease in wages. This view was widely accepted at the time, and the Speenhamland System, which provided such relief for the poor, was consequently condemned. When Mark Blaug examined the relevant statistics, however, he found that in fact there was no clear evidence that the system had had the predicted results. Populations increased in areas without the Speenhamland system as well as in those with it; and wages in areas where the system was applied were not uniformly lower than those in areas where it was not. The generalization derived from Malthus's theory has now, therefore, been abandoned (Blaug, 1963; and Deane, 1965, pp. 143–4). Malthus's theory is not so strongly respected that its apparent implications are given more credence than fairly reliable statistical data warrant. Interestingly, Blaug argued that the conclusions drawn by the Poor Law Commissioners in 1834 from Malthus's theory would not have been drawn if they had been using a more sophisticated modern theory (Blaug, 1963, p. 153).

Statistical justification of law-like generalizations

A common empiricist assumption has been that generalizations about the world can be justified by observations which exemplify them. The difficulty of providing an entirely compelling justification of this sort for law-like generalizations is now seen to be almost insuperable. Nevertheless in many cases there are observations which justify belief in the truth of law-like generalizations, even though they do not prove them true beyond all possibility of error.

One thing which prevents us from proving the truths of inductive inferences, be they to singular or general conclusions, is the impossibility of proving the reliability of the inductive procedures we employ. This difficulty has been discussed before. However, there is another difficulty in justifying inductive arguments to general, law-like conclusions which is prior to the one just mentioned, and that is the difficulty of stating the rule for warranted inferences of this kind. Extensive philosophic discussion of this problem has revealed several sources of difficulty. Our natural tendency, as Hume pointed out, is to think, after seeing several As associated with Bs, that all As are Bs. This procedure is unreliable, however, unless the observed cases are truly representative of the whole population. It is important, therefore, to establish the representativeness of the observed sample. In the case of accidental generalizations, about a known finite number of cases, this can be done by an appropriate method of sampling. Law-like generalizations, however, are about unknown as well as known cases. The limits of the population to which they refer are indefinite, and so the problem of proving that any sample is representative of the whole is sometimes insuperable. It is clearly insuperable when the population is infinite, as the population referred to by some natural generalizations is. If Boyle's law is true, relating the pressure of a gas to its volume and temperature, it is true of all time and space, in an infinite number of possible cases. There is no way of knowing what a representative sample of these would be.

Because generalizations based upon observations are usually conditional, depending for their truth upon the presence or absence of certain conditions besides those mentioned in the protasis of the generalization, investigators have rightly concluded that the greater the variety of circumstances under which a generalization is found to be exemplified, the more likely it is to be true. They conclude that if a generalization is exemplified by a large variety of cases, and has been found false in none, it is likely to be true. But this leaves unanswered the question of how large a variety of cases must be examined before it is rational to accept a generalization as true.

There are some, like Sir Karl Popper, who deny that it is ever reasonable to believe generalizations true, and who argue that all that scientists can do is check that they are not false. This is done by testing their implications, to see whether they are borne out by observation. Positive results may not verify the generalization, but negative ones would falsify it, or at least throw serious doubts upon it. Much can and has been said about Popper's views. Here it is only necessary to point out that if historical generalizations are statistical, describing a relation which holds in only a certain proportion of cases, occasional negative results do not falsify them. Indeed if they are statistical and about an infinite population, it is quite impossible to infer a finite set of observation statements whose falsity would falsify them. The problem of finding a representative sample is not avoided by turning to Popper and adopting his hypothetico-deductive approach.

There are other difficulties about the inductive justification of law-like generalizations, but these are of less practical significance to historians. N. Goodman pointed out that frequent observations of green emeralds up until the present time, T, equally well supports the generalizations that all emeralds are green, and that all emeralds are 'grue', that is, green until time T and blue thereafter. This fact seems to suggest that generalizations should not be more complex than is necessary for instances of them, so far observed, to be true. It has also been remarked that instances of a generalization do not necessarily confirm all logical equivalents of that generalization. Evidence that whatever is not black is not a raven does not necessarily confirm the logically equivalent generalization that all ravens are black. (These difficulties are discussed by Swinburne, 1973, chs 7 and 10, where relevant references are given. See also Hesse, 1974, chs 3 and 7.) These points are unlikely to concern historians, however, as much as the problem of deciding upon a representative sample of the population referred to by a law-like generalization.

In practice, historians do not think of the populations referred to by their law-like generalizations as infinite, but as limited to certain historical societies. Often they even have a rough idea of the conditions which might affect the exemplification of the generalization, and know, again roughly, the homogeneity of a society with respect to those conditions. They can check these estimates by taking large samples of the population, and noting the frequency with which one variable is related to the other in those. If several large samples yield similar results, they are generally taken to be representative of the population as a whole. Clearly the larger the samples, and the more numerous and diverse they are, the more reliable this procedure is. (See Floud, 1973, pp. 166–7 for slightly more sophisticated methods, used when the variables can each have a range of values.) The argument at this point appears to be an argument to the best explanation: what would better explain similar results among several different samples than the hypothesis that they represented the whole population from which they were drawn? Such similarity is unlikely to be the result of chance factors – indeed, if the variables were not related, the chance of such a correlation being found in a sample can often actually be estimated. If that chance is very small, then the correlation is regarded as significant. The smaller the chance, the more significant it is (see Blalock, 1972, pp. 155–65 and also Floud, 1973, ch. 7).

Statistical arguments embodying these approaches are often quite complex and sophisticated, but the heart of such arguments is sometimes easy enough to grasp. Robert A. McGuire (1981), for example was interested to discover whether a significant relationship existed between agrarian unrest in late nineteenth-century America and economic instability. So he correlated variations in the price, yield and income of wheat, corn and oats, with the degree of agrarian protest through various farmers' associations for four different periods, 1867–74, 1874–81, 1883–90, 1890–97, as well as for the entire period 1866–1909. In each period, and for each kind of economic instability, McGuire got a large number of significant correlations and this, he said, 'strongly supports the conjecture that economic uncertainty in agriculture was a major factor in fomenting farmer discontent' (McGuire, 1981, p. 848).

To justify the claim that a correlation is law-like, one has to show that it was not a matter of chance. If the chance of a very high correlation occurring between two variables which are not causally related is very small, then by demonstrating such a high correlation one has done all one can, statistically, to justify the claim that the correlation is law-like. Still, this justification by itself is not entirely compelling. There remains the possibility, however slight, that the high correlation is simply a matter of chance. Even McGuire did not conclude that his figures definitely proved a law-like relation between economic uncertainty in agriculture and farmers' discontent – only that they strongly supported such a conjecture. The possibility of a high correlation occurring by chance is only set aside when the generalization, as well as being supported by statistics, can also be derived from other accepted generalizations. If a highly significant correlation cannot be explained by other generalizations, then there remains some reason for thinking it might have been a matter of chance.

Of course, when few generalizations are available in a field, it may not be possible to derive one generalization from others. Only as higher level generalizations are developed, does this become possible. Higher level generalizations derive superior law-like status from their superior explanatory scope. They entail more facts which can be established by observation than lower generalizations do, for they usually explain several different lower level generalizations, and all the observations which exemplify them.

Law-like habitual behaviour

The law-like statements most frequently used by historians, either implicitly or explicitly, are those about people's habitual responses. Whether people have free will or not, there is no doubt that much of their behaviour is regular and predictable, and that this regularity and predictability is not just a matter of chance, but exemplifies commonly accepted higher level generalizations about human behaviour. It is important to acknowledge these generalizations, in case the preceding discussion has given the impression that the only generalizations which historians can use for inference or explanation are those implied by theories developed by social sciences such as economics, sociology, anthropology and politics. In fact some of the high level generalizations appealed to by historians are entirely commonplace. Here are a few examples.

Historians often draw inferences upon the basis of their knowledge of an individual's habits. Having observed a certain pattern of behaviour, they expect it to be repeated on the basis of the generalization that once people have acquired a habitual pattern of behaviour, they normally conform to it, so long as nothing happens which is likely to alter it. Habits are usually identified by observing a pattern of behaviour and employing an argument from criteria. Thus when W. L. Warren wanted to defend his claim that King John of England 'seems to have been at least conventionally devout', he listed a large number of his actions which could be taken as instances of his religious devotion, explaining away reports to the contrary as the distortions of embittered monks whose monasteries had suffered at his hands (Warren, 1961, pp. 171–2).

People's habits can also be inferred from a knowledge of their general intentions, using the generalization that people generally act in a way which they believe will bring about what they strongly wish for as efficiently as possible, so long as the action has no likely consequences which they would deplore. By means of this generalization Warren inferred that one of the chief sources of King John's reign, Roger of Wendover, was disposed to exaggerate the vices and virtues of the people he described rather than present only well-authenticated knowledge of them. For Wendover confessed that his purpose in writing a chronicle was not merely to record what had happened, but to provide examples of virtue for his readers to imitate and of vice for them to shun. Warren concluded, 'Naturally, therefore, he was more interested in the effectiveness of his sermons than the authenticity of the stories with which he illustrated them' (p. 13).

Declarations of intent are not always reliable evidence of a person's practice, however, as people sometimes fail to behave in the way they intend. Like all generalizations, statements of people's dispositions are best supported by observed instances of them. Warren was confident that Wendover was disposed to exaggerate King John's vices because he had detected frequent distortions of the truth in Wendover's chronicle. It was possible that these distortions reflected Wendover's inaccurate sources rather than a desire to exaggerate, as he was a monk of St Alban's, writing some ten years after King John's death, and that abbey was patronized and visited frequently by members of the baronial class hostile to the king. His declaration of intent, however, makes it likely that an inclination to exaggerate played at least a part in determining the character of his chronicle as well. It certainly warranted the generalization which Warren drew from it.

Some habits are not unique or peculiar to individuals, but are shared by almost all members of a society. These are usually habits enforced by legal or social sanctions. In our society there are laws which require people regularly to record births, marriages and deaths, the ownership of land, and the receipt of income. The mere existence of such laws does not ensure their observance, of course, as Robert Brown has pointed out (1973, pp. 97–101). But while strong sanctions are associated with such laws, it is likely that people will comply with them. This generalization itself rests upon a higher level generalization that people will usually act according to their own interests as they perceive them, especially when the reward for doing so and/or the penalty for not doing so is believed to be great. This is a commonplace generalization about human nature.

The conventions most frequently employed by historians are those about the meanings of words, phrases, and sentences, even though these conventions are sometimes difficult to state. The conventional use of language in a society is enforced by certain social sanctions (general disapproval of the misuse of words) and sometimes by authorities (rejection by teachers and later by employers of instances of linguistic misuse). Sometimes generalizations about the appropriate use of certain phrases are enshrined in rigorously observed administrative conventions. For instance, in the twelfth century the Pope never offered 'the full papal greeting "gratiam et apostolicam benedictionem" . . ., except by mistake, in addressing excommunicated persons'. Mary Cheney used this fact as a reason for denying that a mandate containing these words could have been issued to Gilbert Foliot, Bishop of London, on 1 October 1170, since the Bishop was excommunicated at that time, a fact which the Pope was not likely to have forgotten as he had recently written at length to Gilbert explaining the conditions under which he might obtain absolution. Cheney had no doubt that the rule would have been followed on this occasion, even though there was no direct evidence that it had been (Cheney, 1969, p. 476).

Clearly all the instances of habitual behaviour mentioned in this section provide an historian with no more than conditional generalizations, generalizations which are true and law-like of only one person or of a limited group of people for a limited period of time. When a habit is broken, or a rule is revoked or is left unenforced, then the conditions necessary for the truth of the generalization relating to it will no longer exist, and the generalization will no longer be true. But the fact that, for one reason or another, habits die is no reason for denying that while they exist people usually conform to them with law-like regularity.

One final point. If a generalization is implied by a higher level generalization, then it may not need strong statistical support in order to be credible. Thus, if it is known that a community strictly enforced a uniform practice in the spelling of words, then one would need only a few instances of the spelling of a given word to know how it was generally spelt in that community. This fact often enables historians to acquire an accurate knowledge of social conventions quite quickly, without having to use careful statistical arguments.

4 The justification of causal generalizations in history

Before closing this chapter, more should be said about the justification of causal generalizations in history. In the next chapter it will be argued that causes are conditions necessary for the occurrence of their effects. Causal generalizations, then, state the kinds of circumstance generally necessary for certain kinds of effect, that is, the kinds of circumstances without which such effects would not occur. Many causal generalizations are also explanatory generalizations stating what kinds of conditions were generally sufficient as well as necessary for a certain kind of effect. Like other generalizations, causal generalizations can be categorical or conditional, law-like or accidental. Categorical causal generalizations are the basic laws of nature, like the law of gravitation mentioned before. Conditional causal generalizations are true whenever and wherever the necessary conditions exist. In certain societies it is a law-like generalization that if the government registry office has an official register of someone's birth, marriage or death, then the person named on the form was born, married or died on the date recorded. The truth of that generalization, however, depends upon certain conditions, such as that the enforcement of the policy of registering births, marriages and deaths is carried out with quite severe sanctions. Accidental causal generalizations describe what was generally the cause of a particular kind of event at a particular time, without implying that such an event would have such a cause on another occasion. Thus the claim that most of those who voted for a certain party at a certain election did so for religious reasons would be an accidental causal generalization, implying nothing about what would cause people to vote for that party on other occasions.

Statistical justifications of causal generalizations can be very persuasive, but they are not entirely convincing unless supplemented with arguments either from higher level generalizations or from rational considerations. This is true, no matter whether the generalization be law-like or accidental.

The limitations of statistical evidence can be readily understood. The fact that in large random samples two variables are highly correlated is good evidence of some causal connection between them – for what else could account for the correlation as well – but it leaves quite uncertain the nature of the relation between them. If the existence of one of the variables preceded that of the other, then it may well have been the cause of the other; but it might have been just a symptom of the real cause. The appearance of gunsmoke and a loud bang might regularly precede the arrival of a shell, yet not be the causes of its arrival. They are but the perceptible results of the explosion which launched it on its way. Alternatively, the apparent cause might in fact be a complex thing, only part of which is causally efficacious. Self-raising flour will make cakes rise, but it is only the baking powder in it which causes that effect. Plain flour, containing no baking powder, will not produce the same result. So a high correlation between variables does not imply a simple causal relation between them.

There are two tests which an historian can carry out to check whether a suspected cause was an actual cause, was really necessary for a certain kind of effect. One is to try to find a significant number of cases in which instances of the effect occurred without that kind of cause being present. If he can find such cases, then he has shown that what was thought to be a common cause, really was not. For example, it has often been thought that international peace is generally caused by a balance of power among nations. Geoffrey Blainey (1973) has pointed out, however, that lasting peace has occurred, not when there is a balance of power, but when a decisive victory has given one nation or group of nations a preponderance of power, as after the defeats of the French armies in 1815 and 1871, and of the German armies in 1918 and 1945. 'Those years of extreme imbalance', he wrote, 'marked the first stage of perhaps the most pronounced periods of peace known to Europe in the last three or more centuries' (p. 113).

A generalization which passes this test is not necessarily true, however. There are several reasons why an historian might fail to find cases in which a certain effect was achieved without a suspected cause being present. Certainly that could happen because the suspected cause was indeed a cause of the kind of effect being studied. But the suspected cause might really be spurious, and the historian simply have failed to detect instances of the effect being produced in isolation from it.

Another way to test a causal generalization is to compare situations which it correctly describes with situations which resemble it in almost all respects except that the suspected cause is absent. If the effect is absent too, then the suspected cause might be the actual one. If two cakes are made in exactly the same way, except that one contains baking powder and the other does not, and the former rises but the other does not we can confidently say that the baking powder caused the first cake to rise. Stanley Elkins used this form of argument to strengthen his case for the generalization that American negro slaves acquired what he called a 'Sambo' type of personality, which was essentially childlike, because they were put in a tightly closed society, the plantation, in which their life and well being depended totally upon the whim of their owner. To add credence to this generalization he contrasted the slaves in Latin America, where slaves from the same background, transported in the same way, enjoyed a slightly freer existence, being allowed private relations with their family and with priests, and being protected to some extent by the law. Latin American slaves did not have the 'Sambo' type of personality, and Elkins argued that that was because they were not interred in a totally closed institution (Elkins, 1968, chs 2 and 3).

Again, however, it must be pointed out that arguments of this sort do not ensure that the cause has been identified correctly. The cause might be only part of that which stands out as the relevant difference; or indeed it might be something else which distinguishes the cases being compared but has not been identified at all.

Tests to determine whether a cause was generally sufficient for an effect are predictably simple. If many cases can be found in which instances of the cause were not accompanied by instances of the effect, then its explanatory adequacy will be in doubt. This is how Lee Benson came to discredit the generalization that working-class affiliation caused most of the Democratic vote in the 1844 election in the state of New York. He found some working-class areas, which were inhabited by a large proportion of native Americans with a Protestant background, such as the Fifth, Eight and Tenth wards of New York City, in which the Democrats did not receive a large share of the vote (Benson, 1961, pp. 144–5). Benson found that support for the Democrats was much more regularly related to the religion and ethnic background of the voters than to their economic class. Roman Catholics and people of Irish and German descent were particularly prone to vote Democrat. He concluded that these factors were more likely to have been causally significant.

Given the tentativeness of conclusions based upon statistical data, historians normally look for support for their causal generalizations from their general knowledge. If a causal relation suggested by the data can be explained by some higher level generalization, then they can have more confidence in it. Elkins, for example, found his generalization that membership of a totally closed, authoritarian society produces a childlike personality supported by psychological theories, and used these in its defence. Freudians accounted for it in their theory of infantile regression, which involves identification with the authority who threatens one's existence. H. S. Sullivan's 'interpersonal theory', which explains personality as the result of internalizing the attitudes of 'significant others', accounted for it. Finally, role theory, which sees personality as a function of the social roles adopted by the subject in order to survive, also supports it (Elkins, 1968, pp. 115–55). Clearly such theoretical support adds much to the credibility of Elkins' generalizations. If plantations were as closed as Elkins assumed and slaves as childlike and docile as he said, the causal relation between these two can scarcely be doubted. Critics have argued that conditions on plantations were not as uniform as Elkins said, but they have not challenged the appropriateness of his appeal to theory (Lewis, 1967).

Generally the theories assumed by historians as justifying their causal generalizations are commonplace ones. They normally indicate a disjunction of likely possible causes necessary for the occurrence of the kind of event being explained, and are based upon the historian's knowledge of similar cases. This is particularly true of general theories about the range of possible motives for various kinds of human behaviour. If, on a certain occasion, an historian finds just one of the possible motives for an action to be highly correlated with instances of that action, then he is justified in claiming that it was generally the cause of people acting in that way on that occasion. The rational adequacy of a motive in explaining an action is, of course, no proof of its causal efficacy, because people can often produce reasons which rationally justify their actions but did not in fact cause them. The justification of causal judgements is more fully discussed in the next chapter.

Conclusion

Observed regular relations provide the basis of all our general knowledge. If two variables are found to be regularly related in a large variety of cases, we infer that such a relation generally holds between such variables, even when we do not know all the cases to which such a generalization refers. There is a leap of faith involved here, which empiricists happily make, assuming regularity in nature.

When several generalizations have been formed, they are checked against one another for consistency, on the assumption that the true laws of nature are rationally consistent. Often several generalizations are contemplated to see whether they themselves exemplify a higher level generalization. Sometimes they are contemplated in the hope of imagining a theoretical process which will account for the regular relations they describe. Thus, for example, molecular theory explains the regular connection between the pressure of gas and its temperature and volume. The whole edifice of laws and theories rests upon observations of regular relations. As new observations are made, the edifice is adjusted to accommodate them. The laws and theories are qualified, sometimes even abandoned. In history, as in other sciences, observation statements, or statements readily inferred from observation statements, are given maximum credence. Of course observation statements employ concepts, but the concepts do not presuppose or imply the truth of the laws and theories which are derived, modified or rejected on the basis of the observation statements which use them.

Accidental generalizations can be true in a correspondence sense. They refer to identifiable sets, though an historian's idea of the characteristics of members of those sets may be very sketchy. 45.7% of those who voted in the Fifth ward in New York City in 1844 voted Democrat (Benson, 1964, p. 145). The description is of a finite number of people, though the number is not mentioned, doing an identifiable thing in an identifiable place at an identifiable time. A range of possible truth conditions of this generalization can be envisaged, and if part of reality resembled one of them, then the generalization is true.

The truth of law-like generalizations, referring to unknown as well as known cases, is trickier to understand, because law-like generalizations are not purely descriptive. Consider the generalization 'Most negro slaves in America had childlike personalities'. It does describe the personalities of most actual negro slaves in America, so it is descriptive in that respect. But if we interpret the statement as law-like, we take it to mean something more, namely that being a negro slave in America was sufficient to make it probable that a person had a childlike personality. This suggests that the relationship between the two variables, far from being accidental, is explicable, that it can be explained, either by reference to a more general law or, as Elkins did, in terms of a theory about the process by which the variables are related.

Thus law-like generalizations are in part descriptions about all actual members of their reference classes, with the implied admission that what those members are is not entirely known. In this respect, as descriptions, they can be true or false. But they are also used to suggest that the relation between the two variables, between being a member of one class and being a member of another, is explicable. It is because the relationship is explicable, because we have reason to think that being a member of the one class is sufficient to make it probable that something is also a member of the other, that we can say that the generalization applies to all possible as well as all actual members of the reference class. The suggestion that a relationship between variables is explicable can be true or false as well, but what is true or false in this case is that the relationship is explicable, not the description of that relationship provided by the generalization. One must distinguish the truth of the description provided by a law-like generalization, and the truth of the implication that the relationship it describes is explicable.

7

Justifying singular causal judgements in history

Causal judgements are expressed in many different ways in historical writing. They are not all of the form 'Event A caused event B'. There are other words which may indicate a causal relation: 'consequently', 'as a result', 'therefore', and so on. Many active verbs imply a causal judgement too. Take this sentence for example:

The establishment of some semblance of order in Normandy, and in particular the introduction of a system of landholding which, to a considerable extent, concentrated an inheritance in the hands of an eldest son, and left the younger children landless, raised serious problems for many Norman warrior families; problems which the traditional Viking love of adventure and of wandering helped to solve. (Brooke, 1964, p. 219)

There appear to be four causal judgements here: the establishment of order in Normandy by the Norman dukes in the eleventh century, together with their system of landholding caused the eldest sons to inherit most, and caused younger children to remain landless; the latter caused worries for many Norman warrior families; and the resolution of these worries was partly the result of the traditional Viking love of adventure and of wandering.

Sometimes the mere juxtaposition of events in a sentence is clearly intended to indicate a causal relation between them.

From 1103 to 1154 Sicily was ruled by Roger II, Roger 'the Great'. For some years his rule was nominal, since he was a child at the time of his father's death. From 1112, when he officially came of age, or perhaps rather from 1113, when his mother went off to be queen of Jerusalem, Roger was effective ruler of Sicily. (Ibid, p. 222)

In the second sentence the word 'since' refers explicitly to the causal relation between Roger II's minority and his nominal rule. But in the third sentence no less, a causal relation is clearly suggested between his coming of age in 1112, or the departure of his mother in 1113, and his independence as a ruler. The causal relation between these events is so easy to imagine that it does not even have to be mentioned.

Because causal judgements are not always expressed in statements which make them entirely explicit, this chapter is entitled an inquiry into causal judgements, not merely causal statements, in history.

At present there is considerable uncertainty among philosophers as to what we mean when we say one event caused another. One commentator has usefully described the main views as Leibnizian (the idea that objects really have causal powers to bring about changes in certain circumstances), Humean (the belief that causal relations are attributed to events by people on the basis of observed invariate relations between them, but are not to be discovered in natural things themselves) and Kantian (the view that causal relations have to be assumed as real, though they cannot be observed, if nature is to be understood) (Wartofsky, 1968, p. 311–15). To these three should be added what Tom L. Beauchamp has called 'the manipulability theory' espoused by R. G. Collingwood and others, that causes are events or states of affairs by which we can produce or prevent other events or states of affairs (Beauchamp, 1974, Part IV). Much can be said in defence of each position, and of variations of them, as well as in favour of the view that our concept of cause is indefinable, as Michael Scriven has argued (1971b). No attempt will be made here to pick out and defend a particular interpretation of the word 'cause' as the only correct one.

Although there is considerable disagreement as to what the word 'cause' means, there is much less disagreement about when one thing may be called a cause of another. Intuitions are not entirely certain even about this, but people are generally much more agreed about the assertion conditions of causal statements than about their truth conditions, at least in history. The assertion conditions being referred to here are those relations which exist between things in virtue of which we are warranted in saying that those things are causally related, that one was a cause of the other. Indeed these assertion conditions may be regarded as minimum truth conditions of a statement of a causal relation. If one thing is a cause of another, then at least the first is related to the second in the ways stipulated by the assertion conditions of such a statement. It is even possible that the assertion conditions are the only truth conditions of causal statements which we are justified in believing to exist. But whether that is so, whether in particular we are obliged to postulate the existence of natural necessity or causal powers of some sort, is a question which will be left unanswered here. In what follows, when it is said 'Conditions $C_1 \ldots C_n$ are sufficient for the occurrence of event E', what is meant is just that whenever $C_1 \ldots C_n$ occur, so does E; and when it is said 'Condition C is necessary for E' all that is meant is that whenever E occurs, so does C. Why such invariable sequences exist, if they do, is for metaphysicians to speculate.

The relations between an historical cause and its effect will be presented in terms of singular and general statements about the past. The possibility of justifying belief in the truth of such statements has already been discussed, so it need not be further discussed here. The task in this chapter is to set out the minimum truth conditions of causal statements as clearly as possible, and to defend them against objections. Once these truth conditions are known, then the possibility of justifying belief in the truth of singular causal descriptions of the past can be inferred.

1   The independence of causes and effects

There are several different conditions which have to be satisfied before historians are justified in believing a causal relationship to exist. To begin with, the relationship must be between events or states of affairs (which are taken to include among other things relations, dispositions and even the absence of these) which are not identical, where one does not include the other, and where the relation between them is not merely, if at all, a logical one.

The claim that causes and effects are always distinct, in the senses just indicated, has been challenged by Maurice Mandelbaum in *The Anatomy of Historical Knowledge* (1977). There he has argued that in many cases 'cause and effect are not to be construed as distinct events, but are to be regarded as components within some single ongoing process' (p. 63). It is his belief that in many everyday and scientific contexts causal relations can be observed, and cause and effect are found not to be separate but to be either identical, or such that the effect includes the cause, or at least and most commonly, such that the cause overlaps the effect in the course of an ongoing process.

Mandelbaum has defended his opinion with a large variety of examples. We might say, for instance, that the writing of a sentence with chalk on a blackboard caused the sentence to be written; but the cause is not 'some separate and distinct precedent event', said Mandelbaum, but is rather just part of the effect (p. 56). Historians, he said, typically explain events (effects) by describing their constituent parts (as causes).

To take an example from Michael Scriven, when the historian seeks to explain the rise of the City of London as a financial center, he appeals to changes included *within* that rise, which together account for it. Since no one of these changes, taken by itself, was identical with the rise of the City's power, that rise (which one seeks to explain) is to be regarded as the effect of a concatenation of individual changes that, together, account for it. (p. 111)

For evidence that people commonly regard cause and effect as overlapping, Mandelbaum referred to the reports of subjects involved in A. Michotte's 'entraining' experiment. In this experiment one square form was made to move towards another square form of a different colour, and after the first had met the second they both moved on together in the same direction that the first had been travelling. Michotte recorded that most subjects reported such a visual experience as of one square causing the other to move. Mandelbaum pointed out that although the subjects could distinguish the two squares, they did not perceive each as having a different motion once they had met. In other words, the motion of the first was not perceived as independent of the motion of the second (p. 198). So, he concluded, the causal relation was not considered to have been between two separate, independent events. Finally, Mandelbaum pointed out that causes and effects whose relation is described in scientific laws such as Boyle's Law, which states that under any conditions the pressure of a given volume of gas varies inversely with its volume, are not independent events, the one occurring before the other, but are mutually dependent factors which occur at the same time (pp. 98–9).

These examples are representative of the range offered by Mandelbaum, and the only way to criticize his theory is to discuss them in turn. The sentence-writing example and many like it depend upon the ambiguity of descriptions like 'the writing of a sentence' to make Mandelbaum's point. Such a phrase can refer to a bodily *action*, for example the motion of arm and hand which causes a chalk to move and thus a sentence to be written, and in this sense the writing of a sentence certainly does cause a sentence to be written. But the phrase can also refer to the *act* of writing a sentence, which is a sequence of events beginning with the agent's bodily movements and concluding with the chalked sentence appearing on the blackboard. In this sense the writing of a sentence includes a sentence being written, but is not the cause of that event. I have elaborated the distinction between actions and acts elsewhere (1976). We can agree that the action of writing a sentence occurs at the same time as the appearance of the sentence. But the fact that two events are contemporaneous does not mean they are not distinct.

Michael Scriven's example of the 'causes' of the rise of the City of London as a financial centre is one in which, Scriven said, 'cause and effect are physically identical and only conceptually distinct' (Scriven, 1966, p. 243). Mandelbaum, a little more precisely perhaps, said that in this case the causes were, severally, part of the effect and so not distinct from it. This example trades upon the ambiguity of 'accounting for'. One can explain an event by showing *how* it occurred, or explain it by showing *why* it occurred. In explaining how a change occurred one describes the steps of that change. But this does not explain why it occurred, or what caused it. (This point is elaborated in McCullagh, 1969.) The changes which constituted the rise of the City of London as a financial centre explain how its financial activities increased. But they do not, by themselves, explain why they increased; they do not, in other words, provide the causes of that increase. They do nothing but describe the ways in which that increase occurred. The passage in question makes this plain:

At the same time the significance of the City of London as a financial centre was enhanced by the transactions of the business involved in the provision of British subsidies, the supplying of British armies and the raising of government loans as well as by the eclipse of the financial power of Amsterdam. The growth of British exports, . . . was very rapid and entailed a similar growth in merchant shipping . . . (Scriven, 1966, pp. 242–3)

Each of the activities listed here – the provision of British subsidies, the supplying of British armies and so on – contributed to the increase in financial business in London. However the passage does not explain why financial business increased in these various ways; it does not tell us what gave rise to the various activities listed here. It simply documents the rise of the City by mentioning them.

There are some occasions on which explaining how a change occurred also helps to explain why it occurred. This happens when the stages of a change are causally related to one another, in the manner described for instance in W. H. Dray's 'model of continuous series' (1957, pp. 66–72) or in C. G. Hempel's model of 'genetic explanation' (1965, pp. 447–53). In these cases most of the events in the causal chain are both effects and causes, but even so the causes and effects are distinct in the relevant respect: no event is an effect of itself or a cause of itself. Each is always caused by another distinct event and itself causes another.

The result of Michotte's entrainment experiment does not support Mandelbaum's position as much as he thought. We may agree, for the sake of argument, that the perception of the movement of each of the two squares was not distinguishable after they had met. In discussion, however, Mandelbaum quite explicitly allowed that we can think of the motion of each without the other, that is we can have an idea of their motions as separate even though we cannot perceive them to be such (Mandelbaum, 1977, pp. 197–8). The question then becomes whether the doctrine that causal relations are between distinct events should be taken to imply that causal relations are between events which can always be perceived to be distinct. There is no reason, it seems, to think that this is so, even though, as Mandelbaum has pointed out, Hume assumed the contrary (see Mandelbaum, 1974). So long as they actually are distinct, in the senses stated at the start of this section, that is enough. The motions of the two squares were in fact distinct and not identical when they travelled together, even though they might not have been perceived to have been so, since they were motions of quite distinct objects.

Finally, when scientists show that one state of a system is a function of another state of the system, it would appear that the two are causally related yet not at all distinct, because the one state cannot obtain without the other. But the fact that two states of affairs are constantly related does not mean they are not distinct. So long as the states they refer to are not identical, and one does not include the other nor merely conceptually imply the other, then they can be causally related. I do not think that Mandelbaum has proved that events or states of affairs which are generally taken to be causally related are ever not distinct in these ways. As will be seen later, it is important to insist upon these distinctions between cause and effect if certain counter-examples to the proposed analysis are to be successfully deflected.

Historians judge one event or state of affairs to have been a cause of another, I suggest, only if they believe the occurrence of the first to have been necessary in the circumstances, contingently necessary, for the occurrence of the second. Whether the shape of Cleopatra's nose influenced Roman history or not, depends, as W. H. Dray correctly observed, upon whether that history would have been different had her nose been less attractive (1957, p. 103). Dray was inclined to doubt that it would have, though Cleopatra's fascination for Mark Antony is indisputable. Roughly speaking, one event or state of affairs is a cause of another if, had the former been different in some way and everything else remained the same, the latter would not have occurred as it did. In that sense we can say that the occurrence of the first was necessary in the circumstances for the occurrence of the second, and therefore a cause of it.

Before elaborating and defending this proposal, let me briefly explain (1) why it will not be claimed that historians must be convinced that the occurrence of one event was sufficient for the occurrence of another before judging them to have been causally related; and (2) why causes are not held to be always universally necessary for their effects, but may be just contingently necessary for them.

2   The sufficiency of causes

One event can be sufficient to make the occurrence of another very probable yet not be a cause of it. A sudden considerable fall in a normal barometer reading is sufficient to make the occurrence of a storm very likely, but would not be considered a cause of that storm. An abnormally high body temperature might be sufficient to ensure the presence of an infection, but would not be considered a cause of the infection. In short, many events are symptoms of other events from which one could infer their occurrence with confidence, but are not causes of them. So it is not enough for the occurrence of one event to have been sufficient for the occurrence of another for them to have been causally related.

But are events which we do regard as causes always sufficient for their effects nevertheless? It is widely accepted now that many events which historians judge to be causes were not by themselves sufficient for their effects (thanks largely to the work of Michael Scriven, e.g. 1966, pp. 246–50). For example some historians have said that none of the causes of the First World War was by itself sufficient to have produced it, though they remained causes nonetheless.

In the forty years following the Franco-Prussian War, ... there developed a system of alliances which divided Europe into two hostile groups. This hostility was accentuated by the increase of armaments, economic rivalry, nationalist ambitions and antagonisms, and newspaper incitement. But it is very doubtful whether all these dangerous tendencies would have actually led to war, had it not been for the assassination of Franz Ferdinand. (Fay, 1930, p. 21)

And A. J. P. Taylor has expressed a similar opinion: 'It would be wrong to exaggerate the rigidity of the system of alliances or to regard the European war as inevitable. No war is inevitable until it breaks out' (Taylor, 1954, p. 56). Of course some historians have thought the economic causes of the war were sufficient for its occurrence (e.g. K. Zilliacus, 1946); others have thought the spirit of national rivalry was sufficient (e.g. P. Renouvin, 1955).

As Taylor's comment suggests, historians can identify causes of an event without knowing conditions sufficient to have brought it about. A more generally acceptable example, perhaps, is A. G. Dickens's discussion of Martin Luther's attack on the papacy. Historians know a number of reasons for it, but these go nowhere near explaining its vehement and utterly uncompromising nature. E. H. Erikson, in his *Young Man Luther* (1959), offered a psychological explanation of it, suggesting among other things that in attacking the Pope as he did Luther was trying to win independence from his own father. Dickens doubted whether Erikson's interpretation could be made to square with the evidence: Luther remained on affectionate terms with his parents to the end of their long lives, and they were devoted to his welfare. But Dickens concluded:

Even if, despite all the objections, we proclaim this evidence enough to justify a diagnosis, we end by 'explaining' singularly little about Luther's enormous achievement, his amazing energy and versatility, his immense and lasting impact upon the German people, upon the Christian world. There have been hosts of manic-depressives, many young men subject to identity-crises, yet there has been only one Luther. A mere manic-depressive is not led by his psychiatric problems into propounding and setting forth with demonic energy a system of ideas which tears a whole civilisation asunder and alters the course of western history. (Dickens, 1967, p. 14)

Some would hold that Luther's energy was not demonic but divine! But whether Dickens's comments upon Erikson's theory and its significance are justified or not, we have here an example of an historian who insists that what might have been a cause of Luther's revolt was far from sufficient to account for it.

It is sometimes thought that although causes are not individually sufficient for the occurrence of an effect, they must nevertheless always belong to a set of causes which is sufficient for the effect's occurrence. This view is particularly popular with those who see some form of natural necessity as essential to our notion of cause. If one is prepared to reject or remain sceptical about natural necessity, however, there is no need to assert that for every event there are sufficient causes of its occurrence. The advantage of abandoning natural necessity, or at least of omitting it from an account of causation, is that one thereby leaves room for the possibility of indeterminacy in nature. Causes might make the occurrence of events probable without necessitating them. A cause, then, might have been contingently necessary for the occurrence of an event, so that the effect would not have occurred without it, yet not be a member of a set of conditions sufficient for the occurrence of that effect. No such set might exist. One certainly does not have to know of a set of sufficient conditions of an event in order to identify one of its causes. One can know that generally certain sorts of conditions, or disjunctions of conditions, are necessary for the occurrence of a certain kind of event, without knowing any set of conditions to be strictly sufficient for it, necessitating the occurrence of that kind of event. This is typically all that historians do know about the causes of the kinds of events they study. As Taylor said: 'No war is inevitable until it breaks out.' (The most thorough attack upon historical inevitability remains Sir Isaiah Berlin's book of that title, 1954.) It is interesting to recall that some causes do not even combine to make an event probable: the bombardment of an alpha particle may cause the nucleus of a uranium atom to break, without making that event at all probable. But without the action of the alpha particle, the uranium atom would not have decayed. (G. E. M. Anscombe attacked the connection between causation and necessity in *Causality and Determination*, 1971.)

One is loath to abandon all reference to sufficiency in an account of causation, however, because an explication of contingent necessity in terms of sufficiency, while not entirely necessary, does have practical value. If one allows that a condition C is contingently necessary for an event E if in the circumstances, without C there were no sufficient conditions to bring about E, then one can justify a claim that C was contingently necessary for E by pointing out that without C, E would not have occurred. This is not the only way of establishing the contingent necessity of C, as will be seen, but it is a useful way, and the one frequently adopted by historians. The notion of sufficiency in history can be retained and made compatible with indeterminism by allowing that although conditions may never necessitate the occurrence of an event, they can sometimes be said to make its occurrence highly probable.

3   The necessity of causes

Historical causes are usually not universally necessary for their effects, that is they are not always necessary for the occurrence of events like their effects. Scientists have proved quite successful in finding universal causes for natural events. But historians are constantly reminded that similar effects do not always have similar causes. There are numerous different reasons why a king might lose his head, a religious group acquire popularity, or an economy become depressed. What historians seek are not universal causes for such events, for they know of none, but the causes which were necessary in the particular circumstances for the occurrence of those events. The causes they find are typically not universally but only contingently necessary for their effects.

In his important article 'Causes, Connections and Conditions in History' (1966), Michael Scriven argued that causes in history are often contingently necessary for their effects, but he stopped short of saying that they are always so in the face of what appeared to him to be convincing counter-instances. These were all instances of overdetermination, in which it seemed that a cause was not necessary in the circumstances for its effect because there was more than one set of conditions present sufficient to have produced that effect. I believe that these counter-instances can be met, however, by refining the notion of contingent necessity a little. Scriven described three kinds of overdetermination, 'independent', 'simultaneous' and 'linked', which will now be considered in turn.

If two or more events occur, one event following upon another, and each is sufficient in itself to make a further event very likely, then that further event is said to be 'independently overdetermined'. For example, if a shipload of gelignite blew up a bridge from below and thirty seconds later a large bomb dropped on it, the collapse of the bridge would have been independently overdetermined. In such a case, although we would unhesitatingly say the exploding gelignite caused the bridge to collapse, it would seem that the gelignite blast was not necessary in the circumstances for the collapse to have taken place. The bomb would have destroyed it if the gelignite had not.

Is it true that the blast of gelignite was not contingently necessary for the bridge's collapse? Only if the event being accounted for is regarded under the general description 'the collapse of the bridge'. A collapse of the bridge would truly have occurred even if the shipload of gelignite had not exploded, so that this blast was not contingently necessary for its collapse. But there are other descriptions of this particular, individual collapse which would not have been true if the gelignite had not exploded. The collapse would not have begun at the time it did, and the structure would not have crumpled in the manner it did, if the gelignite had not exploded when and as it did. Its explosion was not necessary for *a* collapse to have taken place. But it was necessary in the circumstances for this particular, individual collapse to have happened when and as it did. And this, surely, is why we identify it as a cause of that event.

The causes of singular events, then, are contingently necessary for the events they cause under some descriptions, but not under any or every description. The fact that there is one description of an event for which an antecedent condition was not contingently necessary does not imply that that condition cannot have been contingently necessary for that event. If there is at least one description of the event for which it was contingently necessary, that is enough. That description is not, of course, always the description by which the event is identified.

Moreover, it can be seen that not every feature of the blast of gelignite was contingently necessary for the subsequent collapse. The noise it made, for example, did not contribute to it. So we can conclude that one event is contingently necessary for another if the occurrence of an event having at least one of the possible descriptions of the first is necessary in the circumstances for the occurrence of an event having at least one of the possible descriptions of the second.

If this account of contingent necessity is accepted, then independent overdetermination never provides grounds for saying that a cause was not contingently necessary for its effect, that is, for its effect under at least one description, namely one specifying the time of its occurrence. But this is not the case with simultaneous overdetermination, for here each cause is sufficient to bring about a certain event at the same time. Scriven offered the example of a firing squad, where several bullets are fired simultaneously into a person's head, each sufficient to cause his death. None, it would seem, was necessary in the circumstances to bring about his death. Yet surely all caused it. In this case, though none was contingently necessary for 'that person's death at that time', i.e. for an event under only this description, each was necessary in the circumstances for the particular event which took place, for its features would have been different had any bullet not hit the person.

Trickier examples of simultaneous overdetermination are those in which a person has more than one motive sufficient to drive him to a certain action. In these cases, it is supposed, the event, his action, would not be different if any motive were absent. So none can be held contingently necessary for what happens. If it is true that causes are contingently necessary for their effects, then in such a case no single motive can be said to have caused the action. (J. L. Mackie has adopted the line taken here, 1974, p. 47.) But one could say that they all had brought it about, for if none of the motives had been present, then, the circumstances being what they were, the action would not have been performed. And this, I think, is what we find. Was the gift given through generosity or in the hope of gain? Where both motives are strong, it is genuinely hard to say. All one can say is that both prompted it. The fact that we cannot confidently say of either motive that it caused the action in such cases confirms the theory that for us to judge an event to be a cause of an effect we must believe it to have been at least contingently necessary for that effect.

Scriven has briefly acknowledged many of the things which have been said here about independent and simultaneous overdetermination. The example he sets most store upon for showing that causes are not always contingently necessary conditions is a case of linked overdetermination.

The example which follows is one Scriven has used in seminars. (A similar one is to be found in Scriven, 1971b, p. 54.) Cases of linked overdetermination have also been referred to as cases of 'pre-emption' (see D. Lewis, 1973; and T. A. Climo and P. G. A. Howells, 1976, pp. 12–14). The illustration Scriven has offered is a little complicated, but as telling as can be. Imagine a large dam of water high in some hills, feeding two rivers each of which has been walled near its source to hold back the water in the dam. One river flows down the back of the mountain and meanders about before being joined by the other and flowing through a town. The other river runs directly down the front of the hill to join the first and flow through the town. One day a tremor creates great waves washing back and forth in the dam, great enough to break the retaining walls. It happens that the back wall gives, and an enormous bank of water rushes off and after travelling some miles, eventually reaches the town and floods it. Clearly the breach of the back wall caused the flood in the town. But that breach was not contingently necessary for that effect, Scriven argued, for had the wave not broken the back wall when it did, it would have broken the front one on the rebound, and the water flowing down the shorter front river would have reached the town at the same time and in the same quantity as it in fact did, such being the geography of the place.

Whether one agrees with Scriven's conclusion or not depends upon one's notion of contingent necessity. I would suggest that we do judge the breach of the back wall contingently necessary for the flooding, because taking into account all the events which actually did occur prior to that flooding, it was one without which there would not have been sufficient conditions for the flooding to have occurred. There was no other event among those which in fact occurred which made the flooding at all likely. The breaching of the back wall was not of practical necessity for the flooding of the town since, if it had held, the front wall would have collapsed and brought it about. But it was of causal necessity in the circumstances, since of all the events and states of affairs which did in fact occur prior to the flooding of the town, the breaching of the back wall was one without which there were insufficient conditions for that flooding to have occurred.

So instead of saying A is contingently necessary for B when the circumstances are such that had A not occurred then B would not have, which is the definition Scriven has accepted, I would prefer to say, roughly, A is contingently necessary for B if A is such that had it not occurred, and everything else except B had happened precisely as it did, then B would not have occurred. This, I think, comes much closer to the notion of contingent necessity by which we identify what is a cause and what is not. (A similar critique of Scriven's discussion of cases of linked overdetermination has been formulated by John A. Barker, 1975, pp. 43–55.)

To be entirely adequate, my definition must be further modified. As it stands it covers some cases, but not all. It fits those circumstances which are immediate causes of events, but not those which only indirectly cause them. It satisfactorily defines what we mean when we say that the surge of a great quantity of water down the longer of the two rivers was contingently necessary for the flooding of the town. If it had not occurred, and everything else except that surge had happened precisely as it did, then the flooding would not have occurred as it did. But this definition does not adequately express what we mean when we say that the breaching of the dam wall was contingently necessary for the flooding of the town. Because if the dam had not burst, and everything else except the flooding had occurred precisely as it did, the town would in fact have been flooded – by the great body of water which rushed down the river in the time between the breaking of the dam and the flooding of the town.

The breaching of the dam was contingently necessary, in the sense defined, for the onrush of water, which in turn was contingently necessary for the flooding of the town. To allow for such cases of indirect causation, the definition of contingent necessity should be extended. One could say that an event or state of affairs was contingently necessary for another event either if it was so directly according to the definition, or if it was contingently necessary in this sense for any other condition which itself was directly contingently necessary for that event. Presumably a causal chain may have an unlimited number of links. The poor design of the dam was contingently necessary for the flooding of the town; as was the bad training of the design engineer, and so on.

Consideration of these cases of overdetermination has yielded several insights into the nature of contingent necessity, insights which should be brought together in a comprehensive definition of the term. It would appear that one event or state of affairs (C) is contingently necessary for another (E) either (i) directly, when the situation is such that had an event having at least one possible description of C not occurred, and everything else except E had happened precisely as it did, then an event having at least one possible description of E would not have occurred; or (ii) indirectly, when C is contingently necessary in the sense just defined for another event (D), which is contingently necessary either for E or for another event (F) which is contingently necessary for E, and so on indefinitely. One should recall that even if it is true that had C not occurred, an event having at least one possible description of E would have occurred, this does not imply that C was not contingently necessary for E. It only implies that it was not contingently necessary for E under that description. So long as there is one possible description of E which would not have been true but for C, then C is contingently necessary for E.

If the relation of contingent necessity is understood along these lines, then cases of overdetermination do not provide counter-examples to the theory that causes are at least contingently necessary for their effects. We shall look at a group of other alleged counter-examples in a moment. But before doing so, let us apply the present analysis of contingent necessity to justify a causal judgement in the historical example of linked overdetermination or 'pre-emption' offered by Climo and Howells (1976). Climo and Howells suggested we consider alternative possible worlds to decide the actual causes in such cases, but, as will be seen, this is not necessary. (The problem of justifying judgements of contingent necessity is discussed below.) During World War II prices in Britain rose substantially because the war severely reduced imported supplies, thus forcing prices up. However, had there not been a war it is possible, apparently, that an increase in employment and consequent increase in purchasing power, unlimited by government controls, would have caused an increase in prices. So the actual cause, it seems, was not necessary in the circumstances for the effect, since the effect would have happened anyway in its absence.

This is a poor example of pre-emption because the rise in prices which might have occurred in the absence of the war would doubtless have differed in some details – in extent, and in the goods affected, for instance – from the actual rise which took place; so the actual cause was clearly contingently necessary for the effect under some description. But our discussion of linked overdetermination suggests another basis for a judgement as to the actual cause. The war was contingently necessary in an indirect way for the rise in prices, and thus its cause, because it was contingently necessary for the restriction on imports, which in turn was contingently necessary for the rise in prices. The judgement of causes proceeds from the effect, back, step by step. If there had been no restriction on imports during the war, but everything else remained the same (so that there was no increase in people's purchasing power), prices would probably not have risen. And if there had been no war, indeed there would probably have been no restriction on imports. The war was an actual cause of price rises in Britain, even though other circumstances such as an increase in purchasing power might have brought about price rises had the war not occurred.

I have suggested that in every case where one event or state of affairs is contingently necessary, in the sense defined, for another event or state of affairs, then the first is a cause of the second – so long as the two are not identical, and one is not part of the other, and one is not merely logically implied by the other. The importance of these caveats becomes clear when one encounters Jaigwon Kim's list of events or states of affairs contingently necessary for other events or states of affairs which are yet not causes of the latter (Kim, 1973).

Kim has given four examples to show that 'counterfactual dependency is too broad to pin down causal dependency'. They are as follows:

(1) 'If yesterday had not been Monday, today would not be Tuesday.'

(2) 'If I had not written "r" twice in succession, I would not have written "Larry".'

(3) 'If I had not turned the knob, I would not have opened the window.'

(4) 'If my sister had not given birth at *t*, I would not have become an uncle at *t*.'

In the first and fourth of these examples, the antecedent state of affairs (in (1)) or event (in (4)) logically implies the consequent, implies it, that is, according to linguistic convention, but does not empirically imply it, that is imply it according to a generalization whose truth or falsity can be established by observation. In the second and third examples, the antecedent event is part of the consequent. Writing 'r' twice is part of writing 'Larry'; and turning the knob, in the third example, is explained as part of the act of opening the window, for it was 'by turning the knob, I open the window'. (The 'by-relation' is discussed in McCullagh, 1976.)

These and similar counter-examples to an analysis of causal relations in terms of contingent necessity are met when the further conditions are added that causes are not part of their effects, nor do they merely logically imply them.

4   The temporal relations between causes and effects

There are other counter-examples to an analysis of causal relations in terms of contingent necessity which are met by pointing out that historians regard causes as occurring before or at the time of their effects, but not after them. For sometimes one event can be contingently necessary for another yet occur after it, and then it is not normally accepted as a cause of the latter. It seems to be true, for instance, that wood cannot burn without emitting smoke, in which case the emission of smoke is necessary for the burning of wood – the burning would not happen unless the smoke were emitted. (The proverb 'Where there's smoke there's fire' goes further in stating that emission of smoke is sufficient for the presence of burning.) But we would not regard the emission of smoke as a cause of wood's burning, even though it is necessary for it, because it is subsequent to that event.

It has been argued that sometimes we may want to allow backward causation and so it is wrong to insist that causes cannot follow their effects (see Mackie, 1974, ch. 7). The difficulty then of distinguishing causes from non-causes becomes much greater. It is certain that historians do not look for cases of backward causation, but adopt the everyday analysis of causation which excludes this possibility.

The stipulation that causes do not follow their effects enables one to exclude counter-instances to the present account which would otherwise allow that sometimes they do. These counter-examples, like that of smoke causing fire, David Lewis discussed briefly as 'the problem of effects'. What Lewis did not appreciate was that the same stipulation also enables one to avoid other counter-examples which he called 'the problem of epiphenomena'. He expressed this problem succinctly as follows:

Suppose that e is an epiphenomenal effect of a genuine cause c of an effect f. That is, c causes first e and then f, but e does not cause f. Suppose further that, given the laws and some of the actual circumstances, c could not have failed to cause e; and that, given the laws and others of the circumstances, f could not have been caused otherwise than by c. It seems to follow that if the epiphenomenon e had not occurred, then its cause c would not have occurred and the further effect f of that same cause would not have occurred either. We have a spurious causal dependence of f on e, contradicting our supposition that e did not cause f. (Lewis, 1973, p. 190)

These relations can be represented diagrammatically thus, the arrows indicating material implication:

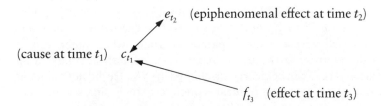

e_{t_2} (epiphenomenal effect at time t_2)

(cause at time t_1) c_{t_1}

f_{t_3} (effect at time t_3)

Lewis pointed out that we cannot deny that e caused f in cases such as these by stipulating that causes must precede their effects, since e does in fact precede f. But suppose we stipulate, not only that causes do not succeed their direct effects, but also that if a cause is indirect, it must not succeed any of the other causes by which it is related to its effect. Epiphenomena such as e in Lewis's example are related to effects like f only via events like c, which preceded them. So such epiphenomena could not, on this account, be called causes of events like f, even though they were indirectly contingently necessary for their occurrence.

From the foregoing discussion we can conclude that one event or state of affairs is causally related to another if and only if (1) the former is not identical to the latter, or part of it, and does not merely logically imply it; (2) the former is at least contingently necessary, in the sense defined, for the latter; and (3) the former does not succeed the latter. Once an historian has found two events or states of affairs which satisfy these conditions, he then is justified in asserting that the former was a cause of the latter.

5   Judgements of contingent necessity

The question which naturally arises now is how can an historian tell when one event was contingently necessary for another? Our careful analysis of that relation makes the answer to this question pretty obvious. But some philosophers have thought the answer far from obvious, and indeed have almost despaired of answering it at all. William Todd, in his book *History as Applied Science* (1972), saw the problem of proving that one event was contingently necessary for another as the same as the problem of proving any counterfactual statement to be true, whereas, as we shall see, statements of the form 'If *c* had not happened then *e* would not have occurred' are counterfactuals of a special, limited kind. Todd considered two different ways of verifying counterfactuals, neither of which proved of much use for historians.

His first suggestion was that the counterfactuals used by historians should be inferred from universal causal laws. For a law of the form 'Conditions of the kind $C_1 \ldots C_n$ are both necessary and sufficient for an event of the kind E' implies that 'If any of the conditions of the kind $C_1 \ldots C_n$ is absent, then an event of the kind E will not occur'. The only type of history in which anything like universal causal laws are employed extensively is economic history. For this reason Todd suggested that 'economic history may well serve as a sort of paradigm around which other sorts of history will congregate in the future' (p. 99). In economic history he said 'all sorts of general laws can be clearly formulated' (p. 98). He did not point out that such laws are true only of ideal economic systems, and assume very wide *ceteris paribus* conditions. But, granting this, his example demonstrates that such laws and their implied counterfactuals do exist and can be of use in deciding the causes, the necessary conditions, of historical events. Todd's example is taken from E. G. Campbell's *Reorganization of the American Railroad System, 1893–1900*, and is a discussion of the causes of the collapse of the Norfolk and Western railroad company (pp. 91–9). The company was well managed and had good prospects, but after an expensive expansion programme suffered from a marked drop in general freight rates, and so in income, from 1892 during a time of general economic depression. It incurred deficits from 1893 and failed altogether in 1896. One might concede that it is a law of a normal capitalist society that 'If and only if (C_1) a company is well managed, (C_2) has good prospects, and (C_3) does not suffer from an unexpected large drop in income, then (E) it will remain prosperous.' (This can probably be expressed better in technical terms, and made more specifically applicable to railroad companies.) This law implies a universal counterfactual of the form 'In a normal capitalist society, if not C_1 and/or not C_2 and/or not C_3, then not E.' If true, this would prove that the unexpected great drop in income suffered by the company (not C_3) was sufficient to bring about the company's failure (not E), there being no extraordinary circumstances not found in a 'normal' competitive capitalist society, like support for the company from the government, which would prevent it from doing so. (For further discussion of how counterfactuals can be derived from laws see Murphy, 1969.)

The trouble is, as Todd repeatedly bewailed, that at present the general laws which he thought necessary to justify historians' causal judgements are simply not to be found in other forms of history. At one point Todd found himself forced to conclude that, because historians do not know any appropriate general laws, they cannot formulate, or at least justify, counterfactuals at all. But this observation was made in a discussion about the counterfactuals which a writer of 'general history', C. L. Mowat, had in fact been prepared to assert. Todd remarked that in the passage in question 'Mowat's most important assertion is that of a causal connection between two pieces of legislation', the Housing and Town Planning Act of 1919, known as the Addison Act, and the Unemployment Insurance Act of 1920, 'and later social and economic developments' in Britain, namely a vast increase in government housing and poor-relief (p. 60). The counterfactual implied by this assertion is that had these acts not been passed, those increases in social welfare would not have occurred as and when they did. The problem which Todd had to face, given his belief that the counterfactual must be of universal form, was how such a counterfactual can be justified when no even remotely acceptable laws relating such a cause to such an effect are known. His conclusion was this:

Of course, for there to be a causal explanation at all there do have to be general laws, whether they are explicitly mentioned or not, and once there are laws there will be counterfactuals that can be derived from them. If we had here a general law which specified a connection between the passage or non-passage of an act such as the Addison Act and the appearance or non-appearance of housing such as the council houses at a certain later date, we could then deduce a counterfactual which might, for example, say that if the Addison Act or something similar had not been passed then there would have been no council houses or anything similar before a certain date, perhaps the beginning of the Second World War. Since we do not have this law we cannot derive the counterfactual statement. We know that some counterfactuals could be legitimately asserted since there must be some laws which are presupposed [by such a causal judgment] but since we do not know exactly which laws are involved we cannot specify these counterfactuals with any precision. Thus it is that the historian does not really know what to do about counterfactual statements. (p. 65)

Given historians' general inability, outside economic history, to derive the counterfactual statements which justify their causal judgements from general laws, Todd turned to another method of proving them, namely that of considering the course of events in a hypothetical world in which the antecedent of the counterfactual is true, to see whether the consequent would be true also. Following Nelson Goodman, Todd assumed that to do this the hypothetical world constructed by the historian must be coherent, one in which the truth of the antecedent of the counterfactual is compatible according to the laws of that world with everything else which occurred in it (p. 219). Thus, to take his own example, to test the assertion that 'if chivalry had not been a dominant factor at the time, the

later crusades would not have taken the form they did', Todd said the
historian must envisage 'a world which is sufficiently different from the
actual one so that chivalry need not have occurred in medieval times' and
then work out whether, in such a different world, 'the later crusades
would either not have occurred or would have had a different goal'
(p. 206).

The difficulty with this method of verifying counterfactuals, as Todd
clearly explained, is that the historian cannot be sure what the coherent
counterfactual world he is required to hypothesize would really contain.
For instance, in testing the proposition that chivalrous ideals caused the
later crusades to take the form they did, Todd imagined we would have to
reason as follows:

Since it was not supposed that the occurrence of chivalry was a chance event, we
have to ask under what conditions chivalry might not have arisen. One's first
intuition might be that it had a good deal to do with feudalism. Suppose, then,
that we set feudalism aside in the hypothetical world so as to make possible the
non-occurrence of chivalry. We then have to ask what to put in its place: something akin to modern democracy, the totalitarian rule of societies such as Nazi
Germany or the ancient China of the Emperor Ch'in Shih Huang-ti or something
entirely different? Having chosen one alternative we then ask whether it would
have been likely to have resulted in an invasion of Palestine. Along the way we
have to ask such questions as, for example, whether any European society would
have been well organized enough to have mounted invasions and whether the
different countries could have cooperated enough to have participated in a joint
undertaking of that size. There seems to be no rational way of answering these
questions. (p. 213)

Todd was on the right track in thinking that causal judgements in
history are justified either by causal generalizations or by imagining the
implications of the absence of a possible cause. But his account of those
processes can be improved.

The causal generalizations to which historians customarily appeal in
making causal judgements are seldom universal statements of conditions
necessary and sufficient for an effect. As Todd said, very few true laws of
this kind exist. Indeed there are even fewer than he realized: the law he
cited governing the prosperity of a company is far from universal, being
true only in certain kinds of capitalist economies and, even within those,
capable of being falsified. Rather, the causal generalizations which historians use are often statements of a disjunction of conditions necessary
for a certain kind of event in a certain kind of situation. These can be
represented schematically, as 'If E, then probably either C_1 or C_2 . . . or
C_n'. Michael Scriven, discussing their use in history, called them 'back-
ward-looking generalizations'. As Scriven said, we all have a fund of
general knowledge about the kinds of possible causes of various kinds of
events, knowledge which we have not always articulated, and we draw
upon it when searching for causes. Doctors use a special set of these

generalizations in diagnosing the causes of illness, and motor mechanics use another set in identifying the causes of a malfunction in a car. Similarly, historians acquire law-like general knowledge of the kinds of things which can cause the kinds of events they study and use it to direct their search for causes (Scriven, 1966, pp. 250–4; and Scriven, 1969).

What distinguishes the general knowledge used by historians in making causal judgements from that used by doctors and mechanics, is that historians' general knowledge is seldom very specific about the nature of possible causes whereas that of doctors and mechanics often is. What would an historian say, for example, were the possible causes of the 1911 revolution in China, in which a large number of provinces freed themselves from imperial authority by setting up their own revolutionary governments? He would probably say that for this to happen a large number of influential people must have wanted it to happen, probably because of some predicament for which they blamed the imperial government; or alternatively it might have happened because the revolutionaries in those provinces had sufficient force to drive off the imperial authorities and compel obedience to themselves. The historian could not be much more specific than this. He could not, for instance, list all the possible grievances which might have driven the people to rebellion in the detail which Scriven sometimes suggests, for the possibilities are almost limitless. Rather, having formulated his general ideas of the sorts of conditions necessary for such a revolution, the historian would then examine the events preceding the revolution to see if he could find instances of the types of causes he had in mind. Thus there was widespread dissatisfaction with the Ch'ing government in China prior to 1911, thanks largely to the advertising of its inadequacies by the constitutionalists through newspapers, speeches in provincial and national assemblies and petitions circulated for signatures. But there was not widespread fear of the revolutionary groups prior to 1911. So popular discontent probably caused the rejection of imperial authority in 1911 (Chang, 1968).

Someone might object to this account of how historians discover the existence of causal relations as follows. There are perhaps some kinds of events like revolutions concerning whose causes historians have the sort of general knowledge which according to the above account is required. But many events in history are actions so uncommon that no such general knowledge of their causes is available to the historian. To discover their causes, historians simply examine the process of events which led up to them and, as Mandelbaum said, regard that process as their cause (Mandelbaum, 1977, e.g. pp. 93, 119). If an historian were to ask, for instance, what caused Yuan Shih-k'ai to become president of the Chinese Republic in 1912, he would not begin by thinking of possible general causes. He would rather straight away examine the chain of events which led to Yuan's accession. What Mandelbaum called 'spatial continuity, correspondence (between the kind of change in the cause and the kind of change in the effect) and instantaneous succession' (ch. 3) would guide his choice as to what was causally relevant and what not.

It is a mistake, however, to think that the causal judgements in cases such as these are not justified by appeal to general knowledge. Mandelbaum's criteria are not adequate in distinguishing causal relations from non-causal relations. Cars travelling bumper to bumper along a crowded road on the speed limit might satisfy all his criteria, yet the movement of one need not cause the movement of another. Ironically enough, even the movement of the square images in Michotte's experiments, which appeared to be directly causally related, were not. A person can be requested to act in a certain way, and then immediately act that way, but not because he was requested. To distinguish real causal relations from merely apparent ones it is necessary to show that the apparent cause was contingently necessary for the apparent effect.

If an historian is studying a unique action he knows that it could have been caused by conscious or unconscious desires and beliefs which rationalize it (which make it a reasonable thing for the agent to have done), or done because it was desired for its own sake, or possibly caused by an inadvertent bodily movement. These are the alternative conditions necessary for any human action, and knowledge of these directs historians in their search for causes of unique actions. As for Yuan Shih-k'ai, it seems that the revolutionary leaders Sun Yat-sen, Li Yuan-hung and the majority of their followers invited him to lead the republic after he had been appointed Prime Minister by the Manchu government in November 1911, partly to encourage him to arrange for the abdication of the Manchu dynasty and partly to establish peaceful republican government over the whole of China. And Yuan accepted the invitation, partly perhaps to bring peace to China but mostly because he desired the power it gave him as ruler of China, power which he later tried to increase by proposing to become emperor himself. But for these hopes and desires, neither side would probably have acted as it did (see esp. Young, 1968).

The method of justifying causal judgements explained so far appeals to general knowledge of conditions necessary for an effect of a certain kind. There is a second method of justifying causal judgements, which employs general knowledge of conditions sufficient for a certain kind of effect. Having identified a possible cause of an effect, an historian can establish whether it was a cause or not by seeing whether the remaining conditions would have been sufficient to make the effect likely. If they would not have sufficed without it, but would have been sufficient with it, then the possible cause was necessary for the occurrence of the effect in the circumstances, and so may be identified as one of its causes. This method of justifying causal judgements is of more limited application than the last, for it applies only in cases where historians know kinds of conditions sufficient to make the occurrence of an event highly probable. It is of no use in establishing causes of improbable events. Only the first method, appealing to general knowledge of kinds of causes, is of use in establishing the causes of improbable events. However, historians often do know the kinds of things which would make the occurrence of the kinds of events they are studying very likely. If an event was very unlikely to have occurred in the absence of one condition but very likely to have occurred given its presence, then that condition may be judged one of its causes. Of course this is not the same as saying that any circumstance which makes an event highly probable is its cause: falls in barometers do not cause storms.

Todd misunderstood this procedure for justifying causal judgements. He believed that it involved substituting something for the condition imaginatively removed from the situation being examined, so that the coherence of that contrary-to-fact world could be restored. He then found the difficulty of deciding what to substitute quite insuperable. But substitution is not necessary. To judge one condition to have been necessary for an event, the historian has only to consider the other conditions which actually did obtain, to see whether or not they were of a kind sufficient to make the effect likely. If they were not, but the effect was likely with the condition restored, then that condition may be regarded as having been necessary for the occurrence of the effect. Huizinga, for instance, pointed out that if European kings had been less dedicated to the ideals of chivalry, they would have concentrated their thoughts upon checking the Turkish advance through the Balkans instead of planning crusades to regain Jerusalem (as quoted in Todd, 1972, p. 102). To reach this conclusion he did not attempt to construct an alternative coherent hypothetical world in the manner Todd suggested. He simply noted the implications of the other concerns of the rulers at that time.

This same method was used also by P'eng-Yuan Chang to show that it was the activities of a large number of politically active gentry, whom he called 'the constitutionalists', which caused the 1911 revolution in China, and which kept it fairly bloodless. He summed up his findings in the following words: 'Without their opposition, the imperial system might have been preserved and renovated. On the other hand, without their leadership of the Revolution, there might have been more and bloodier local upheavals, leading to more sweeping revolutionary change' (Chang, 1968, p. 183). And how were these statements justified? Not by creating an imaginary coherent alternative world, but by looking at the likely outcome of events in China had the constitutionalists not done what they did. Without the support of the constitutionalists, the revolutionary forces were too few and their influence too small to have succeeded in toppling the imperial government. And had the constitutionalists not done so much to set up revolutionary administrations in the

provinces immediately after the revolt had taken place, the revolutionaries would have found it difficult to acquire much control and would
probably have had to resort to much more violence than they did. These
conclusions are based upon historical general knowledge of political
processes.

Neither of the two methods of justifying causal judgements which have
just been described is infallible. Both can yield false results because of an
historian's ignorance. An historian can never prove that he has in mind all
the alternative necessary conditions for a certain kind of effect. In fact he
might be ignorant of one or two, so that what he identifies as necessary
because it is the only one on his list which was present, might in fact not
have been causally related to the effect at all, when, for example, the effect
was caused by the presence of another, unknown necessary condition. If
more than one of a list of alternative necessary conditions is present, it
may be that the effect is overdetermined, or it may be that only one of
them belongs to a set of actual conditions sufficient to make the effect
likely – in which case only it is truly necessary for the effect, and so its
cause. To illustrate the latter case briefly, there might be three possible
causes of a car driving over a cliff: mechanical failure; poor visibility,
resulting in a failure to see a bend in the road; and suicidal depression in
the driver. It is quite possible that the driver did want to commit suicide,
but could not overcome his moral repugnance at the deed, and in fact
drove over the cliff because of a tyre blow-out. The list of alternative
possible necessary conditions is nothing but a guide to possible causes. An
instance of such a condition is truly necessary for an effect, and so truly a
cause, only if the effect would not have occurred in its absence. Since the
car would not have driven over the cliff but for the tyre blow-out, the
latter was indeed a cause of the accident, even though another possible
cause, suicidal depression, was also present.

The second method of establishing a causal relation is fallible too,
because an historian cannot prove that he knows all the possible sets of
conditions sufficient to bring about a certain kind of effect. He might
believe one condition is necessary for a certain outcome simply because he
is ignorant of another set of conditions sufficient for its occurrence. What
he has identified as the causes of an event might be no more than symptoms of the real causes, whose nature is unknown to him.

Because the success of causal analysis depends so largely upon the
general knowledge of the analyst, it is hard for non-experts in a field to
produce reliable causal judgements in it. An historian's causal judgements
deserve the greater respect, the more familiar he is with the kinds of
conditions which cause the kinds of effects he is studying. Here, as
elsewhere, one must defer to expert knowledge.

It is interesting to see that the truth and falsity of causal judgements is a
function of the truth and falsity of statements which are true or false in a

correspondence sense. Their possible truth conditions cannot be simply envisaged, since the relation of one thing being necessary for the occurrence of another is not an observable one, so causal statements are not true of the world in the simple correspondence sense that other descriptive statements are. But the singular and general statements which warrant causal judgements are themselves true in a correspondence sense, so the truth of causal statements is a function of these. One could, perhaps, say that statements whose truth is a function of statements which are true in a correspondence sense, are true in an indirect correspondence sense. Statements that one thing was a cause of another can be true in an indirect correspondence sense.

8

Judgements of 'the most significant cause' in history

It has been argued that causes are events or states of affairs which are at least contingently necessary for their effects. If this is so, then for any given event there is a very large number of causes, indeed a truly infinite number if indirect as well as direct causes are considered. Think of all the events and states of affairs directly contingently necessary for a person to drive a car from one place to another – bodily, mechanical and environmental – and then think of the conditions contingently necessary for these, and so on back in time. The number of causes of any historical event is infinite. So too is the number of effects, allowing for both direct and indirect ones and presuming the world, or rather all matter, is not about to end shortly.

Given that there is an infinite number of causes which an historian could cite for any event, what does he mean when he nominates one or more as 'the cause(s)'? When historians isolate one or more causes in this way, they often speak of the remaining causes as mere 'conditions' for the occurrence of the effect. But to speak of a cause as a 'condition' is not to deny its causal status. It is merely to deny it the additional status which goes with the title 'the cause'. When can 'a cause' also be called 'the cause' of an event?

When historians designate one or more causes as 'the causes' of an event, they generally mean one of three things: (1) the cause selected was the most important for the occurrence of the effect; (2) the causes selected help to explain the occurrence of the effect, explaining either how it was possible or why it was probable; or (3) the cause selected was 'responsible' for the effect. In practice, when historians describe one or more events and states of affairs as 'the cause(s)' of an event they seldom mention the basis of their selection, and indeed, one suspects they are sometimes unsure of it. But on examination it is usually found that the causes have been selected upon one of these three criteria. These could indeed be considered the three main meanings of the phrase 'the cause(s)'.

Analysis of these senses of the phrase 'the cause' reveals that not all statements which use it are simple descriptions of the past. Statements which use the phrase in the first sense, to refer to the cause which was most important in producing a certain effect, are capable of being justified simply by reference to the evidence, without any reference to the context of the discussion or any appeal to the historian's interests and values. Statements about the cause of an event in this sense are just true or false descriptions of the past. However, when an historian identifies certain causes in the second sense, as the ones which explain the occurrence of an event, then whether or not they are 'the causes' of that event depends upon their adequacy in providing an explanation. One condition for an explanation being adequate is that the historical descriptions it contains are true. But there are other conditions besides this, as will be seen. The description of the causes selected must help to correct or complete the reader's understanding of what made the event being explained possible or probable. If a description of.certain causes is true, and does provide the kind of understanding required, then it is an adequate explanation. In that case, the claim that those causes were 'the causes' of the event, meaning the causes which explain the event, is indeed true. But the claim that certain causes were 'the causes' of an event in this sense is not simply a description of the past. Rather it is a statement about the explanatory adequacy of the historian's description of those causes. Finally, judgements of responsibility can often be justified by reference to agreed facts about a case. But when an historian selects from among several people responsible for an event just one or one group as especially praiseworthy or blameworthy, then he is often not describing what was thought in the past, but rather is making a judgement of his own upon the morality of their actions. Statements of 'the cause' of an event in this third sense, therefore, are not always descriptions of the past, but are often evaluations of who deserves most praise or blame for what happened. All these points will be amplified and illustrated in what follows.

1 The most important cause

Sometimes historians find that one cause made an event highly probable whereas the other contributory causes were of much less consequence. In such cases historians are prone to call the cause which made the effect most likely to occur 'the most important' of its causes, its 'principal' cause, or something similar.

One of the things for which the new economic historians have been admired is the way in which they have made explicit the methods by which the relative importance of causes should be judged. They claim to have exposed the assumptions and arguments involved in such judgements, thereby making them easier to assess.

In the by now voluminous discussions of the achievements of the new economic historians, Robert W. Fogel's study of the significance of the American railways in the prosperity of America in 1890 has been hailed almost universally as a paradigm of how the significance of causes is to be judged. Fogel himself presented it as such (1966, pp. 332–3) and both his admirers and his critics have accepted his judgement. For example, in a critical discussion of Fogel's work, E. H. Hunt described it as 'the best example' of how the significance of causes is assessed (Hunt, 1968, pp. 5–7).

I have said that Fogel's study has been taken to be a paradigm for assessing 'the significance of causes'. But precisely what is meant by that last phrase? Most have understood it to refer to the amount which a cause can be said to have contributed to the production of a certain effect in certain circumstances. Hunt said Fogel had revealed how an historian estimates the influence of 'an event or institution . . . in bringing about a historical situation' (ibid., p. 6). Similarly Peter D. McClelland cited Fogel's work as an example of how historians estimate 'the importance of a particular causal factor that actually was operative in the situation under consideration' (McClelland, 1975, p. 149). And finally Fogel himself at one point referred to it as an example of an attempt 'to establish the net effect of innovations, institutions or processes on the course of economic development' (1966, p. 332).

What has to be said, however, is that Fogel's study of American railways is not even an example, far less a paradigm, of how historians estimate the actual causal importance of an event or state of affairs in bringing about a certain effect. Albert Fishlow once pointed this out, but the significance of his argument has been completely overlooked it seems. Fishlow's argument will be explained in what follows, and a correct method of weighting causes suggested by him will be outlined. It is a relief to find that it requires much less counterfactual speculation than does Fogel's.

But even the method recommended and adopted by Fishlow is not the only one historians can use for estimating the relative importance of causes. It is of use in comparing more or less concurrent causes, but a different method is used to compare the importance of causes which follow one another in bringing about an event. Like Fishlow's, this method involves some counterfactual speculation, but not very much.

The two methods mentioned in the last paragraph, however, are not the only ones available to historians. There are other methods which can sometimes be used which require no reference to a counterfactual world at all. These have not been noticed in the literature on this subject, but have been used with justified confidence in historical practice. Each of these methods will be described in turn.

Estimating the comparative significance of concurrent causes

In his book *Railroads and American Economic Growth: Essays in Econometric History* (1964) Robert Fogel was not measuring the causal significance of railways, that is the amount they actually contributed to the gross national product of the U.S.A. in 1890; rather he was trying to estimate their practical significance, that is whether it was necessary to have developed railways for America to have achieved the prosperity it had in 1890. He did this by estimating the extent to which the G.N.P. would have been different in 1890 had other methods of transport been developed instead. Albert Fishlow recognized this distinction from the start. Comparing his book *American Railroads and the Transformation of the Ante-Bellum Economy* with Fogel's, he wrote:

The two books approach the question of the importance of the railroad somewhat differently, and, not surprisingly, yield different answers. Fogel's principal interest is in the necessity of the innovation: could the United States have developed without it? The question I ask, rather, is how much of a stimulus did the railroad afford and by what means? We both may be correct, therefore, when he affirms that the railroad was not 'important' and I that it was. (1965, pp. ix–x)

This interpretation of Fogel's work is confirmed by Fogel's own careful description of the problem he was facing, which he described as the need to test the axiom that railways were 'indispensable' to American economic prosperity in 1890.

The axiom of indispensability is not primarily a description of the performance characteristics of a particular innovation. The crucial aspect of the axiom is not what it says about the railroad; it is what it says about all things other than the railroad. The crucial aspect is the implicit assertion that the economy of the nineteenth century lacked an effective alternative to the railroad and was incapable of producing one.

  Evaluation of the axiom of indispensability thus requires not only an examination of what the railroad did but also an examination of what substitutes for the railroad could have done. Railroads warrant the title of indispensability only if it can be shown that their incremental contribution over the next best alternative directly or indirectly accounted for a large part of the output of the American economy during the nineteenth century. (Fogel, 1964, p. 10.)

To judge whether railroads were indispensable to American prosperity in the late nineteenth century, of course it is necessary to consider what prosperity would have been, or could have been, achieved without them. As Fogel said, that requires the historian to speculate about 'the next best alternative', in this case transport by road and water, and the level of prosperity it would have permitted. The counterfactual, hypothetical world being considered in this case is very different from the actual one, and its contents are very difficult to determine. Without railways, would settlement in the United States have been in different places; would different industries have developed as a consequence; and would markets for goods produced have been very different too? Estimates of the G.N.P. of such a different country can be little more than educated guesses. Yet that is what Fogel had to estimate to discover how much the American economy benefited from the development of railways instead of the development of alternative methods of transport. To measure the 'social saving' involved, Fogel said, he had to calculate 'the difference between the actual level of national income in 1890 and the level of national income that would have prevailed if the economy had made the most efficient possible adjustment to the absence of the interregional railroad' (1964, p. 20, n. 10).

To judge the actual contribution of railways to the American economy, however, requires much less counterfactual speculation, as Fishlow and Fogel have both acknowledged (Fishlow and Fogel, 1971, p. 16). To judge the actual causal significance of an event in producing an effect, all one has to judge is the probability of that effect being produced by the remaining causes which existed. As Fishlow explained: 'Strictly speaking, it is necessary to proceed railroad by railroad, specifying exactly the transport services performed by each and reallocating these to the most efficient [actual] alternative route. The difference between the total costs incurred under the two regimes then is a measure of the direct benefits' (1965, p. 32). Using an aggregative method of analysis for convenience, Fishlow found that the saving directly resulting from the use of railways in 1859 was not great, since extensive water transport was available then at little extra cost (pp. 32–8).

By 1890, however, railways had increased dramatically in both size and efficiency, and as there had been no comparable increase in road and water facilities the cost of finding alternative transport for goods carried by rail, or the loss of not carrying them at all, would have been enormous. Fishlow estimated it at at least 15% of the gross national product. This contrasts strikingly with Fogel's estimate of the social saving of railways in 1890 as being less than 5%. But as Fishlow reminded his readers, Fogel and he were not measuring the same thing. In Fogel's case

The contribution of the railroad sector no longer is reckoned as the transport savings it provided in historical fact, but as its potential advantage in a very special, and nonexistent, world. The difference in conception has large implications. It is sufficient to transform 1890 benefits in the transport of agricultural commodities from $410 to $214 million, with a proportional reduction in the aggregate estimate based on this result.

There is nothing wrong with building such hypothetical worlds as can be imagined as likely without the innovation of the railroad. But their juxtaposition with the actual circumstances of 1890 then measure the unique attributes of the innovation rather than the realized consequences of the investment in railroads that actually occurred. (Fishlow, 1965, pp. 57–8)

I do not know where Fishlow got the figure of $410 million. Fogel's final estimate of 'α' – the difference between the cost of transporting goods by rail and by other actually available means in 1890 – was $337 million; after making allowance for the construction of new canals and roads, he reduced this to $214 million (Fogel, 1964, pp. 91–100, 214–18).

To compare the actual historical significance of roughly simultaneous causes of an event, one does not need to imagine a world as different from the actual one as Fogel envisaged. Rather one has to imagine what would have happened if the world had been without the event or state of affairs whose causal significance is being assessed. There is no need to imagine a substitute for that event or state of affairs. Its actual significance is found by comparing what would have happened, as far as one can imagine, without it and what actually did happen with it. The difference between these two outcomes is a measure of the importance of the event in producing the outcome of interest. When one is studying the importance of a cause in a system, like a transport system, one has to judge how the system would have operated in the absence of that cause, with only the remaining elements present, and compare that with the actual performance of the system when it included the cause being assessed. Again, the difference in the performance is a measure of the importance of that element in the system.

Estimating the consequences of a set of counterfactual conditions will involve imagining counterfactual events, of course, following from the counterfactual set of causes. But the room for error, especially in calculating the significance of causes which occurred close to their effects, is much less than in the sort of estimate Fogel made. The most important cause is the one whose absence would have resulted in the greatest alteration in the effect.

Consider, for example, A. J. Youngson's judgement of the relative significance of pegged prices and the fall in the level of industrial production upon coal production between 1929 and 1933. The 1930 Coal Mines Act in Britain provided the means of putting quotas upon the production of coal and of fixing minimum prices for it.

Coal prices were extraordinarily stable from 1930 to 1933, falling by only 3 per cent while the general price level fell be about 15 per cent; and after 1933 they rose. There can be no doubt that this peculiar behavior of coal prices was a result of the working of the 1930 Act. But, as critics of the Act have pointed out, production fell catastrophically: from 262m. tons in 1929 it fell to 210m. tons in 1933 (the lowest figure since 1898, excepting the strike years 1921 and 1926); gradually recovering thereafter to 245m. tons in 1937. Was the fall in output a consequence of the maintenance of prices? Prices may have had some influence, but beyond question the major factor in the demand for coal in these years was the level of industrial production. In Great Britain, this was 17 per cent lower in 1933 than in 1929. Inevitably, the demand for coal fell; price reductions could have done little, if anything, to maintain it. To argue about the price elasticity of demand in these circumstances is like attending to nice adjustments in the rigging while the ship is filling with water. (Youngson, 1967, p. 100)

Youngson first looked at what would probably have happened had, contrary to fact, coal prices been allowed to fall instead of remaining fixed in the economy of the time. In his opinion 'price reductions could have done little, if anything to maintain' the demand for coal; so price pegging, a consequence of the 1930 Act, was not an important cause of the drop in coal production. That left the 17% drop in industrial production, which in Youngson's judgement made a large drop in the demand for coal 'inevitable'. So he picked upon it as 'the major factor' determining the level of the demand for coal and consequently of coal production during that period. Indeed he likened it to a leak which causes a boat to fill with water and presumably sink, thereby clearly suggesting that had industrial production not fallen, production levels of coal would not have sunk so low.

This method of judging the comparative significance of causes is effective when the causes involved are relatively independent, but impossible to apply when they are not. Michael Hammond has provided an illustration of this fact in pointing out that one cannot compare the causal significance of the following four causes of the American Civil War because they are not independent of each other (Hammond, 1977, pp. 119–22). These are the causes which Peter J. Parish has said are most commonly cited as the chief causes of the Civil War: (i) the social and cultural incompatibility between the North and the South; (ii) economic rivalry; (iii) constitutional disagreement, e.g., over states' rights and the amount of southern representation in Congress; and (iv) controversy over Negro slavery. Parish judged that if there had not been a large population of Negro slaves in the southern states, then the Civil War would not have occurred (Parish, 1975, ch. 4). This does not prove that slavery was the most important cause of the war, however, as Parish seemed to think it did, but merely shows it was necessary for its occurrence. As Hammond said, it simply justifies 'a primitive causal judgment' (1977, p. 120). To show that it was the most important cause, Parish would have to have compared in turn the probability of the war occurring if slavery had been absent and the other causes present with the probability of its occurring had each of the other causes been absent and the remaining causes present; and that is impossible, Hammond argued, because the other causes all relate to slavery. The constitutional disagreements which took place, for example, would not have occurred in the absence of slavery. One cannot isolate these causes, so one cannot compare their causal significance.

I entirely agree with Hammond that when causes are dependent on each other, their individual significance cannot be compared. I would disagree with Hammond's further conclusion that one cannot show slavery to have been the most important cause of the Civil War, however, because there are other causes independent of slavery with which it can be compared. The industrial North wanted tariffs on industrial imports, whereas the rural South did not; northerners wanted public land to be given away to new settlers whereas southerners wanted it conserved and sold only at good prices; the North wanted a national banking system, but the South did not; northerners preferred democratic social institutions, whereas the leaders of the South were more oligarchic in outlook (Nevins and Commager, 1966, pp. 218–20). Attitudes on these issues can, I think, be distinguished from attitudes over Negro slavery; and most historians would agree, I imagine, that the probability of war in the absence of slavery was much less than in the absence of any of the other causes.

Estimating the comparative significance of sequential causes

In political history, usually written in narrative style, causes are often depicted as following upon one another, some remote in time from their effect and some more nearly preceding it, some indeed precipitating its occurrence. Here the historian weighs the significance of each cause by seeing what difference the addition of each would have made to the probability of the effect's occurrence. The most important cause is that which increased the probability of the effect the most. Thus, as Raymond Aron explained in his discussion of the causes of the First World War, if the remote causes made the war highly probable, then the immediate causes would have been of little importance.

The historian, concerned to show the causes of an event, puts two questions, both legitimate, but which must be carefully distinguished. First of all, why did war come at that particular time; and given the situation, who were the men, or what were the circumstances, that precipitated war? Secondly, how was the situation which led to the war created? The first question refers to what are generally called the immediate causes, the second to what are called the remote origins. Historians attribute to the former more or less importance according to their philosophy and also to the results of their inquiry. If they come to the conclusion that the situation led inevitably to war, the immediate causes obviously lost importance. (Aron, 1954, pp. 67–8)

Aron did not think the remote causes of the war made it very probable. 'The division of the principal nations of Europe into two camps did not necessarily make for war. It only made it inevitable that any conflict involving two great powers would bring general war' (ibid., p. 71). He was inclined, however, to think that the next set of causes which by 1911 had created tension between the two camps, that is between the German–Austrian alliance and the Triple Entente between Britain, France and Russia, did make war highly probable, and so was more important than the final events in the Balkans which triggered it off.

The growing tension centered about three principal difficulties: the rivalry between Austria and Russia in the Balkans, the Franco-German conflict over Morocco, and the arms race – on sea between Britain and Germany, and on land between all the powers. The two last causes had produced the situation, the first one kindled the spark.

There are doubtless those who contend that the immediate cause matters little, and that war might have broken out just as easily in 1911 as in 1914. The contention readily suggests itself and is not easily disproved. (Ibid., p. 71)

The two intermediate causes he thought were important, for they 'spread the conviction of approaching disaster', and did seem to make the outbreak of hostilities very likely. The immediate cause, the conflict in the Balkans, added just that little degree of probability needed to make a large-scale war inevitable. It was a necessary cause of its outbreak, but probably not the most important.

Judgements involving historical rather than counterfactual contrasts

Although the counterfactual worlds involved in estimating the relative importance of causes in these ways, so typical of economic and political histories respectively, are not as fanciful as the one Fogel employed, there is a measure of uncertainty about them just the same. Precisely what increase in demand for coal might have followed a drop in its price? It is hard to be sure, though reasonable estimates are perhaps possible. And precisely what was the probability of war given the tension between the great powers in 1911? Here estimates are much harder to make, since relevant general knowledge relating such tension to the outbreak of war is scarce if not entirely lacking, and the period between the cause and its effect is so great that there is more chance of detailed predictions about the possible course of events being falsified by unexpected happenings. As Peter McClelland pointed out when discussing this method of weighting causes, if covering laws are used to judge the probability of an effect given certain causes, then there is no need to employ counterfactual speculation at all (1975, pp. 157–8). Very seldom, however, are the necessary covering laws available.

It is not always necessary to use one of these counterfactual methods to judge the significance of causes. Sometimes, instead of comparing an actual course of events with a counterfactual, hypothetical one, it is possible to compare one actual course of events with another historical sequence which resembles the first but lacks one or two of its causes and consequently has a different outcome. The significance of the causes which are present in the first case but absent in the second is indicated by the difference between the outcome in the first case and the outcome in the second.

For example, what were the most important causes of the rapid expansion of the woollen industry in the West Riding of Yorkshire in the eighteenth and nineteeth centuries? To answer this question P. J. Perry compared the woollen industry in Yorkshire with that in East Anglia and the West of England, where it had not expanded, and noted the differences. The two causes apparent in Yorkshire and lacking in the other areas were a pushing, hardworking attitude in the north which led to the introduction of machinery to manufacture woollen products almost a generation before this happened in the south; and concentration on the production of cheaper, coarser goods which attracted a much larger market than the quality goods produced in the other areas. (Shoddy was one kind of cloth produced then in Yorkshire!) These, therefore, Perry judged to have been 'the two principal elements in the triumph of the West Riding' (Perry, 1975, pp. 83–5).

Historical comparisons can sometimes also be used when judging the importance of causes which occurred in sequence. Pierre Renouvin used this method to judge the importance of rivalry for colonial empires between the great power blocks as a cause of the First World War. By examining other cases of such rivalry and noticing that they did not lead to war he was able to conclude that imperial rivalry alone was not a very important cause of the war.

Rivalries between colonial imperialisms have often reached the critical point where the adversaries seemed to have said their 'last word'; and yet the conflicts have not gone beyond threats: the Afghanistan question was regulated in 1885 by an Anglo-Russian compromise; the English Cabinet, in spite of the importance of Far Eastern markets for the British economy, left Port Arthur to Russia in 1898; and the French government, as much as it wanted to reopen the 'Egyptian question', recoiled at the time of Fashoda before the prospect of an armed conflict. Fundamentally governments and peoples have been conscious that these clashes over material interests were not worth a war, at least a 'great war'. (Renouvin, 1955, p. 54.)

What was present in 1914 and not on those other occasions, Renouvin argued, was a strong sense of national rivalry which greatly increased the chance of war. So this, he believed, was the most important cause of hostilities (ibid., p. 55).

The calculation in these cases is quite straightforward in theory, if sometimes difficult to make in practice. If one set of causes makes a certain kind of event fairly improbable, and that set plus one or two additional causes then make that kind of event highly probable, the additional causes were more important than all the others – so long as the difference between the two probabilities exceeds the initial low probability. Thus if the probability of war, given imperial rivalry was, say, about 30%, and the probability of war given imperial rivalry plus fierce national feeling was very high, say 80%, then national feeling was a more important cause than imperial rivalry, contributing 50% to its 30% of the cause.

Undoubtedly this sort of comparative analysis can yield convincing conclusions, though the degree of conviction depends upon the degree of similarity between the situations compared. Were the imperial rivalries mentioned by Renouvin really equivalent to those between European powers prior to World War I? If not, then his conclusion is doubtful. Outside economic history, uncertainty can also attend estimates of the probability of a certain kind of effect following upon a certain set of causes. In political history one can hope for little more than a very rough approximation. But this can be enough to range two or three causes in order of importance, even if it is not enough to specify precisely the degree to which they contributed to their effect.

Enough has now been said to see that Fogel's study of American railways should not be taken as a paradigm for judging the relative importance of causes, and to see how such judgements are, and should be, made. Sometimes they may require some counterfactual speculation, though much less than Fogel envisaged. But occasionally they can be made with no counterfactual speculation at all.

The basic cause

Occasionally the causes which historians isolate as being of special importance they refer to as 'the basic cause(s)'. Does this mean something other than the most important cause?

There is a feature of basic causes which has not been captured in the analysis of the most important cause. Basic causes are usually causes which were common to the causal antecedents of each of a cluster of activities being regarded by an historian as a whole. Thus David Potter argued that 'slavery was basic' to the cultural, economic and ideological differences, concern for which motivated the American Civil War (Potter, 1976, pp. 41–3). It is as a common cause that slavery can be identified as the basic cause of the American Civil War. The different points of serious conflict, Potter suggested, all involved the institution of slavery.

However, that was not all that Potter claimed. He also said that polarization over the institution of slavery made people lose sight of the realities and complexities of the issues, and thus helped to quicken hostility between North and South.

Thus in cultural and economic matters, as well as in terms of values, slavery had an effect which no other sectional factor exercised in isolating North and South from each other ... The slavery issue structured and polarized many random, unoriented points of conflict on which sectional interest diverged. It transformed political action from a process of accommodation to a mode of combat. (Ibid., p. 43)

As well as being a common cause of hostility, Potter might here be suggesting that slavery did much to produce the hostility between North and South. As well as being a common cause of the Civil War, it was a very important one.

In most instances, the cause which an historian identifies as basic is both common and very important. The revival of interest in classical art and literature was long thought to have been the basic cause of the Italian Renaissance. Notice how J. C. Jebb put it in the old *Cambridge Modern History*: 'The Revival of Learning, by which is meant more especially the resuscitated knowledge of classical antiquity, is the most potent and characteristic of the forces which operated in the Renaissance' (vol. I, p. 532). There are the two characteristics, side by side: 'the most potent and characteristic'.

Assertions that a cause was both a common and a very important cause of a complex effect can be justified by reference to the evidence, and may be taken to be an historical description which is either true or false. There is another interpretation of 'the basic cause' which cannot be so justified or interpreted. It is possible to use the phrase 'the basic cause' to refer to the first step in a causal process which an historian believes best explains the occurrence of an effect. In this sense, one may say that the basic cause of war is human greed. In cases such as this, the cause singled out as basic is part of an explanation, and the acceptability of explanations depends upon other facts besides the truth of the descriptions they contain, as will be seen in the next section. For this reason, a statement about the basic cause of an event in this sense is not a description of the past; rather it describes a feature of an adequate explanation of a past event.

It is interesting to see that when Wallace K. Ferguson argued that the classical revival was not the basic cause of the Italian Renaissance, he argued both that it was not common to all manifestations of the new culture, and that it was not the first cause in the process which produced it. He noted that 'even where the classics exerted no direct influence, as in music, the Renaissance broke new ground and exhibited enormous vitality' (Ferguson, 1951, p. 108). And he also suggested that what produced the great cultural creations of the Renaissance was not the availability of classical models, but the needs of the new Italian cities, which were urban and lay, rather than feudal and ecclesiastical, and which were prospering thanks to their commerce and industry while other agrarian economies were withering. The cities needed new models to inspire them, and it was this need, satisfied by the classics, which was the root cause of their cultural activity (1951, p. 108; cf. Ferguson, 1940, pp. 75–7).

2   Causes which help to explain the occurrence of events

Probably the most common ground for selecting causes in history is the belief that they help to explain a certain event, their effect, most satisfactorily. There are two senses of 'explain' which must be considered here. Sometimes causes are selected to show how an effect was possible, to explain 'how-possibly' as W. H. Dray has called it (1957, ch. 6). And sometimes causes are selected to show why an event was probable, explaining 'why-probably' we might say. (Dray suggested 'why-necessarily', but it seems unlikely that historians can explain why any historical events were necessary, that is show why they could not possibly have been otherwise. The most they can show is that they were probable, to some degree.) Here is an example of each sort of explanation, drawn from

Helen Cam's book *England before Elizabeth* (1967). The first is an explanation of how it was possible for Henry VI to regain the throne from Edward IV for a few months in 1470–1.

Edward IV's reign was interrupted by two battles in 1464, and a brief restoration of Henry VI for seven months in 1470–71, a 're-adoption' made possible by the defection of Edward's brother, Clarence, and his leading supporter, the 'king-maker' Warwick. (p. 147)

Next, here is a list of causes judged by Cam to have been sufficient to make the revolt of English barons against King John quite probable.

The king's hand lay heavily on his subjects; but extortionate taxation would not alone have produced revolt. It was seizure of Normandy by his French overlord in 1204, and John's failure to recover it in subsequent campaigns, that laid him open to the attacks of a baronage with many private as well as public grievances. (p. 90)

Clearly it was Cam's intention here to list causes which made the revolt probable. Sometimes by mentioning a cause an historian can perform both functions, can show both how an event was possible and why it was probable. Consider, for example, the following explanation of how and why the parliament under Richard II did not speak with an independent voice, but represented the interests of aristocrats through the factions which they controlled.

The peerage had by 1376 become a well-defined and steadily narrowing ring of hereditary magnates, and the elected members of parliament had only a few weeks in which to acquire the common consciousness that would enable them to act for themselves in a political issue. So the factions led by great earls, royal dukes, and even, at times, by the king himself, formed currents guiding the stream of public opinion in different directions. (pp. 136–7)

Given the existence of parliamentary factions, the short sitting time made it both possible and probable that no common parliamentary consciousness would develop.

When historians attempt to explain the possible or probable occurrence of an event, they do so because the knowledge of the world which they assume the reader of their work to possess is such as to render its occurrence improbable, or at least unexpected. If this were not the case, the reader would not be interested in an explanation designed to show the occurrence of such an event to have been possible, or indeed probable. One function of causal explanations is to add to the reader's knowledge enough information to allow him to see that an event being explained (an *explanandum*) was possible, or probable.

Some writers have suggested that causal explanations are usually of abnormal events, and that these are explained in terms of abnormal conditions. Judgements as to what is normal vary, as Gorovitz put it, both with the context of inquiry (that is, with what the inquirer regards as normal) and with the context of the occurrence of the event (that is, with the normal state of the system in which the event occurred) (Gorovitz, 1965, p. 239; and see Hart and Honoré, 1958, pp. 228–9). Because the selection of causes is relative to the context of inquiry, and this can be shown to be a function of the inquirer's interests, it seems that the selection of causes is relative to the inquirer's interests. However Morton White, while adhering to the view that the causes selected by historians are selected because they are judged to be abnormal (White, 1965, p. 107), has argued that although often what is regarded as normal and abnormal depends upon an historian's point of view and interest, '*sometimes* the cause is uniquely and absolutely determined without reference to an historian's interest' (p. 129; and see p. 123), but his reasons are not convincing. His argument, in brief, is as follows. Suppose

  (i)   whatever is P and R is Q;
  (ii)   most Ps are not Q;
  (iii) it is not the case that most Rs are not Q; and
  (iv)   an individual a is P and R and Q.
  Then (v) a is Q because a is R.

Why is this so? 'Because we cannot even frame the question that will elicit as an answer "The cause of a's being Q is a's being P"' (p. 129). But a well-known example of Hart and Honoré's which White accepted (p. 118) refutes this. Let

  P = a person eating parsnips
  Q = a person suffering from indigestion
  R = a person having a gastric ulcer.

Then (i) is true: whoever eats parsnips and has a gastric ulcer suffers from indigestion. And (ii) is true: most people who eat parsnips do not suffer from indigestion. And (iii) is true: it is not the case that most people with gastric ulcers do not have indigestion. And (iv) could be true, namely that a certain individual eat parsnips, having a gastric ulcer and having indigestion. But not everyone would find (v) a satisfactory explanation. It would satisfy the doctor, to whom having gastric ulcers is much rarer among people than their eating parsnips. He would explain the patient's indigestion in terms of his ulcer. But it would not satisfy the man's wife, who was familiar with his having an ulcer and still wished to know what caused his indigestion. She could frame the question which would elicit as an answer 'The cause of the man's indigestion is his having eaten a parsnip.'

Hart and Honoré used this example in support of their claim that people isolate as causes of events those which appear to be abnormal in the context as they perceive it (1958, pp. 229–30). In fact the example supports just as well the theory that people isolate as causes those which, when added to what they already know, make the effect appear possible or probable. In fact, though, what appears crucial to the identification of causes in these cases is not whether they are judged to be abnormal, nor whether they provide information which was previously unknown. What is crucial is whether the cause makes the occurrence of an event of a certain kind possible or probable which, relative to a certain body of information about the circumstances, appeared to be either not possible or not probable. In some cases the assumed set of circumstances will be one which there is reason to believe normal, but not always. It might be just the state of affairs as far as it has been revealed to the reader at a certain point in a narrative.

To explain why an event was possible or probable, then, an historian provides information which he wishes the reader to add to the facts which make an event of that kind seem to have been impossible or improbable. This additional information is what he may refer to as 'the cause' of the event. The additional information need not refer to the most important cause of the event being explained – that might already have been revealed in the course of the narrative. The cause which is mentioned may well be, for example, just the precipitating cause.

Explaining how an event was possible

The way in which an historian explains how the occurrence of an event was possible depends upon the reasons he thinks a reader might have for doubting it. Sometimes a reader will doubt the possibility of an event's occurrence simply because in his opinion it is very unusual; but more often he will doubt it because his beliefs about what happened prior to its occurrence make the probability of its occurrence very small indeed. A reader familiar with the dominance of the House of Commons in the British parliament over the last two hundred years might be surprised to read that it was not an independent body in the fourteenth century, and wonder what made its subservience to the aristocracy possible. He is surprised simply because this state is not what he assumed to be the usual one. But a reader's doubt that Henry VI could regain the throne in 1470–1 would probably stem from his knowledge that Edward IV had completely defeated the Lancastrians at Towton in 1461 so that it did not seem possible for the Lancastrian king, Henry VI, to be king again. The following three different kinds of case cover those most commonly found in historical writing.

Where scepticism is based on general knowledge of what usually happens, then historians explain the possibility of an apparently unusual event by pointing out that one of the causes necessary for the occurrence of what usually happens was absent in the apparently unusual case in question. One condition for the independence of the House of Commons, according to Cam, has been the fairly long sessions which have allowed members to form a common consciousness. Its subservience to the aristocracy in the fifteenth century was possible because this condition was lacking.

When scepticism is based upon knowledge of an event prior to the *explanandum* and an assumption that the course of events which would probably have flowed from it would not have included the *explanandum*, then the historian shows the *explanandum* to have been possible by describing those events at which the actual course of events departed from those which the reader might well have envisaged. And the description of the actual events will proceed far enough for the reader to see that the *explanandum* was not so very improbable after all.

For example, having read in Cam's book that 'King Edward IV in 1461, defeated the Lancastrian forces utterly at Towton, and obtained from parliament a full endorsement of his claims as the lawful heir of Richard II', the reader might imagine that Edward IV would then have kept the Lancastrians well under control, thereby securing his position on the throne. How then was it possible for the Lancastrian Henry VI to supplant King Edward in 1470–71? Where the actual course of events departed from the envisaged story was at the point where some of King Edward's own Yorkist supporters turned against him, namely his brother, the Duke of Clarence, and the most powerful member of the nobility, the Earl of Warwick. Once it is realized that this had happened, Edward's throne certainly does not appear so secure against the Lancastrians.

Notice that the events mentioned in explaining how an event was possible will vary with the particular ground for doubt. Suppose someone knew of the treachery of Clarence and Warwick, and indeed knew that in 1469 Warwick had planned to put Clarence on the throne; given that information he might still doubt that Henry VI would ever retain it. On the contrary, he would probably have expected that either Warwick would have got Clarence to replace his brother on the throne, or have been prevented and probably executed in the attempt. To convince someone who knew this much of the story that Henry VI could have become king again, the historian would have to tell the events which caused Warwick to drop his support for Clarence and rally support for Henry VI. These events would include the discovery and suppression of Clarence and Warwick's rebellion in March 1470 by King Edward, their flight to France, and the formation of a new plan by Warwick to put Henry VI on the throne with the help of King Louis XI of France, who expected English assistance against the Duke of Burgundy, Edward IV's strong ally, in return. Thus as the background events which are thought to have made a given *explanandum* unlikely vary, so too will the information which the historian must provide to show that the *explanandum* was indeed possible.

The third way of explaining how an event could possibly have happened is a response to scepticism which is based upon an assumed event or state of affairs which in fact did not exist. In cases like this the historian explains that the *explanandum* was possible by showing that the assumption which made it appear improbable was false. Assumptions of this sort are usually based not on fancy, but upon some knowledge of human affairs, even on knowledge of the period in question. To convince the reader that an assumed event or state of affairs did not occur, therefore, the historian will often explain why it did not happen the way the reader might have assumed.

A good example of this way of explaining how an event was possible is provided by F. W. Maitland's essay 'English Law and the Renaissance', in which he explained how it was possible for a post-Renaissance lawyer like Sir Edward Coke to admire statements of the law by a pre-Renaissance lawyer, Sir Thomas Littleton, remembering the widespread reception of Roman law and disparagement of traditional common law in Europe during the sixteenth-century Renaissance. Maitland posed the problem thus:

Perhaps we should hardly believe if we were told for the first time that in the reign of James I a man who was the contemporary of Shakespeare and Bacon, a very able man too and a learned, who left his mark deep in English history, said, not by way of paradox but in sober earnest, said repeatedly and advisedly, that a certain thoroughly medieval book written in decadent colonial French was 'the most perfect and absolute work that ever was written in any human science'. Yet this was what Sir Edward Coke said of a small treatise written by Sir Thomas Littleton, who, though he did not die until 1481, was assuredly no child of the Renaissance . . .

[There is] a question which Coke's words suggest: How was it and why was it that in an age when old creeds of many kinds were crumbling and all knowledge was being transfigured, in an age which had revolted against its predecessor and was fully conscious of the revolt, one body of doctrine and a body that concerns us all remained so intact that Coke could promulgate this prodigious sentence and challenge the whole world to contradict it? (Maitland, 1901, p. 136)

As Maitland said, Coke's admiration of Littleton's writing is surprising given the great changes in belief and knowledge which occurred during the sixteenth century, and more particularly given the widespread admiration for Roman law which grew in Europe during that period. To explain how it was possible, Maitland pointed out that although Roman law was received and accepted in Italy, France and Germany during the sixteenth century, it is a mistake to assume that it was also received in England. Thanks largely to the teaching at the Inns of Court, English lawyers did not accept Roman law but continued to be schooled in English common law. (As well as this essay, see ibid., pp. 108–13, and 126–7, for a statement of this fact.) Consequently it was possible for Coke and other lawyers at the end of that century still to venerate English common law as expounded, for instance, by Littleton.

In each case, the causes selected by an historian to explain how an event was possible are selected to correct the reader's presumed misunderstanding of what had happened. So a statement of 'the cause' of an event meaning 'the cause which made that event possible', is not simply a description of a cause. It is, more particularly, an explanation of why that event was possible. To be acceptable it must be not only true but also successful in convincing the reader that the occurrence of an event like that being explained was indeed possible in the circumstances, in the sense of being more probable than not.

Explaining why an event was probable

Explaining why an event was probable is no simple matter, as the large quantity of literature on explanation over the last forty years or so has shown. An adequate explanation of an event is one which produces adequate understanding of it, and a thorough analysis of the conditions of historical understanding would take us far from questions of truth in history. That being so, a mere sketch will be offered of what historians mean by 'the causes' in the sense of 'those which help to explain why the occurrence of an event was probable'.

(i) To show that event was possible one has to provide information which enables the reader to see that the occurrence of such an event was not improbable in the circumstances, that it was more probable than not. As was seen, this is usually done by countering assumptions to the contrary. To show that an event's occurrence was more probable than not, however, is not to show that it was very probable. To show that an event was probable, and not just possible, usually requires the historian to show that it was very probable. For to show that an event was probable the historian has normally to show that the occurrence of such an event was more probable than that of some other event, when that other event might well have occurred in the circumstances.

The causes selected and described to explain why an event was probable depend very much upon the contrast state which the historian has in mind. For example, one who asks 'Why was the monarchy replaced by a republic in France in 1792?' could have several contrasts in mind, and the answer to the question will depend upon which is being considered. He might mean 'Why was there a change of constitution and not just a change of government?', or 'Why was the republic set up in 1792 and not earlier?' The fact that the people represented at the General Assembly had lost faith in obtaining justice under a feudal monarchy might suffice to explain why a constitutional change was more probable than a political one. And the fact that faith in the crown did not entirely fail until the defeats of the royal army and the attempted flight of Louis XVI in 1792 might explain why the inauguration of a republic was more likely that year than earlier. But these facts do not suffice to answer another interpretation of the question, namely 'Why was the establishment of a republican government in France in 1792 more likely than any other form of government?' A republic was not the only known alternative to a feudal monarchy. A limited constitutional monarchy, with perhaps a new king, would seem to have been a possible solution, on the English model. More has to be said to show that the setting up of a republic was more probable than this alternative.

(ii) Showing that the occurrence of one kind of an event was more probable than the occurrence of another kind, or more probable than the occurrence of an event of any other kind, is but a minimum requirement of explanations of this sort. There are often several different causal histories which will do this. Hugh Stretton has illustrated this point fully in the first part of his book, *The Political Sciences* (1969). The causal story which historians select, he said, usually is of a kind which they wish to publicize in support of political or social interests. Stretton illustrated this fact vividly by contrasting different explanations of the outbreak of the First World War, relating them to the political convictions of the historians concerned. Left-wing historians, said Stretton, attributed it to capitalism, which they hated, largely for its other effects – injustice and social disintegration.

While the Left tried thus to establish an unbreakable causal chain from capitalism to war, the Right insisted that any such chain was either longer or shorter. 'Longer' or 'shorter' would serve equally well to destroy the implication that war could be prevented by tampering with capitalism. One sort of conservative saw a chain like this:

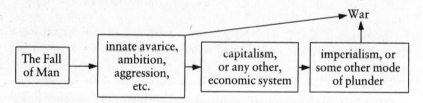

'Man is born to trouble as the sparks fly upward.' Either the chain by-passes capitalism, or capitalism is as unbreakable as any of its other links, or any other economic system in place of capitalism would serve as an equally effective link: do not tribal, feudal or riverine economies organize the same material rapacities as express themselves through capitalism?

Meanwhile other conservatives and many unradical liberals preserved the innocence of capitalism by attaching war to a much shorter chain of causes. If war could be sufficiently explained by some avoidable mistakes of government or diplomacy, then we could satisfy the universal desire to rid society of war while preserving intact the remainder of society's more controversial fabric. These reasons prompted some of the many explanations of World War I which confined themselves to the diplomacy of July 1914 or at least to questions of the national and personal guilt of particular governments. (Stretton, 1969, pp. 56–7)

Stretton was particularly interested in the political bias of causal histories. His point can be extended, however, by saying that historians often have in mind a preconception of a kind of process of events which normally produces an event of the kind they wish to explain, and the causes they select in their explanation are usually those which illustrate their general preconception of how the *explanandum* probably came about. An historian's preconception of the normal process by which events of the kind being explained usually occur, is generally one which is closely related to his values and interests, as Stretton demonstrated.

These observations draw attention to the fact that for an historical explanation to be acceptable, it must refer to causes of a sort which interest the reader. It will not be false for being uninteresting, but it will be deemed inadequate. When people seek an explanation of an event, they usually have certain kinds of causes in mind, and they want historical information about those, if possible. An explanation is judged adequate only if it is in terms of those kinds of causes which interest the reader, or if it shows that those sorts of causes did not operate in the case in hand and explains the event in terms of another acceptable theory instead.

(iii) For an explanation to be acceptable, it must be based upon generalizations about the process of historical change which are both well supported by previous discoveries and are relevant to the particular case in question. Sometimes historians insist upon representing the causes of an event in terms of a general theory which is not exemplified by the facts of the case, and when that occurs the explanation is generally rejected for including false statements about the past. Christopher Hill, for example, has offered a Marxist explanation of the outbreak of the English Civil War, and of the defeat of the Royalists in it, which critics have said is inadequate. Hill described the outbreak of the war as the result of an increasingly powerful capitalist, bourgeouis class having its economic growth thwarted by the Crown and the 'semi-feudal landed aristocracy' which supported it. The thesis is most bluntly stated in the Introduction to *The Good Old Cause*, edited by Christopher Hill and Edmund Dell (1949); and it is retained in Hill's later works. In *The Century of Revolution, 1603–1714*, (1972) Hill wrote: 'The issue [was] between the monarchy as the champion of the established economic order, and the rising middle class as its assailant' (p. 131). Hill is here quoting E. Lipson with approval. But critics have objected that the Civil War was fought between parties, not classes.

Mr. Hill seems to take for granted, that class solidarity based on economic interest is the natural state of affairs in seventeenth-century England. In reality the world of seventeenth-century politics was one of multiple factions, based on personal, family and local sympathies and antipathies. These tended to polarize round a two-*party* organization, an entirely different matter from a two-*class* organization. (Wilson, 1962, p. 86)

Hill's explanation of the outbreak of the Civil War as caused by the discontents of a group of people whom he identified as 'a bourgeois, capitalist class', clearly depended upon the Marxist theory that growing capitalist classes would inevitably challenge ruling feudal classes which inhibited their growth. As Hill put it: 'The middle-class struggle to shake off the control of this group was not merely selfish; it fulfilled a progress-ive historical function . . . It was necessary for the further development of capitalism' (1955, p. 9). But once it is agreed that the Parliamentarians did not represent a class at all, this Marxist theory becomes irrelevant to the Civil War, and Hill's explanation in terms of it is correspondingly inadequate. The need to describe the parties to the war as 'classes' for the Marxist theory to apply made it easy for critics to see that the explanation being offered was inadequate.

It is interesting to note that Wilson also found Hill's explanation of the defeat of the Royalists inadequate, not because it included false state-ments but because it did not make the *explanandum* probable. Hill, in true Marxist fashion, attributed it to the poorer material resources of the Royalists, whose support lay in the northern and western counties of England, whereas the Parliamentarians had the support of London and the southern and eastern counties (Hill, 1972, pp. 112–13). But Wilson objected that these causes did not make the *explanandum* very probable, and so did not provide an adequate explanation of it. 'The theory that the unequal distribution of resources and support doomed the Cavaliers to inevitable failure must be rejected. Economic resources do not, by them-selves, win wars' (Wilson, 1962, p. 85). Wilson placed much of the blame for the Royalist defeat on 'the continuous indecision' of King Charles I, which lost them many early advantages and gave the Parliamentarians time to organize and train. In this case the generalization appealed to by Hill was relevant but false. For a causal explanation to be satisfactory, the generalization it assumes, which states what usually suffices to produce events like the *explanandum*, must be true, particularly of the period in question.

(iv) As was mentioned before, an adequate explanation does not have to state all the information necessary to make the occurrence of an *explanandum* more probable than the occurrence of something else; it need only state those facts which, taken together with what the reader already knows, will make the outcome appear probable.

Sometimes the historian assists the reader in recalling the relevant facts which have already been stated, by summing them up. Thus, for example, Cam (1967) summed up the reasons for the baron's revolt against King John. The king's extortionate taxation was not enough in feudal times to produce such a revolt. What made it likely were the additional facts that the barons were angry and dismayed at the loss of Normandy, fearing the growing power of the French king, Philip Augustus; and the fact that the barons resented the king's illegal, unjust and often monstrous acts of brutality against his subjects at home. Given all those attitudes, Cam believed, revolt was probable (p. 90).

Occasionally an historian has not only to state the causes which make an *explanandum* probable, but add information which enables the reader to see quite clearly how those causes are related to the *explanandum*. This might involve references to a little-known causal generalization. Or, in the case of rational explanations, it might require the historian to provide more detail about the agent's reasoning, that is, to provide more information about the reasons which caused the agent to act as he did. Take, for example, the following explanation of Walpole's opposition to the land-tax levied in Britain in his day.

Walpole disliked the tax, partly because it was a tax on a limited class and he believed that every man should be taxed in proportion to the benefit he received from the community, partly because he was anxious to conciliate the mainly tory landholders. (Williams, 1952, p. 180)

It is clear enough why opposition to the land-tax would conciliate the tory landholders: it would relieve them of taxation, which would make them pleased with his administration, and even if it were replaced by some other sort of a tax on wealth, that would presumably not discriminate against the landholders as the land-tax did. There is no need for the historian to fill out this pattern of reasoning, for the reader can readily do so himself. But it is not so clear why the fact that Walpole saw the tax to be on a limited class should incline him to oppose it. To make the connection here fully intelligible, therefore, Williams added the information that Walpole believed every man should be taxed in proportion to what he received from the community. Now it is possible to complete the argument. Clearly people who did not own land, like the merchants, received benefits, income, from the community. The tax therefore was not fairly distributed in Walpole's opinion, and consequently he opposed it in favour of something more equitable.

(v) Finally, the causes mentioned must be described in such a way that the reader is likely to see that they make the occurrence of the *explanandum* probable. Consider, for instance, the following explanation of the poverty of the Scottish Highlands in the mid-eighteenth century:

The Highlands . . . were a poor country, dependent chiefly on cattle-raising, but so overstocked and with such bad pastures that the cattle surviving the winters or neighbours' raids were of little value till they had been sent down from the great cattle-marts at Crieff and Falkirk to be fattened on the rich pastures of Norfolk. (Williams, 1952, pp. 263–4)

This is a convincing explanation, since it is common knowledge that cattle raised on overstocked and poor pastures will be lean and so of little value for meat. Williams could have described the causes of the cattle's poor condition more precisely by saying how many head of cattle were, on average, run to the acre, and what kinds of grass they had to feed on. This would give a farmer, perhaps, a more precise idea of the cattle's condition; but it would be of no use to the general reader, ignorant of what number of cattle per acre would constitute overstocking and of what feed value those grasses had. The description of the causes which Williams chose was the appropriate one, for it enabled his reader to see that the causes referred to were indeed likely to have had the effect they did. When a technical explanation is unavoidable, then the technical terms have to be interpreted for the general reader, or else the explanation does not produce the understanding it is meant to provide.

To sum up, for a statement of the causes of an event to explain why the event was probable, the causes must (i) be such as to make the occurrence of such an event appear more probable than the occurrence of a certain contrast state; (ii) be of a kind which is of interest to the reader; and (iii) be accurately described. For the explanation to be entirely satisfactory the historian must (iv) provide the reader with all the information he needs to see that the *explanandum* was probable, bearing in mind what the reader may be assumed to know already and of what he may well be ignorant. Finally, for an explanation to be adequate, (v) the causes must be described in language which enables the reader to appreciate their explanatory significance.

If this is roughly right as an analysis of the conditions which must be satisfied by a statement of 'the causes' offered as an explanation of some event, then obviously such a statement is not simply a description of the past. Such a statement does describe some of the causes of the event whose occurrence is being explained, but it is also meant to satisfy the reader's interests and complete his understanding about the causes of that event in an appropriate way. Notice that, strictly speaking, the causes themselves, being states or events in the world, are not explanatory – only descriptions of them can be. A statement of 'the causes' in this sense, then, is not merely true or false, but more or less adequate as an explanation.

Causes selected as explaining why an event was probable are often those which did most to make its occurrence probable, and so can also be deemed the most important cause of that event. But this is not always the case. Often important background causes for an event such as a war are already known, and the event which explains the war's occurrence, in that context, is the precipitating cause, which made the outcome not merely probable, which it was already, but virtually certain. Then the cause of explanatory value is not the most important cause of the event it explains.

3 Causes which are responsible for effects

Historians often select causes because they believe them to have been responsible for an event, in some sense or other. There are, indeed, three distinct senses in which historians assert that a cause was responsible for a certain effect. In the first sense the assertion means little more than that the cause was the most important cause of the effect, in the sense explained in section 1. 'Responsible' is used in the second sense to suggest that a cause is an action of a person or a group of people who are answerable or accountable for the effect because their action brought it about, though they might not deserve either praise or blame for what they did. And third, the word can be used to refer to an action of a person or a group of people who are not only answerable, but are also worthy of praise or blame for the effect of their action.

To say that a person or a group of people were responsible for an event in any of these three senses is to provide a simple description of them which may be justified by reference to evidence. The kinds of conditions which justify such descriptions are set out in this section. Although only one person or group of people can be responsible for an event in the first sense, several different people or groups of people may be responsible for an event in the second or third senses. In these two senses, therefore, it is possible to select someone as 'the most responsible' for an event. The manner of doing this is described in section 4. Often an historian's account of who was most praiseworthy or blameworthy in bringing about an event is not a description of the past, but is rather a commentary upon the moral value of the events which the historian wants to add to his description of them.

The most important cause

In the following passage it is clear that when the author, John L. Snell, asks who or what was responsible for the Nazi revolution in 1933, he means little more than what was its most important cause.

The central question is the question of causation: How was it possible for the Nazis to come to power in one of the most civilized countries of Europe in the twentieth century, just fourteen years after that country had thrown its monarchical armor on the slag heap of history and wrapped itself in the clothing of democratic republicanism? Did it happen because of unique conditions in Germany? Were other nations chiefly or partly responsible? . . . Was it the fault of one man, Adolf Hitler? Of leading Entent statesmen, makers of the Versailles Treaty? Of the men of German industry or the German army? Of the democratic system? . . . In forming your own explanation, you must first decide which factors were relatively most important in causing the Nazi victory. (Snell, 1959, pp. ix, xvii)

Notice that in this sense of 'responsible', responsibility for an event can be attributed to an institution such as the German system of democracy as easily as to a person like Hitler, though it would be absurd to consider an impersonal institution like democracy accountable in a legal or moral sense. It can only be blamed in a purely causal sense: had it been different then the effect would have been different too.

In blaming a person or an institution for an event in this sense, the historian is doing little more than saying it was the most important cause.

Precisely what little he is saying more than that is hard to specify and probably varies from case to case. Often, it seems, he is expressing some regret over the cause's existence.

The acceptance conditions for statements asserting that one thing was the most important cause of another were described in the first section. Historians usually regret the existence of causes when they judge that it would have been better had they been otherwise. But not every cause is condemned just because its effects were bad. People's intentions are often approved even though their actions had unfortunate consequences. Causes which do not incur the historian's disapproval can be held responsible for an event, in the simple causal sense, without being blamed for it.

Accountability

Occasionally historians hold people accountable for certain events, responsible for them in that sense, without praising or blaming them for what happened. Thus Lord Acton wrote of Pope Sixtus IV, who established the Spanish Inquisition: 'Whether Sixtus is infamous or not depends on our view of persecution and absolutism. Whether he is responsible or not depends simply on the ordinary evidence of history' (Acton, 1956, p. 335). Similarly, Sidney Hook, having reported H. A. L. Fisher's opinion that the Emperor Justinian's extermination of the Arian Goths in Italy was responsible for the subsequent division of Christendom into the Western and Eastern Empires, commented: 'Whether this event should be called an "error" depends, of course, on one's religious predilections. Those who accept the theology of the Council of Nicea call Justinian's crusade a blessing. But error or blessing, the act was fateful for the history of Europe' (Hook, 1943, p. 165).

Clearly historians can and do assign personal responsibility for events yet leave open the question of whether the person responsible for them is to be praised or blamed.

It is generally agreed that two conditions must be satisfied for a person to be held accountable for an event. First the event in question must have been intentionally and knowingly brought about by that person, either directly or indirectly, or if it was an unintended effect of his action, his ignorance of the probability of its occurrence must have itself been culpable; and second, the person's action in bringing about that effect must have been freely done, so that he could have acted otherwise in the circumstances. If a person fails to satisfy either of these conditions, then he is not held answerable for the events he brought about.

The importance of the first of these two conditions becomes apparent when one studies debates about Germany's responsibility for the outbreak of the First World War and Hitler's responsibility for the Second. Although Article 231 of the Treaty of Versailles saddled Germany with sole guilt for the outbreak of the First World War, it was soon agreed by historians that no country had deliberately sought war, but rather that all had 'stumbled into' it, to use Lloyd George's phrase. As S. B. Fay put it, 'None of the powers wanted a European War' (1930, p. 16). Professor Fritz Fischer has challenged this view, however, by providing evidence that many leading Germans in the army, industry and agriculture, in the Prussian nobility and the middle class, wanted war, and that the German Chancellor Bethmann-Hollweg planned for it and was willing to risk it, even provoked it in July 1914, in the desire to make Germany a great world power. 'There can be no talk of any accidental "stumbling into war". Bethmann-Hollweg's actions at the beginning and at the height of the crisis [of July 1914] were not ruled by destiny or a fateful tragedy, but were a conscious political decision' (Fischer, 1964, p. 142). If Fischer is right in his view that some Germans, notably the Chancellor Bethmann-Hollweg, deliberately brought about the outbreak of war between the great powers, then they can be held to some extent responsible, that is accountable, for the war which followed.

The stir caused by Fischer in arguing that Germans intentionally brought about the First World War has been matched by the dismay caused by A. J. P. Taylor when he argued that Hitler had not intended to bring about the Second, and so cannot be really held responsible for it. It was Taylor's belief that Hitler 'did not so much aim at war as expect it to happen, unless he could evade it by some ingenious trick' (Taylor, 1964, p. 12). Taylor played down the significance of the Hossbach Memorandum as evidence of Hitler's intentions (ibid., pp. 20–2, 169–71; and see above p. 121), just as Fischer had insisted upon the importance of Bethmann-Hollweg's Memorandum of 9 September 1914 in revealing the Chancellor's war aims that year (see Joll, 1966, pp. 20–5; and Janssen, 1972, pp. 274–7). Taylor was inclined to blame the Treaty of Versailles, the vacillation of the British government and the timidity of the French for the Second World War, rather than Hitler.

Taylor's critics have argued, however, that, although Hitler may not have formed a detailed plan of the course of the second great war, his general policies of restoring German power and creating a German empire in eastern Europe were bound to result in a general war and he could not have but realized this (see above, p. 121). In pursuing those policies, therefore, he brought about the Second World War and did so quite deliberately. His moral responsibility for it therefore should not be denied. P. A. Reynolds, for example, wrote when reviewing Taylor's book: 'To maintain that each crisis in detail did not develop precisely according to Hitler's plans and intentions is irrelevant to the argument that the succession of crises represented stages in a broad plan the aims of which could not be achieved except by war, and that Hitler recognized this' (1961, p. 217).

The second condition for holding a person answerable for his acts is that they should have been freely done. If they were not freely done but were compelled, then we generally mitigate the agent's responsibility for them. Professor Gerhard Ritter, for example, has tried to mitigate Germany's responsibility for the outbreak of the First World War by arguing that its leaders were not free to act other than the way they did. For him

> the German leaders, and especially Bethmann-Hollweg and (General) Moltke, are the helpless and often anguished victims of circumstances, carried into war against their will by the inexorable unfolding of military plans which they did not devise and whose political consequences had never been properly foreseen. (Joll, 1966, p. 24)

Having noted this, James Joll went on to question whether Ritter's views can be sustained in the light of evidence uncovered by Fischer (ibid., 24–5; see also Janssen, 1972, pp. 260–2). But if Ritter was right and Germany's leaders were not acting freely in bringing about the war, that would certainly mitigate their responsibility for its outbreak.

The opinion that compulsion mitigates responsibility is widely shared. Gordon Leff, for instance, has said: 'Moral responsibility is directly proportional to the lack of antecedents; the less binding they are the greater the freedom of individual action and a corresponding responsibility for such action' (1969, p. 110). But this opinion is supported, often, for quite different reasons. Some think it true because they believe a person is morally responsible only for acts which are chosen by himself and are not determined by physical or psychological events beside himself. This is the view of Sir Isaiah Berlin (1954, pp. 25–33). He admits that sometimes in history people's freedom of choice seems to have been restricted, and the degree of their responsibility for their actions correspondingly reduced. But people's freedom and responsibility is never, in his opinion, eliminated altogether (p. 29).

Ernest Nagel (1960) has carefully criticized Berlin's discussion of responsibility from the point of view of one who believes ascriptions of responsibility are compatible with determinism. He, like all compatibilists, believes that people are responsible for those acts which they perform freely in the sense that they could have acted otherwise had they wanted to. That is, actions are done freely if they are not constrained by physical or psychological forces which would have prevented the agent acting otherwise had he wanted to. If we find that an agent is unable to alter his behaviour when it is clearly in his interests to do so, then, said Nagel, we judge that he is not responsible for it (ibid., p. 377–8).

The debate between libertarians like Berlin, who see categorical freedom of action (the agent's being free to act otherwise unconditionally) as a prerequisite of personal responsibility, and compatibilists like Nagel, who believe conditional freedom of action (the agent's being free to act otherwise if he wants to) sufficient to warrant personal responsibility, has continued a long time and there is no sign of its being concluded. But it is a debate about the truth conditions of personal responsibility, not the acceptance conditions. In practice it seems, if an agent's decision and action appear to have been a product of his wants and beliefs and principles, then he is held responsible for them unless the chance of his acting on other wants was severely reduced by either external factors such as constraints and threats, bodily conditions such as extreme need for food or drugs, or strong psychological compulsions which prevented the agent acting as he would have liked to. (These conditions do not mitigate responsibility, however, in those cases where the agent himself is responsible for their occurrence.) In the absence of excuses such as these, historians do hold people personally accountable for their intentional actions. And they do so without having discovered whether the action in question was freely chosen, as the libertarians require, or entirely determined, as the compatibilists believe it always to be.

Madam de Staël said that to understand all is to forgive all, but in practice few historians would agree with her. An historian can understand, perhaps, why a government preferred one policy a little more than another, why for instance the British government preferred to put off rather than conclude an alliance with Russia in 1939, but if, as in this case, it would not have been difficult to have decided otherwise, then the historian can and does hold that government responsible for what it did (see below, pp. 223–4). Only when one knows of conditions which would have made an alternative decision extremely difficult, and which indeed made it very unlikely, is one justified in excusing an agent for the decision he made.

Sometimes it can be very difficult to tell the strength of a person's desires and fears, both conscious and unconscious, and so it can be difficult to determine how easily that person could have acted otherwise in a given situation. One can get some idea of the strength of people's wants by observing their choices and patterns of behaviour over a period of time. But this knowledge, when available, is not always reliable. People's passions are subject to change, so that in a given situation it can still be difficult to know with much confidence what emotional pressures they were subject to. When there is such uncertainty, any ascription of responsibility must be tentative.

Praise and blame

For a person to be worthy of praise or blame for an effect of his actions, to be responsible for an effect in this third sense, he must not only be personally responsible or answerable for it on the conditions just described, but he must also have been capable of knowing that, by his own community's standards, it was good or bad as the case may be. Some compatibilitists, who see praise and blame as having a purely utilitarian justification, might disagree with this assertion and argue that it is good for historians to praise those whose actions they judge good and blame those whom they think acted badly, so that readers will be encouraged to imitate or avoid similar actions in future. Those who value history for propaganda purposes would be inclined to argue thus. But many historians believe one should not praise or blame people for actions which they did not recognize as having particularly good or bad consequences.

This point was at the heart of Creighton's disagreement with Acton over how historians should judge men of the sixteenth century like Pope Sixtus IV and Calvin, who persecuted those whom they regarded as heretics. Acton thought they should all be condemned for their cruel actions. But Creighton argued that they might not have regarded their actions as bad, indeed they might have thought them good. 'Nowadays people are not agreed about what heresy is; they do not think it a menace to society; hence they do not ask for its punishment. But the men who conscientiously thought heresy a crime may be accused of an intellectual mistake, not necessarily of a moral crime' (in Acton, 1956, p. 344). He concluded that we should not blame people who acted badly according to our values, but well according to their own understanding. 'Surely they knew not what they did' (ibid.) – and should therefore be forgiven.

Most historians would side with Creighton in this debate. Henry Steele Commager, for example, has argued similarly: 'We can agree now, most of us, that slavery was an unmitigated evil, but we cannot therefrom conclude that those who inherited it, were caught in it and by it, supported it and fought for it, were evil men' (1965, p. 67). One should not condemn those who conscientously acted well by the standards of their own community. The most one can do in such cases is condemn the kind of action they did, but not them for doing it.

When people in authority behave cruelly towards others, it is sometimes difficult to tell whether they acted from a genuine intention to do good, or largely out of spite. Butterfield believed we can never know men's motives with sufficient confidence to pass judgement on them: 'The historian can never quite know men from the inside . . . he can never quite carry his enquiries to that innermost region where the final play of motive and the point of responsibility can be decided . . . that innermost region of all, which has to be reached before a personality can be assessed in a moral judgement' (1951, pp. 116–17).

His opinion was endorsed by his colleague, David Knowles: 'The degree of ignorance, the degree of malice, the degree of weakness, the degree of guilt, must always elude us' (Knowles, 1963, p. 13). It is always difficult to be sure whether a person honestly thought he was acting well or badly by his own lights, and so difficult to decide whether a person deserves praise or blame.

Nevertheless, when an historian is well informed about the morality of the society he is studying and knows a person in it to have been intelligent, he is often justified in blaming that person for an action which he could have seen to be bad, whether he actually realized its wickedness or not. Jonathan Glover has provided a vivid illustration of this point in the trial in Jerusalem of A. Eichmann for his part in the Nazi murders of Jews. Eichmann claimed he saw himself as doing nothing more than obeying orders in a dutiful manner. But, as Glover said, even if Eichmann did not fully realize the wrongness of what he was doing, we do not on this account excuse him. For he could without much difficulty have judged how monstrous his behaviour was. Probably few cases of culpable self-deception are as easy to establish as Eichmann's (Glover, 1970, pp. 175–8). But it shows that, *pace* Butterfield, one does not always have to be sure of a person's interpretation of his own action in order to pass moral judgement upon him for it. It is enough that one knows he could easily have seen its wickedness, whether he did so or not.

It is generally agreed that if a person freely and intentionally brings about an event which he judges to be good, he should be praised for it, and if he freely and intentionally brings about an event which he judges to be bad, he should be blamed for it. It is also generally agreed, I think, that if someone acts from good intentions but their action has unpredictable, disastrous results, they should be praised for their intentions and not blamed for the outcome. There is much less agreement, however, as to how we should judge people who deliberately bring about an event which they know the world will judge to be good, but do so for bad motives. What should we say of the wealthy philanthropist who is looking for tax concessions, or the social reformer who is looking for votes? In such cases perhaps the wisest course is to withhold both praise and blame. And since people very often act from mixed motives, it follows that praise and blame should seldom be expressed.

There are other circumstances which historians take as justifying blame for a person's action, namely culpable irrationality in planning and culpable incompetence in the execution of plans. The failure of Britain to secure an alliance with Soviet Russia in 1939 is a well-known example of such a blameworthy action, or inaction. A. J. P. Taylor, in his discussion of it, hesitated in deciding whether it was the result of irrational planning or the incompetent execution of a plan. Britain was repeatedly warned, at that time, that Russia might come to an agreement with Germany. Given Britain's obligations under the Anglo-Polish alliance, it is incredible that the British government could not see the advantage of an alliance with Russia, which the Russians themselves were quite willing to enter. It is in fact so incredible, that Taylor was driven to speculate that perhaps the British did want an alliance with Russia but were not competent enough to secure it (Taylor, 1964, p. 280). On either count the British government could be blamed for failing to negotiate the alliance which was so much in her national interest.

Judgements of this kind rest upon the assumption that people ought to think and act as well as they can. This assumption is held true by historians particularly of people in positions of responsibility, people whose decisions affect many others for good or ill. They expect that such people should decide their goals by the most careful possible consideration of the circumstances and of the principles applicable to them, and that they should decide the means of achieving those goals by carefully considering which possible course of action would be the most likely to achieve them in the circumstances. On Taylor's arguments the British government was culpable in 1939 for failing to satisfy either the first or the second conditions, for not considering their goals carefully enough, or the means of achieving them.

Blaming someone for irrational conduct implies not only that he could have behaved more rationally in the circumstances, but also that he could and should have realized the importance of doing so in the case in question. In matters which affect the peace of a nation, statesmen should exercise, and can be expected to exercise, extreme care in the planning and execution of their policies. In their choice of which horse to back for a dollar at the races, less care is expected.

The grounds upon which historians feel justified in praising or blaming people for their actions have now been stated. But Butterfield has argued strenuously that historians should not make moral judgements about the people they study, even when these conditions are fulfilled. The reasons for which he has objected to moral judgements are both moral and practical. The moral reason is simple: since we are all guilty of some misdemeanours we have no right to condemn others for theirs. Indeed, had we been in their shoes we might have acted similarly. (Butterfield, 1951, p. 104; and 1931, pp. 123–4. Commager argues similarly, 1965, pp. 67–8.) This seems a powerful argument to me. Let us expose people's thoughts and actions as fully as we like. But let us not condemn men for their wickedness, merely bewail it.

Butterfield offered two practical reasons for eschewing moral judgements in history. First he said that moral judgement is often a substitute for full understanding. Those who are quick to blame people for events often do so for political motives and are reluctant to investigate fully the true reasons for the actions of those they condemn (1951, pp. 101–7; see also Bloch, 1954, pp. 138–44). Of course, we must add, although moral judgement can be a substitute for full understanding, it is not necessarily incompatible with it, despite Mme de Staël's opinion to the contrary. And, second, Butterfield suggested that more insight into the morality of an action is provided by a full and detailed exposition of its nature and consequences than by a swift word of condemnation (1951, p. 123).

Lord Acton was quite unsympathetic to arguments such as these. He thought it vital for the morality of the country that historians apportion blame whenever they can, so as to promote higher standards in the conduct of people in authority (Acton, 1956, pp. 48–52, 336). Acton was less interested in justice than in expressing his disapproval of certain forms of behaviour. Calvin's unjustified condemnation of Servetus was enough in Acton's eyes to outweigh all the good things he had done (p. 333). To Butterfield's claim that an historian should not judge people when uncertain about the forces operating upon them in reaching their decisions or about their judgement of its morality, Acton would have replied that instead of withholding sentence the historian should deny those people any benefit of doubt. 'If, in our uncertainty, we must often err, it may be sometimes better to risk excess in rigour than in indulgence, for then at least we do no injury by loss of principle' (p. 51).

Few historians follow Acton now in seeing themselves as defenders of public morality. Most, like Butterfield, avoid moral judgement and simply try to understand and describe the people whose actions they study. However, it is difficult to avoid moral judgements altogether as so many of the words we use have moral overtones, suggesting at least approval or disapproval.

4 Judgements of which cause is the most responsible for an effect

If something is responsible for an effect in the sense of being its most important cause, then it makes no sense to call it 'the most responsible' cause of that effect. There is little more to be said about judgements of responsibility of this kind besides what was said in the last section. The only additional point worth elaborating is the importance that this notion of responsibility has in the identification of heroes in history.

As Sidney Hook has explained, the heroes of history are held responsible for events in precisely this sense. 'The hero in history is the individual to whom we can justifiably attribute preponderant influence in determining an issue or event whose consequences would have been profoundly different if he had not acted as he did' (1943, p. 153). Hook added that the hero is also an 'event-making', not merely an 'eventful', man in that the actions he brings about 'are the consequences of outstanding capacities of intelligence, will, and character rather than of accidents of position' (p. 154).

As Hook pointed out, Marxists are inclined to argue that major historical changes are determined by economic and social factors, and that the importance of particular individuals in bringing them about is always small. There are two senses in which Marxists believe the role of individuals in history to be a minor one. According to George Plekhanov (1940), the most that individuals can determine are the 'individual features' of great historical changes; they are powerless, in his opinion, to alter their general characteristics, which are always determined 'by the development of productive forces and the mutual relations between men in the social – economic process of production' (ibid., ch. 8). Thus, the social and political changes brought about by the French Revolution had to occur, though under different leaders they might have occurred in slightly different ways. Individuals determine only a few, minor aspects of great historical events (ibid., pp. 45–8).

There is another sense in which Marxists argue that individuals are of little importance in bringing about major historical changes: individuals, they argue, are dispensable, for if one group had not led a change, another group would have done so. Plekhanov suggests this in places, and Engels has said so explicitly (quoted by Hook, 1943, pp. 78–9; and see ibid., ch. 5 passim.) Hook has argued impressively against this theory, showing, for example, that the Russian Revolution of 1917 would not have occurred without Lenin's leadership, and that there was no chance of anyone else bringing it about in his absence (ibid., ch. 10).

Historians would, perhaps, be especially confident about attributing responsibility to a person for an event if they knew that he not only contributed most to its occurrence, but was also indispensable for its happening. It is enough, however, for a person's action to have been the most important cause of an event for it to be singled out as responsible for it.

Does it make sense to speak of someone as 'the most responsible' for an event in the second sense described in section 3, in the sense of being the most accountable for it? Given that a person is accountable for an event if it is one which he could have predicted as occurring as a consequence of an action he freely performed, it perhaps does make sense to speak of degrees of accountability. The more confidently the agent could have predicted the event, and the more freely he acted, the greater his responsibility for what happened. But historians seldom compare the relative accountability of people for an event in this sense.

When historians speak of the person or people most responsible for an event, it is almost always in the third sense, as the most praiseworthy or the most blameworthy. They make these judgements of merit in two different senses. Sometimes they judge who was most to be praised or blamed for an event according to the moral standards of the society and at the time in which the event occurred. More commonly, however, historians judge the relative merits of past people in terms of the historians' own moral values. In the latter case the judgement is not simply descriptive, but is clearly an expression of the historians' values. When reading moral judgements in history, it is not always easy to tell which of these two criteria – the values of the agent or those of the historian – is being appealed to.

To illustrate these two methods of judging moral responsibility for an event, let us consider three different historians' accounts of the rebellion of 1381, in which a mob of farm labourers and others from Essex and Kent, led by Wat Tyler, seized control of London for a while and executed rough justice against many of the governing class there, though the young king, Richard II, skilfully avoided their reproach. Mary McKisack blamed the rebellion upon the government of John of Gaunt, Duke of Lancaster, who assumed control during the king's minority. She accused it of failing to carry out its responsibilities, pointing to 'the extravagence of the court and household, the burden of taxation, the weakness of the executive, and the inadequacy of the national defences' as all providing excuses for the uprising which occurred. If the government had been more responsible and efficient, the uprising might not have occurred (McKisack, 1959, p. 422). McKisack is evidently judging the government in terms of the moral standards of its day, saying that its perceived inadequacies served to justify the rebellion.

G. M. Trevelyan, in his *English Social History*, regarded the rebellion as more of a triumph than a disaster. But he quite plainly judged it in terms of his own values. Trevelyan wrote in the Whig tradition of his father G. O. Trevelyan and great uncle, Lord Macaulay, and he saw the rebellion as an early expression of the spirit of liberty in England, a cry for 'freedom and justice for the poor'. He depicted the rebellion as largely the responsibility of priests and friars who had been preaching Christian Democracy among the poor. This was something Trevelyan clearly approved, much as he might have deplored the violence which followed from it. He remarked that 'the spirit that had prompted the rising was one of the chief reasons why serfdom died out in England, as it did not die out on the continent of Europe'. Trevelyan saw the labourers' cause as just, and expressed his cautious approval of their complaints, if not of their acts of violence (Trevelyan, 1946, pp. 12–15).

A third historian, Helen Cam, pointed to certain injustices against the labourers as responsible for their revolt: the poll taxes of 1379 and 1380, which were not graduated and so hurt the poor but not the rich; and the Statute of Labourers (1351), which fixed the wages of labourers at rates which applied before the Black Death, at a time when shortage of labour would otherwise have caused wages to rise.

The magnates who ran the government in his [Richard II's] minority authorised the ill-devised poll taxes of 1379 and 1380 which helped to precipitate the rising of 1381. But the country gentlemen must share responsibility, for they had approved the detested Statute of Labourers, aimed at stabilising wages and prices, and immobilising labour in the confused economic conditions that followed the Black Death of 1349. (Cam, 1967, p. 137)

It is not entirely clear whether Cam believed the magnates and the country gentlemen to have been blameworthy according to their own moral standards or according to hers. Perhaps she thought them at fault from both points of view.

The three positions taken here in ascribing responsibility for the revolt of 1381 are mirrored in the historiography of most revolutions and wars. Some historians will blame those in authority for not doing their duty in a responsible manner; some will hold a belligerent group responsible for what happened, admiring or deploring the principles which motivated them; and some will blame injustices perpetrated against the belligerents as responsible for their actions. The revolutions against Charles I in England, George III in America, Louis XVI in France and Nicholas II in Russia have all been treated from these points of view, to mention only the most familiar examples.

Moral judgements about past human actions, even those based upon the values of the people involved, are not descriptions of the past unless they represent a judgement which was actually formed by someone in the past. If the rebels in 1381 really did judge the government irresponsible, as McKisack said, then her account of that moral judgement is a true historical description. If, on the other hand, nobody in fact drew this moral conclusion which might well have been drawn, then her account of it is not a true historical description, but rather is a commentary upon the morality of John of Gaunt's government. Obviously moral judgements expressing the historian's own values are not historical descriptions but are personal opinions about the value of past events.

5 Judgements about effects in history

One event, *E*, is an effect of another, *C*, if *C* was a cause of *E*. So statements describing events as effects of historical events, like those identifying causes, are true or false in an indirect correspondence sense. Statements about 'the effects', however, which single out some as the most significant, are always value judgements, reflecting the historian's personal interests.

There are several common reasons why historians examine effects. Sometimes it is to notice what consequences of their actions people could be held responsible for. More often it is to draw attention to the important historical changes brought about by an event, thereby establishing its historical significance. Because these changes were not always envisaged by those whose actions produced them, those people cannot always be held responsible for them. Thus Kitson Clark, having pointed out the good and evil effects of the industrial revolution in England, insisted that those who promoted the industrial changes should not be held responsible for their effects. He wrote that the industrial revolution

probably should be considered as nearly void of moral significance as a change in the weather which happens to produce in some year a good harvest; probably the human agents who promoted it were in many cases as innocent of any far-sighted visions for humanity as the human agents who caused the increase in population. (Clark, 1962, p. 93)

The effects which an historian mentions are always those which interest him, but more often than not they are determined by the theme of his book or essay. For instance in *The Tyranny of Distance* (1966), Geoffrey Blainey discussed the problems which distances within Australia and between Australia and other countries imposed on Australia's development. It was understandable, therefore, when describing some effects of the wealth which Australians derived from wool in the mid-nineteenth century, that he should mention what effect it had upon these problems, which were the theme of his book.

Wool enabled settlement to push profitability far from the Australian coast. Without the incentive of wool Australia in 1850 would have consisted of a few ports surrounded by a narrow belt of farmland. Wool not only opened much of the inland but also tied Australia to Europe. Australia's commercial life had been linked strongly to Asia and the Pacific in the first thirty years, but with the mounting strength of the Australian-owned flocks and whaling fleets, Australia produced its main exports for the European markets. Its growth came to depend less on the big sums which the British Government spent on maintaining its convicts and their keepers in Australia, and more on the price of wool and whale oils on the British markets. Australia's economic life was no longer so insulated from the outside world. (p. 133)

Sometimes an event changes things so strikingly that historians regard it as a turning point in the history of a subject. In C. L. Mowat's history, *Britain Between the Wars, 1918–1940* (1955), the failure of the Labour government under Ramsay Macdonald to meet the economic crises of 1929–31, and the formation in August 1931 of the National government under his leadership, is identified as 'the turning point' in the story. The National government was composed almost entirely of indecisive Tories (neither Winston Churchill nor Lloyd George were in it), and after the October election, in which 'Labour was routed, [and] independent Liberalism almost blotted out' (p. 399), it faced an insignificant opposition.

To the extent that the events of August 1931 shaped the form of British government and British policy for the next nine years they did constitute the great turning point in the twenty years between the two world wars. The years ahead were dominated by two things: depression and military aggression. Both, but particularly the latter, were not opposed with strength by the British governments of the thirties. Partly this was because depression breeds not strength, but weakness, retreat. Perhaps, however, a government with a smaller majority and a stronger opposition would have followed firmer policies. (p. 400)

In Mowat's opinion 'The history of the National government was one long diminuendo. From its triumph in 1931 it shambled its unimaginative way to its fall in 1940' (p. 413).

Because statements about the effects of historical events reflect the historian's interests, they are not simply true or false. The claim that certain events were effects of others may be true or false; but to call them 'the' effects, or to identify them as the most important effects, is to express an evaluation of their significance.

◁ 9 ▷

Epilogue:
Truth and interpretation in history

In preceding chapters it has been argued that it is reasonable to believe historical descriptions true if they are justified in accordance with the relevant justification conditions. Doubts may linger in the mind of the reader, however, who is aware that historical descriptions are used to provide interpretations, and that interpretations notoriously express the interests and values of the historian. If historical descriptions are in part at least determined by historians' interests and values, is that not a good reason for doubting their truth, no matter how well they appear to be justified?

To investigate the worry expressed in this line of argument, one must inquire more closely about the nature of interpretation in history, to see whether and in what senses each historical description is, or is part of, an interpretation; and one must also discover whether the historian's own interests, which are reflected in his interpretations, are likely to bias his appraisal of his descriptions of the past, in which case it may not be reasonable to believe them true.

1   Interpretation in history

The word 'interpretation' is used in many contexts. Judges interpret laws; critics interpret poems; actors interpret characters; and musicians interpret scores. Historians are said to interpret a range of things: periods, events, intentions, and evidence, for example. What does the word mean in all these contexts? An interpretation of something is one of several possible, more or less equally well-supported accounts of that thing which could be given. (This thesis was first defended in McCullagh, 1971.)

Interpretations should be contrasted with definitive descriptions. Suppose an historian translated a Latin text, giving its conventional meaning quite correctly in his own tongue, there being no uncertainty involved. Then the translation would not be an interpretation of what the text meant in, say, English, but a definitive statement of what it meant. Interpretations are always accounts of something which are made when different, equally well-supported accounts of it are possible. Similarly, an exhaustive description of the meaning of a term, or the nature of an object, is not an interpretation of those things, but a complete account of them.

From the work of Heidegger and Gadamer can be derived the impression that every description of reality is an interpretation, a product of our historically conditioned concepts and values. Our analysis of interpretation helps to make this view intelligible: inasmuch as any description could be different, were the concepts and values of the person making it different, it can be regarded as an interpretation. This theory of interpretation is too broad for present purposes, however, for it does not allow a distinction between descriptions which are interpretations and descriptions which are not, within a language. The correct translation of a Latin sentence, or the exhaustive definition of a term is not regarded as merely 'an interpretation' of what the sentence or the term mean. Rather, they are definitive statements of what they mean, within our language and culture.

Speaking generally one might say that historians interpret past events and present evidence. Close attention to historical practice, however, reveals many more subjects of interpretation than these two. Often the events which historians interpret are actions, and they can interpret what the agents meant by them, what they meant to contemporaries, what their consequences were, and how they can be understood in terms of present theories. There are often several possible, equally well-supported accounts of each of these things which can be given. Thus Bismarck's famous telegram from Ems can be described as a provocation to war, an insult to France, the cause of the Franco-Russian War, and an act of daring statesmanship. Historians interpret many other things besides actions. They interpret other events, changes in the attitudes of social classes and in the economic prosperity of a group or country for instance. They interpret people and institutions as well as events, sometimes in terms of their intrinsic features, sometimes in terms of their causes or effects. Thus Francis Bacon may be called 'the father of modern science'; Lord Shaftesbury 'the great reformer'; and Kingsford Smith 'the pioneer of Australian aviation'.

There are really as many subjects of historical interpretation as there are subjects of historical description. Historians often interpret not just a single event, but a group of events or a period of history. Groups of events can be interpreted by using colligatory concepts which describe features which the group possessed as a whole (see McCullagh, 1978). They may have constituted 'a democratic revolution' or 'a classical renaissance', for example. Historical periods can be interpreted by stating generalizations about people's beliefs, attitudes or behaviour which characterize large numbers of events which occurred within them.

Thus there are many kinds of past, historical subjects which are subjects of historical interpretation. There is also a variety when it comes to historical evidence. But here an important distinction must be made between interpreting the physical characteristics of the evidence, which is usually easy, and interpreting their historical significance, which can be difficult. It may be easy to see the physical shape of a hard stone, but difficult to decide whether or not it had been shaped by man as a cutting instrument. It may be easy to see the letters of a text on a page, but difficult to decide what the letters meant, or when they were written.

It should now be clear that historical descriptions are all interpretations. They are all interpretations of the historical significance of the evidence from which they are derived. And most are also interpretations of the subject of the description. If the subject is the meaning of a word or text, the description of it may be exhaustive. But in other cases, as in the description of an event, a cause or a period of history, it will be only one of several possible, more or less equally well-supported descriptions which could be given of that subject.

2   Bias in history

Interpreters choose an interpretation of a subject from among several which could be given. The choice is seldom arbitrary. It is usually a choice which the interpreter prefers, for personal or academic reasons. The worry is that historians may choose interpretations of past events because they prefer them for personal reasons, even when they are not really as well supported as alternative accounts of the subject which could be given.

Three important points need to be made in response to this concern. The first is that historians' selection of descriptions of the past is seldom directly determined by their personal values, but is rather determined by the need to provide information relevant to the problem or the hypothesis which they have chosen to investigate. The choice of an initial problem or hypothesis will usually be determined in part by the historian's interests, though to a great extent it is also suggested by the current state of historical understanding, and by the materials available to the historian as evidence of the past. It remains true that historians sometimes prefer one answer to their question to another, or one hypothesis to another, for personal reasons because it accords with their existing beliefs and commitments. But they have usually been trained to consider all available material relevant to their inquiry, and to assess its significance fairly.

The second point is that as historians gain a more precise knowledge of the conditions under which their descriptions of the past are justified, so they may become better able to assess their rational justification. The present book is intended to make historians more conscious of the standards of justification required of historical descriptions before they can be deemed credible.

Some philosophers have thought that an appeal to proven standards of inquiry and argument is a sure way of exposing and correcting prejudice in history. This is the view of K. R. Popper (1966, vol. 2, ch. 23, especially pp. 217–18) and also of Charles Frankel (1955, ch. 7, especially pp. 137–9). An appeal to such standards can certainly help to expose the grosser cases of unwarranted assertion. But a critic can be as biased as an historian, either for or against the conclusions he is examining. Only if a hostile expert critic or a critic of proven impartiality accepts an historical description as warranted by the evidence, can one be reasonably confident that a description which is in doubt is indeed justified.

The third thing to be said is that even scrupulous attention to the standards of justification set out here may not prevent the most prevalent forms of bias in history, namely the failure to consider alternative possibilities as a result of commitment to one's preconceptions. Only methodological procedures can save historians, to a large extent, from this. Instances of bias of this sort have been presented in a fascinating article by Quentin Skinner in which he uncovers 'the extent to which the current historical study of ethical, political, religious, and other such ideas is contaminated by the unconscious application of paradigms whose familiarity to the historian disguises an essential inapplicability to the past' (1969, p. 7). Similarly W. L. Burn has shown how easy it is to find evidence in support of one's preconceived generalizations about Victorian England. There is so much material available, one can discover any 'pattern' or 'trend' one likes (1968, ch.1). Skinner's recommendation is that the historian should try to discover what authors intended by their texts, instead of just stating what the historian supposes that they meant. Burn urges us 'to check the generalizations against the thoughts and actions of particular men and women' (1968, p. 23) to see whether the preconceived generalizations fit the individual cases at all adequately.

It is easy to see that an historical description may be well justified according to the standards of justification set out in previous chapters, but still come to be rejected as false when a hitherto unimagined hypothesis is found to be even better justified. A singular description may provide the best explanation of certain data which has so far been thought of, but it will be discarded when someone thinks of a better one. Similarly the conclusion of a statistical syllogism may be accepted as true only to be denied when another, more qualified or even incompatible description of the same subject is shown to be even more probable. Again, one generalization, like the belief that Democrats voted for economic reasons in New York state in 1844, will be acceptable until an even more strongly supported one, like Benson's thesis that they voted for religious and ethnic reasons, is found. Finally, one cause may be judged the most important, or the best explanation until another is considered which is even better justified than the first. A fertile imagination, therefore, is indispensable to an historian, and there is no doubt that it can be restricted by his interests. They, like all people, are often attached to their preconceptions. This kind of bias is the hardest of all to overcome. It is to correct bias of this kind that most histories are re-written.

Knowledge of the limitations of historians' imaginations, not to mention the limitations of available evidence, provides reason for doubting the truth of even well-supported descriptions of the past. From an intellectual point of view, scepticism seems warranted. But for other practical purposes we need historical knowledge: we need it to understand and assess our social and cultural inheritance. So we are justified, for pragmatic reasons, in believing well-supported historical descriptions just the same. They are at least more likely to be reliable than are poorly supported descriptions of the past.

There are two major senses in which written history can be biased. Historical descriptions are biased when the historian's interests have led him to assert them as though they were well supported when, if he were less disposed to accept them, he could have seen that they were not. This is the only sense of bias which has been discussed so far. History is also biased when the historian's interests result in his descriptions of the past being not necessarily false, but misleading.

Historical descriptions are always partial in that they never describe every detail of their subjects. They are selective and simplifying, describing only those features of their subjects which are of interest. They may still be true, just so long as one set of their possible truth conditions corresponds to what actually happened. Descriptions of a high level of generality are not very informative, of course, as there is such a great range of possible truth conditions which could make them true. But their generality does not prevent their being true.

Even true historical descriptions, however, can be misleading, and they are so when the parts of a subject which they describe give a misleading impression of the whole. For example, an historian could give a misleading impression of a person's character by describing only his good deeds and none of his bad ones, as the authors of biographies are sometimes tempted to do to preserve the good name of their subjects. Misleading descriptions are not true of their subjects in that they imply statements about them which are false. The form of implication involved here has been well explained by J. L. Gorman (1982, ch. 3). It is not a strictly logical form of implication, but rather one which rests upon a convention, in this case the convention that historians should describe historical subjects, however briefly, so as to provide a true impression of them as a whole. The reader, assuming this convention to have been observed, is misled in taking partial descriptions to give an accurate impression of their subject as a whole, when in fact they do not.

This is another kind of bias which is not simply corrected by close attention to the justification conditions of historical descriptions. It can only be prevented by historians being aware of their own tendencies and deliberately compensating for them, for instance by looking for the bad points of those they admire and the good points of those they dislike.

This discussion of bias in history has demonstrated the invaluable role played by expert historical critics in protecting the public from obviously false or misleading accounts of the past. Only they can reveal ignorance or misuse of relevant evidence, failure to consider alternative, more plausible interpretations, and misleading descriptions of historical subjects. While free criticism and open debate among historians continues, the public will be protected from excessive misuse of history for the purposes of propaganda. One can be reasonably sure that historical descriptions which have won the approval of unsympathetic or impartial expert critics are not biased, but are well justified and merit belief.

Bibliography

The bibliography is in two sections: philosophical and reflective works are listed in Part A, and historical works, used almost entirely for illustrative purposes, are listed in Part B. The date given in each case is the date on which the edition used was first published.

A. Philosophical and reflective works

Abel, Theodore, 1948. The operation called *Verstehen*. *The American Journal of Sociology*, 54, pp. 211–18.

Anscombe, G. E. M., 1971. *Causality and Determination*. Cambridge, Cambridge University Press.

Austin, J. L., 1962. *How To Do Things With Words*. Oxford, Clarendon.

Aydelotte, William O., 1971. *Quantification in History*. Reading, Mass., Addison-Wesley.

Ayer, A. J., 1964. *Man as a Subject for Science*. London, Athlone Press.

Barker, John A., 1975. Scriven on the Logic of Cause. *Theory and Decision*, 6, pp. 43–55.

Barzun, Jacques and Graff, Henry F., 1970. *The Modern Researcher*, rev. edn. New York, Harcourt, Brace and World.

Beattie, J. H. M., 1970. On understanding ritual. In *Rationality*, ed. Bryan R. Wilson, pp. 240–68. Oxford, Blackwell.

Beauchamp, Tom L., ed., 1974. *Philosophical Problems of Causation*. Encino, California, Dickenson.

Benson, Lee, 1974. Political power and political elites. In *American Political Behavior: Historical Essays and Readings*, ed. Lee Benson, et al., pp. 281–310. New York, Harper and Row.

Berlin, Isaiah, 1954. *Historical Inevitability*. London, Oxford University Press.

Blalock, Hubert M., Jr, 1972. *Social Statistics*, 2nd edn. New York, McGraw-Hill.

Bloch, Marc, 1954. *The Historian's Craft*, tr. Peter Putnam. Manchester, Manchester University Press.

Bogue, Allan G., 1974. American historians and legislative behavior. In *American Political Behavior: Historical Essays and Readings*, ed. Lee Benson, et al., pp. 99–119. New York, Harper and Row.

Brown, Robert, 1973. *Rules and Laws in Sociology*. London, Routledge and Kegan Paul.

Burns, A. L., 1949–51. Ascertainment, probability and evidence in history. *Historical Studies, Australia and New Zealand*, 4, pp. 327–39.

Butterfield, H., 1931. *The Whig Interpretation of History*. London, G. Bell and Sons.

Butterfield, H., 1951. *History and Human Relations*. London, Collins.

Cebik, L. B., 1978. *Concepts, Events and History.* Washington D.C., University Press of America.

Chomsky, Noam, 1966. *Topics in the Theory of Generative Grammar.* Extracts reprinted in *Chomsky: Selected Readings,* ed. J. P. B. Allen and Paul van Buren, pp. 7–16. London, Oxford University Press, 1971. Page references are to this reprint.

Clark, G. Kitson, 1967. *The Critical Historian.* London, Heinemann.

Climo, T. A. and Howells, P. G. A., 1976. Possible worlds in historical explanation. *History and Theory,* XV, pp. 1–20.

Cohen, G. A., 1978. *Karl Marx's Theories of History, A Defence.* Oxford, Clarendon.

Cohen, Howard, 1973. *Das Verstehen* and historical knowledge. *American Philosophical Quarterly,* 10, pp. 299–306.

Cohen, L. Jonathan, 1977. *The Probable and the Provable.* Oxford, Clarendon.

Collingwood, R. G., 1939. *An Autobiography.* London, Oxford University Press, 1970.

Collingwood, R. G., 1946. *The Idea of History.* London, Oxford University Press, paperback edn, 1961.

Commager, Henry Steele, 1965. *The Nature and the Study of History.* Columbus, Ohio, C. E. Merrill Books.

Danto, Arthur C., 1965. *Analytical Philosophy of History.* Cambridge, Cambridge University Press.

Darwin, Charles, 1872. *The Origin of Species,* 6th edn. New York, Collier, 1962.

Day, John Patrick, 1961. *Inductive Probability.* London, Routledge and Kegan Paul.

Dibble, Vernon K., 1963. Four types of inference from documents to events. *History and Theory,* III, pp. 203–21.

Donagan, Alan, 1956. The verification of historical theses. *Philosophical Quarterly,* IV, pp. 193–209.

Donagan, Alan, 1959. Explanation in history. In *Theories of History,* ed. Patrick Gardiner, pp. 428–43. New York, The Free Press.

Donagan, Alan, 1962. *The Later Philosophy of R. G. Collingwood.* Oxford, Clarendon.

Donagan, Alan, 1964. Historical explanation: The Popper–Hempel theory reconsidered. *History and Theory,* IV, pp. 3–26. Reprinted in *Philosophical Analysis and History,* ed. William H. Dray, pp. 127–59. New York and London, Harper and Row, 1966. Page references are to this reprint.

Donagan, Alan, 1969. Alternative historical explanations and their verification. *The Monist,* 53, pp. 58–89.

Donagan, Alan, 1975. Realism and historical instrumentalism. *Revue Internationale de Philosophie,* 111–12, pp. 78–89.

Dray, William, 1957. *Laws and Explanation in History.* London, Oxford University Press.

Dray, William, 1959. 'Explaining What' in history. In *Theories of History,* ed. Patrick Gardiner, pp. 403–8. New York, The Free Press.

Dray, William H., 1964. *Philosophy of History,* Englewood Cliffs, N. J., Prentice-Hall.

Eggleston, Richard, 1978. *Evidence, Proof and Probability.* London, Weidenfeld and Nicolson.

Elton, G. R., 1967. *The Practice of History.* Sydney, Sydney University Press.

Elton, G. R., 1970. *Political History. Principles and Practice.* London, Allen Lane.

Feyerabend, Paul K., 1975. *Against Method.* London, Verso, 1978.

Fleming, Stuart, 1976. *Dating in Archaeology: A Guide to Scientific Techniques*. London, Dent.

Floud, Roderick, 1973. *An Introduction to Quantitative Methods for Historians*. London, Methuen.

Frankel, Charles, 1955. *The Case for Modern Man*, paperback edn. Boston, Beacon Press, 1959.

Galbraith, V. H., 1964. *An Introduction to the Study of History*. London, Watts.

Gallie, W. B., 1964. *Philosophy and the Historical Understanding*. London, Chatto & Windus.

Gardiner, Patrick, 1952. *The Nature of Historical Explanation*. London, Oxford University Press.

Gellner, Ernest, 1962. Concepts and society. *The Transactions of the Fifth World Congress of Sociology*. Reprinted in *Rationality*, ed. Bryan R. Wilson, pp. 18–49. Oxford, Blackwell, 1970. Page references are to this reprint.

Gershoy, Leo, 1963. Some problems of a working historian. In *Philosophy and History: A Symposium*, ed. Sidney Hook, pp. 59–75. New York, New York University Press.

Geyl, Pieter, 1946. Toynbee's System of Civilizations. Reprinted in his *Debates with Historians*, pp. 112–54. London and Glasgow, Collins Fontana Library, 1962.

Gibson, Quentin, 1960. *The Logic of Social Enquiry*. London, Routledge and Kegan Paul.

Glover, Jonathan, 1970. *Responsibility*. London, Routledge and Kegan Paul.

Goldstein, Leon J., 1962. Evidence and events in history. *Philosophy of Science*, 29, pp. 175–9.

Goldstein, Leon J., 1976. *Historical Knowing*. Austin and London, University of Texas Press.

Gorman, J. L., 1982. *The Expression of Historical Knowledge*. Edinburgh, University of Edinburgh Press.

Gorovitz, Samuel, 1965. Causal judgments and causal explanations. *Journal of Philosophy*, 62, pp. 695–711. Reprinted in *Philosophical Problems of Causation*, ed. Tom. L. Beauchamp, pp. 235–47. Encino, California, Dickenson, 1974. Page references are to this reprint.

Gottschalk, Louis, 1950. *Understanding History*. New York, Alfred A. Knopf.

Gottschalk, Louis (ed.), 1963. *Generalization in the Writing of History*. Chicago, University of Chicago Press.

Hammond, Michael, 1977. Weighting causes in historical explanation. *Theoria*, 43, pp. 103–28.

Handlin, Oscar, 1979. *Truth in History*. Cambridge, Mass., Belknap Press.

Harman, Gilbert H., 1965. The inference to the best explanation. *Philosophical Review*, 74, pp. 88–95.

Hart, H. L. A. and Honoré, A. M., 1958. *Causation in the Law*. An extract of this is reprinted in *Philosophical Problems of Causation*, ed. Tom L. Beauchamp, pp. 222–35. Encino, California, Dickenson, 1974. Page references are to this reprint.

Helmer, Olaf and Rescher, Nicholas, 1959. Exact or inexact sciences: a more instructive dichotomy? *Management Science*, 6, pp. 25–52. Reprinted in *The Nature and Scope of Social Science*, ed. L. I. Krimerman, pp. 181–203. New York, Appelton-Century Crofts, 1969. Page references are to this reprint.

Hempel, Carl G., 1962. Explanation in science and in history. Reprinted in *Philosophical Analysis and History*, ed. William H. Dray, pp. 95–126. New York and London, Harper and Row, 1966.

Hempel, Carl G., 1965. *Aspects of Scientific Explanation*. New York, The Free Press.

Hesse, Mary, 1974. *The Structures of Scientific Inference*. London and Basingstoke, Macmillan.

Hexter, J. H., 1961. The historian and his day. In his *Reappraisals in History*, pp. 1–13. London, Longmans.

Hollis, Martin, 1967a. The limits of rationality. *Archives Européenes de Sociologie*, VII, pp. 265–7. Reprinted in *Rationality*, ed. Bryan R. Wilson, pp. 214–20. Oxford, Blackwell, 1970.

Hollis, Martin, 1967b. Reason and ritual. *Philosophy*, XLIII, pp. 231–47. Reprinted in *Rationality*, ed. Bryan R. Wilson, pp. 221–39. Oxford, Blackwell, 1970.

Hollis, Martin and Skinner, Quentin, 1978. Action and context. *Aristotelian Society*, supp. vol. LII, pp. 43–69.

Hook, Sidney, 1943. *The Hero in History; A Study in Limitation and Possibility*. Boston, Beacon Press, 1955.

Horton, Robin, 1970. African traditional thought and western science. In *Rationality*, ed. Bryan R. Wilson, pp. 131–71. Oxford, Blackwell, 1970.

Hume, David, 1777. Of miracles. In *An Enquiry Concerning Human Understanding*, ed. L. Selby-Bigge, pp. 109–31. Oxford, Clarendon, 1962.

Hurst, B. C., 1981. The myth of historical evidence. *History and Theory*, XX, pp. 278–90.

Iggers, George G., 1968. *The German Conception of History: The National Tradition of Historical Thought from Herder to the Present*. Middletown, Conn., Wesleyan University Press.

Karlman, Roland, 1976. *Evidencing Historical Classifications in British and American Historiography 1930–1970*. Studia Historica Upsaliensia 80. Uppsala, University of Uppsala.

Keep, John, ed., 1964. *Contemporary History in the Soviet Mirror*. London, Allen and Unwin.

Kim, J., 1973. Causes and counterfactuals. *Journal of Philosophy*, 70, pp. 570–2.

Knowles, David, 1963. *The Historian and Character, and other essays*. Cambridge, Cambridge University Press.

Lakatos, I., 1970. Falsification and the methodology of scientific research programmes. In *Criticism and the Growth of Knowledge*, ed. Imre Lakatos and Alan Musgrave, pp. 91–196. Cambridge, Cambridge University Press.

Lazarsfeld, Paul F., 1959. Problems in methodology. Reprinted in *Continuities in the Language of Social Research*, ed. P. F. Lazarsfeld, A. K. Pasanella and M. Rosenberg, pp. 17–24. New York, The Free Press, 1972.

Lazarsfeld, P. F., Pasanella, A. K. and Rosenberg, M., eds., 1972. *Continuities in the Language of Social Research*. New York, The Free Press.

Lazarsfeld, P. F. and Rosenberg, M., eds., 1955. *The Language of Social Research*. New York, The Free Press.

Lazarsfeld, Paul F., and Thielens, Wagner, Jr, 1958. Comments on the nature of classification in social research. An extract is reprinted in Lazarsfeld, Pasanella and Rosenberg, 1972, pp. 62–5.

Leff, Gordon, 1969. *History and Social Theory*. London, Merlin Press.

Lewis, David, 1973. Causation. *Journal of Philosophy*, 70, pp. 556–67. Reprinted in *Causation and Conditionals*, ed. Ernest Sosa, pp. 180–91. London, Oxford University Press, 1975. Page references are to this reprint.

Lipset, Seymour Martin, 1968. History and sociology: some methodological considerations. In *Sociology and History: Methods*, ed. Seymour Martin Lipset and Richard Hofstadter, pp. 20–58. New York and London, Basic Books.

Lukes, Steven, 1967. Some problems about rationality. *Archives Européenes de Sociologie*, VIII, pp. 247–64. Reprinted in *Rationality*, ed. Bryan R. Wilson, pp. 194–213. Oxford, Blackwell, 1974.

Maas, Paul, 1958. *Textual Criticism*, tr. Barbara Flower. London, Oxford University Press.

McClelland, Peter D., 1975. *Causal Explanation and Model Building in History, Economics, and the New Economic History*. Ithaca, N.J., Cornell University Press.

McCormick, Richard P., 1960. New perspectives on Jacksonian politics. *American Historical Review*, LXV, pp. 288–301. Reprinted in *Quantitative History*, ed. Don Karl Rowney and James Q. Graham, Jr, pp. 372–84. Homewood, Illinois, The Dorsey Press, 1969. Page references are to this reprint.

McCullagh, C. Behan, 1969. Narrative and explanation in history. *Mind*, LXXVIII, pp. 256–61.

McCullagh, C. Behan, 1971. Interpretation in history. *The Australian Journal of Politics and History*, XVII, pp. 215–29.

McCullagh, C. Behan, 1973. Historical instrumentalism. *History and Theory*, XII, pp. 290–306.

McCullagh, C. Behan, 1976. The individuation of actions and acts. *Australasian Journal of Philosophy*, 54, pp. 133–9.

McCullagh, C. Behan, 1977. The nature of historical inferences. *Revue Internationale de Philosophie*, 121–2, pp. 351–9.

McCullagh, C. Behan, 1978. Colligation and classification in history. *History and Theory*, XVII, pp. 267–84.

McCullagh, C. Behan, 1980. Historical realism. *Philosophy and Phenomenological Research*, XL, pp. 420–5.

McCullagh, C. Behan, 1984. The intelligibility of cognitive relativism. *The Monist*, 67, forthcoming.

Mackie, J. L., 1974. *The Cement of the Universe*. Oxford, Clarendon.

Mandelbaum, Maurice, 1974. The distinguishable and the separable: a note on Hume and causation. *Journal of the History of Philosophy*, 12, pp. 242–7.

Mandelbaum, Maurice, 1977. *The Anatomy of Historical Knowledge*. Baltimore, The Johns Hopkins University Press.

Marrou, Henri-Irénée, 1966. *The Meaning of History*, tr. Robert J. Olsen. Dublin, Helicon.

Mill, John Stuart, 1872. *A System of Logic, Ratiocinative and Inductive*. 8th edn. London, Longmans, Green & Co., 1949.

Murphey, Murray G., 1973. *Our Knowledge of the Historical Past*. Indianapolis and New York, Bobbs-Merrill.

Murphy, George G. S., 1969. On counterfactual propositions. *History and Theory*, Supplement 9, pp. 14–38.

Nagel, Ernest, 1960. Determinism in history. *Philosophy and Phenomenological Research*, 20. Reprinted in *Philosophical Analysis and History*, ed. William H. Dray, pp. 347–82. New York, Harper and Row, 1966. Page references are to this reprint.

O'Connor, D. J., 1975. *The Correspondence Theory of Truth*. London, Hutchinson.

Peirce, C. S., 1934. *Collected Papers*, vol. VII, ch. 3: The logic of drawing history from ancient documents, ed. C. Hartshorne and P. Weiss. Cambridge, Mass., Harvard University Press, 1965.

Plekhanov, George, 1940. *The Role of the Individual in History*. New York, International Publishers.

Pocock, J. G. A., 1972. *Politics, Language and Time*. London, Methuen.

Popper, Karl R., 1963. *Conjectures and Refutations: The Growth of Scientific Knowledge*. London, Routledge and Kegan Paul.

Popper, K. R., 1966. *The Open Society and Its Enemies*, 5th edn. London, Routledge and Kegan Paul.

Popper, Karl R., 1968. *The Logic of Scientific Discovery*, rev. edn. London, Hutchinson.

Popper, Karl R., 1974. Replies to my critics. In *The Philosophy of Karl Popper*, ed. P. A. Schlipp, vol. 2, pp. 961–1197. La Salle, Ill., Open Court.

Quine, Willard van Ormond, 1965. *Elementary Logic*, rev. edn. New York, Harper and Row.

Reynolds, L. D., and Wilson, N. G., 1968. *Scribes and Scholars: A Guide to the Transmission of Greek and Latin Literature*. London, Oxford University Press.

Rorty, Richard, 1972. The world well lost. *Journal of Philosophy*, 69, pp. 649–66.

Rorty, Richard, 1976. Realism and reference. *Monist*, 59, pp. 321–40.

Rorty, Richard, 1980. *Philosophy and the Mirror of Nature*. Oxford, Blackwell; and Princeton, N.J., Princeton University Press.

Ryle, Gilbert, 1949. *The Concept of Mind*. Harmondsworth, Middlesex, Penguin, 1963.

Salmon, Wesley C., 1966. *The Foundations of Scientific Inference*. Pittsburgh, University of Pittsburgh Press.

Salmon, Wesley C., 1975. Confirmation and relevance. *Minnesota Studies in the Philosophy of Science*, VI, pp. 3–36, ed. Grover Maxwell and Robert M. Anderson Jr., Minneapolis, University of Minnesota Press.

Schiffer, S., 1972. *Meaning*. London, Oxford University Press.

Scriven, Michael, 1959a. Truisms as the grounds for historical explanations. In *Theories of History*, ed. Patrick Gardiner, pp. 443–75. New York, The Free Press.

Scriven, Michael, 1959b. The logic of criteria. *The Journal of Philosophy*, 56, pp. 857–68.

Scriven, Michael, 1963. New issues in the logic of explanation. In *Philosophy and History, A Symposium*, ed. Sidney Hook, pp. 339–61. New York, New York University Press.

Scriven, Michael, 1966. Causes, connections and conditions in history. In *Philosophical Analysis and History*, ed. William H. Dray, pp. 238–64. New York and London, Harper and Row.

Scriven, Michael, 1969. Logical positivism and the behavioral sciences. In *The Legacy of Logical Positivism*, ed. P. Achinstein and S. F. Barker, pp. 195–209. Baltimore, The Johns Hopkins University Press.

Scriven, Michael, 1971a. Verstehen again. *Theory and Decision*, 1, pp. 382–6.

Scriven, Michael, 1971b. The logic of cause. *Theory and Decision*, 2, pp. 49–66.

Scruton, Roger, 1976. Truth conditions and criteria. *The Aristotelian Society*, supp. vol. L, pp. 193–216.

Skinner, Quentin, 1969. Meaning and understanding in the history of ideas. *History and Theory*, VIII, pp. 3–53.

Skinner, Quentin, 1970. Conventions and the understanding of speech acts. *Philosophical Quarterly*, 20, pp. 118–38.

Skinner, Quentin, 1971. On performing and explaining linguistic actions. *Philosophical Quarterly*, 21, pp. 1–21.

Skinner, Quentin, 1972a. 'Social meaning' and the explanation of social action. Reprinted in *The Philosophy of History*, ed. Patrick Gardiner, pp. 106–26. London, Oxford University Press, 1974. Page references are to this reprint.

Skinner, Quentin, 1972b. Motives, intentions and the interpretation of texts. *New Literary History*, 3, pp. 393–408.

Sober, Elliott, 1975. *Simplicity*. Oxford, Clarendon.

Strawson, P. F., 1964. Intention and convention in speech acts. *The Philosophical Review*, LXXIII, pp. 439–60. Reprinted in *The Philosophy of Language*, ed. J. R. Searle, pp. 23–38. London, Oxford University Press, 1971. Page references are to this reprint.

Stretton, Hugh, 1969. *The Political Sciences*. London, Routledge and Kegan Paul.

Swierenga, Robert P., ed., 1970. *Quantification in American History: Theory and Research*. New York, Atheneum.

Swinburne, Richard, 1973. *An Introduction to Confirmation Theory*. London, Methuen.

Thernstrom, Stephan, 1968. Quantitative methods in history: some notes. In *Sociology and History: Methods*, ed. Seymour Martin Lipset and Richard Hofstadter, pp. 59–78. New York and London, Basic Books.

Thompson, E. P., 1978. *The Poverty of Theory and Other Essays*. London, Merlin Press.

Todd, William, 1972. *History as Applied Science; A Philosophical Study*. Detroit, Wayne State University Press.

Toynbee, Arnold J., 1960. *A Study of History*, abridged by D. C. Somervell, 2 vols. London, Reader's Union edition, Oxford University Press.

Van Evra, James W., 1971. On Scriven on 'Verstehen'. *Theory and Decision*, 1, pp. 377–81.

Wartofsky, M. W., 1968. *Conceptual Foundations of Scientific Thought*. New York, Macmillan.

Wedgwood, C. V., 1967. *The Sense of the Past*. New York, Collier.

White, Morton, 1965. *Foundations of Historical Knowledge*. New York, Harper and Row.

Wise, Gene, 1973. *American Historical Explanations*. Homewood, Illinois, The Dorsey Press.

Yamane, Taro, 1967. *Elementary Sampling Theory*. Englewood Cliffs, N.J., Prentice-Hall.

B.   Historical works

Acton, J. E. E. D., 1956. *Essays on Freedom and Power*. London, Thames and Hudson.

Aron, Raymond, 1954. Causes and responsibilities, an extract from his book *The Century of Total War*. Reprinted in *The Outbreak of The First World War; Who Was Responsible?*, ed. Dwight E. Lee, pp. 67–72. Boston, D. C. Heath. Page references are to this reprint.

Aydelotte, William O., 1963. Voting patterns in the British House of Commons in the 1840's. *Comparative Studies in Society and History*, V, pp. 134–63. Reprinted in *Quantitative History*, ed. Don Karl Rowney and James Q. Graham Jr, pp. 415–42. Homewood, Illinois, The Dorsey Press, 1969.

Aydelotte, William O., 1972. The disintegration of the conservative party in the 1840's: a study of political attitudes. In *The Dimensions of Quantitative Research in History*, ed. William O. Aydelotte, Allan G. Bogue and Robert William Fogel, pp. 319–46. Princeton, Princeton University Press, 1972.

Barlow, F., 1970. *Edward the Confessor*. London, Eyre and Spottiswoode.

Benson, Lee, 1961. *The Concept of Jacksonian Democracy*. New York, Atheneum Press, 1964.

Benson, Lee, 1967. An approach to the scientific study of past public opinion.

Public Opinion Quarterly, XXXI, pp. 522–67. Reprinted in his book, *Toward the Scientific Study of History*, pp. 105–109. Philadelphia, J. B. Lippincott, 1972. Page references are to this reprint.

Blainey, Geoffrey, 1966. *The Tyranny of Distance*. Melbourne, Sun Books.

Blainey, Geoffrey, 1973. *The Causes of War*. London and Basingstoke, Macmillan.

Blaug, Mark, 1963. The myth of the old Poor Law and the making of the new. *The Journal of Economic History*, XXIII, pp. 151–84.

Bloch, Marc, 1965. *Feudal Society*, 2nd edn. London, Routledge and Kegan Paul.

Bogue, Allan G., 1967. Bloc and Party in the United States Senate: 1861–1863. *Civil War History*, XIII, pp. 221–41. Reprinted in *Quantification in American History: Theory and Research*, ed. Robert P. Swierenga, pp. 131–48. New York, Atheneum, 1970. Page references are to this reprint.

Brooke, Christopher, 1963. *The Saxon and Norman Kings*. London, Batsford.

Brooke, Christopher, 1964. *Europe in the Central Middle Ages 962–1154*. London, Longmans.

Bullock, Alan, 1955. *Hitler, A Study in Tyranny*. London, Odhams Press.

Bullock, Alan, 1967. Hitler and the origins of the second world war. *Proceedings of the British Academy*, LIII. Reprinted in *The Origins of the Second World War*, ed. Esmonde M. Robertson, pp. 189–224. London, Macmillan, 1971. Page references are to this reprint.

Burckhardt, Jacob Christoph, 1949. *The Age of Constantine the Great*, tr. Moses Hadas. London, Routledge and Kegan Paul.

Burn, W. L., 1968. *The Age of Equipoise*. London, Unwin University Books.

Cam, Helen, 1967. *England before Elizabeth*, 3rd edn. London, Hutchinson.

The Cambridge Modern History, 1902. Vol. I., The Renaissance, ed. A. W. Ward, G. W. Pothero, and Stanley Leathes. Cambridge, Cambridge University Press.

Chadwick, John, 1967. *The Decipherment of Linear B*, 2nd edn. Cambridge, Cambridge University Press.

Chang, P'eng-yüan, 1968. The constitutionalists. In *China in Revolution: The First Phase 1900–1913*, ed. M. C. Wright, pp. 143–84. New Haven, Yale University Press.

Cheney, Mary, 1969. The recognition of Pope Alexander III: some neglected evidence. *English Historical Review*, 84, pp. 474–97.

Clark, G. Kitson, 1962. *The Making of Victorian England*. London, Methuen.

Clarke, M. V., 1931. The Wilton Diptych. Reprinted in her book, *Fourteenth Century Studies*, ed. L. S. Sutherland and M. McKisack, pp. 272–92. Oxford, Clarendon, 1937 and 1968.

Collingwood, R. G., 1937. *Roman Britain and the English Settlements*, 2nd edn. Oxford, Clarendon.

Cooper, J. P., 1956. The counting of manors. *Economic History Review*, 2nd ser., VIII, pp. 377–89.

Cowling, Maurice, 1967. *1867, Disraeli, Gladstone and Revolution. The Passing of the Second Reform Bill*. Cambridge, Cambridge University Press.

Cowling, Maurice, 1971. *The Impact of Labour, 1920–1924*. Cambridge, Cambridge University Press.

Deane, Phyllis, 1965. *The First Industrial Revolution*. Cambridge, Cambridge University Press.

Denholm-Young, N., 1969. *Collected Papers*. Cardiff, University of Wales.

Dickens, A. G., 1967. *Martin Luther and the Reformation*. London, English Universities Press.

Dymond, D. P., 1974. *Archeology and History*. London, Thames and Hudson.

Elkins, Stanley, 1968. *Slavery; A Problem in American Institutional and Intellectual Life*, 2nd edn. Chicago, University of Chicago Press.

Elkins, Stanley M., 1971. Slavery and ideology. In *The Debate over Slavery: Stanley Elkins and His Critics*, ed. Ann J. Lane, pp. 325–78. Urbana, University of Illinois Press.

Elton, G. R., 1955. *England under the Tudors*. London, Methuen.

Elton, G. R., 1962. *The Tudor Revolution in Government*. Cambridge, Cambridge University Press.

Erikson, E. H., 1959. *Young Man Luther*. London, Faber.

Evans, C. F., 1970. *Resurrection and the New Testament*. London, S.C.M.

Evans, John, 1950. On the date of British coins. Reprinted in *Man's Discovery of His Past: Literary Landmarks in Archaeology*, ed. Robert F. Heizer, pp. 40–7. Englewood Cliffs, N.J., Prentice-Hall, 1962. Page references are to this reprint.

Eyck, Erich, 1958. *Bismarck and the German Empire*, 2nd edn. London, George Allen and Unwin.

Fay, Sidney Bradshaw, 1930. *Origins of the World War*, 2nd edn. An extract of this book is reprinted in *The Outbreak of the First World War*, ed. Dwight E. Lee, pp. 16–21. Boston, D. C. Heath, 1958. Page references are to this reprint.

Ferguson, Wallace K., 1940. *The Renaissance*. New York, Henry Holt.

Ferguson, Wallace K., 1951. The interpretation of the Renaissance: suggestions for a synthesis. *Journal of the History of Ideas*, XII, pp. 483–95. Reprinted in *The Renaissance, Medieval or Modern?*, ed. Karl H. Dannenfeldt, pp. 101–9. Boston, D. C. Heath, 1959. Page references are to this reprint.

Fischer, Fritz, 1964. World policy, world power and German war aims. *Historische Zeitschrift*, CXCIX. Reprinted in *The Origins of the First World War*, ed. and trans. by H. W. Koch, pp. 79–144. London, Macmillan, 1972. Page references are to this reprint.

Fishlow, Albert, 1965. *American Railroads and the Transformation of the Ante-Bellum Economy*. Cambridge, Mass., Harvard University Press.

Fishlow, Albert and Fogel, Robert W., 1971. Quantitative economic history: an interim evaluation, past trends and present tendencies. *Journal of Economic History*, 31, pp. 15–42.

Fogel, Robert W., 1964. *Railroads and American Economic Growth: Essays in Econometric History*. Baltimore, The Johns Hopkins University Press.

Fogel, Robert W., 1966. The new economic history, its findings and methods. *Economic History Review*, XIX, pp. 642–56. Reprinted in *Quantitative History*, ed. D. K. Rowney and J. Q. Graham Jr, pp. 320–35. Homewood, Illinois, The Dorsey Press, 1969. Page references are to this reprint.

Fromm, Erich, 1941. *Escape from Freedom*. An extract is reprinted in *Hitler and Nazi Germany*, ed. Robert G. L. Waite, pp. 25–8. Hinsdale, Illinois, The Dryden Press, 1969. Page references are to this reprint.

Gay, Peter, 1971. *The Party of Humanity, Essays in the French Enlightenment*. New York, W. W. Norton.

Gershoy, Leo, 1962. *Bertrand Barère, A Reluctant Terrorist*. Princeton, N.J., Princeton University Press.

Grant Michael, 1970. *Nero*. New York, American Heritage Press.

Greenstein, Fred I., 1964. New light on changing American values: a forgotten body of survey data. *Social Forces*, XLII, pp. 441–50. Reprinted in *Sociology and History: Methods*, ed. Seymour Martin Lipset and Richard Hofstadter, pp. 292–310. New York and London, Basic Books.

Hanham, Alison, 1972. Richard III, Lord Hastings and the historians. *English Historical Review*, 87, pp. 233–48.

Hexter, J. H., 1958. Storm over the gentry. *Encounter*, X, No. 5, pp. 22–34.

Largely reprinted in *Social Change and Revolution in England*, ed. L. Stone, pp. 33–45. London, Longmans, 1965. Page references are to this reprint.

Hill, Christopher and Dell, Edmund, eds., 1949. *The Good Old Cause*. London, Lawrence and Wishart.

Hill, Christopher, 1955. *The English Revolution, 1640*, 3rd edn. London, Lawrence and Wishart.

Hill, Christopher, 1972. *The Century of Revolution, 1603–1714*, 2nd edn. London, Sphere Books.

Hodgkin, R. H., 1952. *A History of the Anglo-Saxons*, 3rd edn. London, Oxford University Press.

Hunt, E. H., 1968. The new economic history: Professor Fogel's study of American railways. *History*, 53, pp. 3–18.

Janssen, Karl-Heinz, 1972. Gerhard Ritter: a patriotic historian's justification. In *The Origins of the First World War*, ed. H. W. Koch, pp. 257–86. London, Macmillan.

Jessup, R., 1965. *The Story of Archaeology in Britain*. London, Michael Joseph.

Joll, James, 1966. The 1914 debate continues: Fritz Fischer and his critics. *Past and Present*, 34. Reprinted in *The origins of the First World War*, ed. H. W. Koch, pp. 13–29. London: Macmillan, 1972. Page references are to this reprint.

Kendall, P. M., 1955. *Richard the Third*. London, Allen and Unwin.

Knowles, David, 1963. The *Regula Magistri* and the Rule of St. Benedict. In *Great Historical Enterprises. Problems in Monastic History*. London, Nelson.

Lewis, Mary Agnes, 1967. Slavery and personality. *American Quarterly*, 19, pp. 114–21. Reprinted in *The Debate over Slavery, Stanley Elkins and His Critics*, ed. Ann J. Lane, pp. 75–86. Urbana, University of Illinois Press, 1971.

Locke, John, 1690. *Two Treatises of Government*. ed. Peter Laslett, 2nd edn. Cambridge, Cambridge University Press, 1967.

Macaulay, Thomas Babington, 1857. *The History of England from the Accession of James the Second*, rev. edn. London, Longmans, Green & Co.

McGuire, Robert A., 1981. Economic causes of late-nineteenth century agrarian unrest: new evidence. *Journal of Economic History*, XLI, pp. 835–52.

McKisack, Mary, 1959. *The Fourteenth Century, 1307–1399*. Oxford, Clarendon.

Maitland, F. W., 1901. English law and the Renaissance. Reprinted in *Selected Historical Essays of F. W. Maitland*, ed. Helen M. Cann, pp. 135–51. Boston, Beacon Press, 1962.

Marx, Karl, 1845–6. *The German Ideology*. Extracts from this book are reprinted in *Theories of History*, ed. Patrick Gardiner, pp. 126–31. New York, The Free Press, 1959. Page references are to this reprint.

Marx, Karl, 1859. *A Contribution to the Critique of Political Economy*. The Preface to this work is reprinted in *Theories of History*, ed. Patrick Gardiner, pp. 131–2. New York, The Free Press 1959. Page references are to this reprint.

Marx, Karl and Engels, F., 1888. *Manifesto of the Communist Party*. Moscow, Foreign Languages Publishing House, 1959.

Marxsen, Willi, 1970. *The Resurrection of Jesus of Nazareth*, tr. Margaret Kohl. London, S.C.M.

Mason, T. W., 1964. Some origins of the Second World War. *Past and Present*, 24. Reprinted in *The Origins of the Second World War*, ed. Esmonde M. Robertson, pp. 105–35. London, Macmillan, 1971. Page references are to this reprint.

Merritt, Richard L., 1965. The emergence of American nationalism: a quantitative approach. *The American Quarterly*, XVII, pp. 319–35. Reprinted in

Sociology and History: Methods, ed. Seymour Martin Lipset and Richard Hofstadter, pp. 138–58. New York and London, Basic Books, 1968. Page references are to this reprint.

Middleton, Russell, 1963. Alienation, race and education. *American Sociological Review*, 28, pp. 973–7. Reprinted in Lazarsfeld, Pasanella and Rosenberg, 1972, pp. 35–40. Page references are to this reprint.

Momigliano, Arnaldo, 1969. The origins of the Roman republic. In *Interpretation, Theory and Practice*, ed. Charles S. Singleton, pp. 1–34. Baltimore, The Johns Hopkins University Press.

Mowat, Charles Loch, 1955. *Britain Between the Wars, 1918–1940*. London, Methuen.

Neale, J. E., 1963. *The Age of Catherine de Medici and Essays in Elizabethan History*. London, Jonathan Cape.

Nevins, Allan and Commager, Henry Steele, 1966. *America, The Story of a Free People*, 3rd edn. London, Oxford University Press.

Parish, Peter J., 1975. *The American Civil War*. London, Eyre Methuen.

Perry, P. J., 1975. *A Geography of 19th-Century Britain*. London and Sydney, B. T. Batsford.

Potter, David, 1976. *The Impending Crisis, 1848–1861*. New York, Harper.

Pumphrey, Ralph E., 1959. The introduction of industrialists into the British peerage: a study in adaption of a social institution. *American Historical Review*, LXV, pp. 1–16. Reprinted in *Quantitative History*, ed. Don Karl Rowney and James Q. Graham Jr pp. 164–78. Homewood, Illinois, The Dorsey Press, 1969. Page references are to this reprint.

Renouvin, Pierre, 1955. *Histoire des relations internationales*. An extract of this book, translated by the editor, is printed in *The Outbreak of the First World War*, ed. Dwight E. Lee, pp. 52–5. Boston, D.C. Heath, 1958.

Reynolds, P. A., 1961. Hitler's war? *History*, 46, pp. 212–17.

Rose, John Holland, 1919. *The Life of Napoleon I*, 7th edn. London, G. Bell.

Rostow, W. W., 1960. *The Stages of Economic Growth*. Cambridge, Cambridge University Press.

Rupp, Gordon, 1953. *The Righteousness of God*. London, Hodder.

Schoenbaum, David, 1967. *Hitler's Social Revolution, Class and Status in Nazi Germany 1933–1939*. London, Weidenfeld and Nicolson.

Scott, Ernest, 1920. *A Short History of Australia*. Melbourne, Oxford University Press.

Skinner, Quentin, 1978. *The Foundations of Modern Political Thought*. 2 vols. Cambridge, Cambridge University Press.

Snell, John L., ed. 1959. *The Nazi Revolution: Germany's Guilt or Germany's Fate*. Boston, D.C. Heath.

Stone, Lawrence, 1966. Social mobility in England, 1500–1700. *Past and Present*, No. 30. Reprinted in *Quantitative History*, ed. Don Karl Rowney and James Q. Graham Jr, pp. 238–71. Homewood, Illinois, The Dorsey Press, 1969.

Tarlton, Charles D., 1978. A rope of sand: interpreting Locke's *First Treatise of Government*. *The Historical Journal*, 21, pp. 43–74.

Tawney, R. H., 1941. The rise of the gentry. *Economic History Review*, XI, pp. 1–38. Largely reprinted in *Social Change and Revolution in England*, ed. L. Stone, pp. 6–18. London, Longmans, 1965.

Tawney, R. H., 1954. The rise of the gentry: a postscript. *Economic History Review*, 2nd ser., VII, pp. 91–7.

Taylor, A. J. P., 1954. *The Struggle for the Mastery of Europe*. An extract of this book is reprinted in *The Outbreak of the First World War*, ed. Dwight E. Lee, pp. 56–63. Boston, D.C. Heath, 1958. Page references are to this reprint.

Taylor, A. J. P., 1964. *The Origins of the Second World War*. Harmondsworth, Middlesex, Penguin Books.

Taylor, A. J. P., 1965. War origins again. *Past and Present*, 25. Reprinted in *The Origins of the Second World War*, ed. Esmonde M. Robertson, pp. 136–41. London, Macmillan, 1971. Page references are to this reprint.

Thernstrom, Stephan, 1972. Religion and occupational mobility in Boston, 1880–1963. In *The Dimensions of Quantitative Research in History*, ed. William O. Aydelotte, Allan G. Bogue and Robert William Fogel, pp. 124–58. Princeton, Princeton University Press, 1972.

Thompson, E. P., 1963. *The Making of the English Working Class*. Rev. edn. Hammondsworth, Middlesex, Penguin Books, 1968.

Thompson, J. Eric S., 1960. *Maya Hieroglyphic Writing*, Norman, University of Oklahoma Press.

Tilly, Charles, 1963. The analysis of a counter-revolution. *History and Theory*, III, pp. 30–58. It is reprinted in *Quantitative History*, ed. D. K. Rowney and J. Q. Graham, Jr, pp. 181–208. Homewood, Illinois, The Dorsey Press, 1969. Page references are to this reprint.

Trevelyan, George Macaulay, 1930. *England Under Queen Anne*, vol. I: *Blenheim*. London, Longmans.

Trevelyan, G. M., 1946. *English Social History*, 2nd edn. London, Longmans, Green & Co.

Trevelyan, G. M., 1949a. Autobiography of an historian. In his book *An Autobiography and Other Essays*, pp. 1–51. London, Longmans, Green & Co.

Trevelyan, G. M., 1949b. The coming of the Anglo-Saxons. In his book *An Autobiography and Other Essays*, pp. 129–48. London, Longmans, Green & Co.

Trevor-Roper, H. R., 1953. The decline of the mere gentry. *The Economic History Review Supplements*, I, *The Gentry 1540–1640*. Largely reprinted in *Social Change and Revolution in England*, ed. L. Stone, pp. 19–33. London, Longmans, 1965. Page references are to this reprint.

Waite, Robert G. L., 1971. Adolf Hitler's anti-semitism: a study in history and psychoanalysis. In *The Psychoanalytic Interpretation of History*, ed. Benjamin B. Wolman, pp. 192–230. New York, Basic Books, 1971.

Walter, Gerard, 1957. *Nero*. London, Allen and Unwin.

Warren, W. L., 1961. *King John*. London, Eyre and Spottiswoode.

Weiner, J. S., Oakley, K. P. and Le Gros, W. E., 1953. The solution of the Piltdown problem. Reprinted in *Man's Discovery of His Past: Literary Landmarks in Archaeology*, ed. Robert F. Heizer, pp. 30–6. Englewood Cliffs, N.J., Prentice Hall, 1962.

Whately, Richard, 1819. Historic doubts relative to Napoleon Buonaparte. In *Famous Pamphlets*, ed. Henry Morley, pp. 249–90. London, Routledge, 1886.

Whitelock, Dorothy, 1952. *The Beginnings of English Society*. Harmondsworth, Middlesex, Penguin Books.

Williams, Basil, 1952. *The Whig Supremacy, 1714–1760*. Oxford, Clarendon.

Wilson, Charles, 1962. Review article: economics and politics in the seventeenth century. *The Historical Journal*, V, pp. 80–92.

Woodward, C. Vann, 1974. History from slave sources. *American Historical Review*, 79, pp. 470–81.

Young, Ernest P., 1968. Yuan Shik-k'ai's rise to the presidency. In *China in Revolution: The First Phase 1900–1913*, ed. M. C. Wright, pp. 419–42. New Haven, Conn., Yale University Press.

Youngson, A. J., 1967. *Britain's Economic Growth 1920–1966*. London, Allen and Unwin.

Zilliacus, K., 1946. *Mirror of the Past*. An extract of this book is reprinted in *The Outbreak of the First World War*, ed. Dwight E. Lee, pp. 45–51. Boston, D.C. Heath, 1958.

Subject index

Name index